Designing & Building Business Applications: Oracle 9i

Gerald V. Post

McGraw-Hill Irwin

Boston   Burr Ridge, IL   Dubuque, IA   Madison, WI   New York   San Francisco   St. Louis
Bangkok   Bogotá   Caracas   Kuala Lumpur   Lisbon   London   Madrid   Mexico City
Milan   Montreal   New Delhi   Santiago   Seoul   Singapore   Sydney   Taipei   Toronto

Vice president and editor-in-chief: *Robin J. Zwettler*
Publisher: *Stewart Mattson*
Senior sponsoring editor: *Paul Ducham*
Editorial assistant: *Jennifer Wisnowski*
Marketing manager: *Greta Kleinert*
Media producer: *Greg Bates*
Project manager: *Charlie Fisher*
Manager, New book production: *Heather D. Burbridge*
Supplement producer: *Lynn M. Bluhm*
Senior digital content specialist: *Brian Nacik*
Lead designer: *Matthew Baldwin*
Cover designer: *Fuel Visual Media*
Typeface: *10/12 Times Roman*
Compositor: *The GTS Companies/York, PA Campus*
Printer: *Quebecor World Dubuque Inc.*

Brief Contents

Contents

Designing & Building Business Applications: Oracle 9i

Chapter

Introduction

Objectives

- Identify the main elements of the case.
- Structure the work needed for the case.
- Create a feasibility analysis of the case.
- Create a new database.

Case: All Powder Board and Ski Shop

The ski industry has been through many changes in the 50 years since Bill Shimek founded the ski shop that is now run by his grandson. One of the biggest changes is reflected in the prominence of "Board" in the shop name. Snowboards have revolutionized the industry in several respects. They revived youth interest in the sport, brought new designs to equipment and resorts, and increased sales dramatically. On the other hand, the increased changes in ski and snowboard equipment make it more difficult for shops to stock the hundreds of options and combinations that enthusiasts might want. Shops have become larger, forcing small firms out of business. Even large ski shops have had to identify their customers and forecast customer demands carefully to make sure the high-demand equipment is in stock. Tracking sales, trends, and buyer needs has become critical to survival.

Another factor in the industry is that the firms increasingly rely on rentals. Partly because of the rapid changes in the industry, many people prefer to rent equipment so they can avoid having to buy new boards and skis every year. Consequently, the shop buys several relatively standard boards and skis every year and rents them out. At the end of the year, the used equipment is sold at a discount to make room for next year's models.

Inventory

Monitoring inventory is a first critical step in the process of providing the selection demanded by customers. Figure 1.1 shows some of the detailed information needed, as well as the diversity of equipment available. Note that because of the variety of styles, there are many different types of snowboards and skis. Figure 1.1 shows the importance of the skill categories. Manufacturers produce special boards and skis for each of these categories. Of course, it would be impossible to stock all of the required sizes for rental purposes. Rental boards and skis tend to be as generic as

FIGURE 1.1

Inventory							
Snowboards	Manufacturer	Mfg ID	Size	Description	Graphics	List Price	QOH
Freestyle							
Pipe							
Standard							
Extreme							
Skis	Manufacturer	Mfg ID	Size	Description	Graphics	List Price	QOH
Slalom							
Cross country-skate							
Cross country-trad							
Telemark							
Jumping							
Freestyle							
Downhill/race							

possible. Even for sales, some sizes of the high-end skis and boards have to be special ordered.

Within a category, manufacturers tend to sell boards and skis targeted for different levels of skiers—from beginner to intermediate to expert (Type I, Type II, and Type III skier). Even within the type classifications, All Powder salespeople evaluate customers on the basis of their aggressiveness on the slope. Because of the size of snowboards, along with the youthful image of the sport, manufacturers place a high value on the graphics (images and colors) displayed on both sides of the boards. Customers have often been known to choose a board because of the graphics. Some of this emphasis on graphics has filtered down to skis as well.

Sizes of boards and skis are somewhat tricky and definitely present a challenge to keeping adequate inventory. The length of the ski or board is a critical number, but the customer's choice is also based on several other ski measurements. Snowboards revolutionized board and ski design by adding a narrower waist to aid in turning. This concept migrated to most varieties of skis as well. So customers often want to know the waist width, sideout depth, and effective edge length as well. Generally, boards and skis with narrower waists are targeted for more advanced skiers. Additionally, the construction of the board or ski, in terms of materials and thickness, significantly affects its flexibility and handling. Customers generally want to feel the ski to evaluate and compare its flexibility, but measures of stance location (for boards) and the rider weight range provide some estimate of the handling characteristics. Most skis and boards are also designed for a particular riding weight. For cross-country skis it is particularly important to get the proper length for the weight of the skier.

Bindings and Boots

Bindings and boots represent another common problem for All Powder and other ski shops. Each ski and each board can technically be fitted with several types of bindings. Each binding type generally requires a matching style of boot; and some of the boots can work only with some bindings. For example, snowboards can use clincher, strap, or plate bindings. Cross-country skis can use pin, strap, or rod bindings. Most modern skis use the rod binding, but customers sometimes want boots that fit the older pin bindings. Downhill, freestyle, and slalom skis use similar bindings, and they are the most popular so the store usually stocks several models focusing on skill levels.

Figure 1.2 shows an example of the card system that All Powder uses to help salespeople select bindings and boots. Currently, the salespeople are supposed to change the quantity on hand whenever a boot or binding is sold. Of course, the cards are rarely kept up-to-date and the salespeople often have to go search the physical inventory to see if a size needed by a customer is in stock. Note that boots and bindings are specifically matched and a boot for one purpose can rarely be used for a different application. For example, it would not be possible to use a cross-country boot in a downhill binding. The binding is usually listed as a type (rod, step-in, telemark/cable, and so on). On the other hand, it is possible to mount bindings on different types of skis. For instance, you could mount a telemark binding to a downhill ski. Some of the strange combinations should be avoided, but this knowledge will not be needed in the database.

FIGURE 1.2

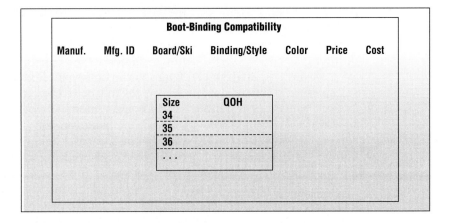

Sales

The sales form shown in Figure 1.3 is fairly standard. All of the hard work in terms of configuration was done by the salesperson. In some cases, the salesperson might ask the customer to initial some items that might present compatibility issues to make sure the customer is aware of the potential problems. Returns are usually accepted on most items as long as they have not been used outside (e.g., scratched or worn boots cannot be returned). The description generally includes the manufacturer's name and style. The SKU (stock keeping unit) is a special number created within the store to code each item. It is important for salespeople to identify the type of boarding/skiing and the skill level. This information is used to send customers mailings about special sales. The owner also has started thinking about keeping customer sizes in a database. This information would be particularly helpful in clearing out last year's inventory of special sizes (very small or very large), because it would help pinpoint customers who could

FIGURE 1.3

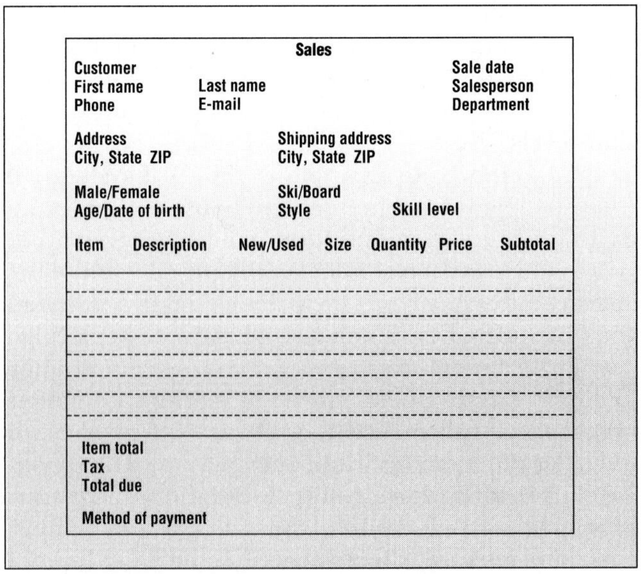

use those special sizes. The catch is that the store owner is concerned about consumer privacy and fears that customers may not want to have their sizes on file at the store. If a customer has already purchased items in a specific category and size, that data will be available. The difficulty lies in having salespeople ask customers their sizes when they are not purchasing these products. For instance, it might appear rude to ask a customer who only came in to buy ski wax for his or her jacket size.

The store evaluates salespeople by the amount of sales they make, so it is important to track sales by each employee. Of course, the database should contain additional information about each employee, such as his or her phone number, address, and primary department assignment. Since, clerks rarely write down the department names properly, it makes sense to have a separate lookup table for the department names.

Also, note that some of the best customers participate in several styles, even crossing between skis and boards. A customer who is an expert at downhill skiing, however, might be a beginner with snowboards.

Rentals

The form to handle rentals is similar to the sales form. But notice in Figure 1.4 that columns have been added for return date, condition, and additional charges. The additional charges are imposed if an item is returned late or if it is damaged. Additionally, customers are required to sign the form to indicate their agreement with the skill level, rental conditions, and the release printed on the back of the form. Katy, the current manager, has talked about capturing the customer signatures digitally and storing them online, but it is not a high priority.

Observe that the current form requires that each rented item be checked off separately when it is returned. Although store clerks often complain about having to mark each row separately, about 20 percent of the time, a customer forgets to return an item and has to bring it back later.

FIGURE 1.4

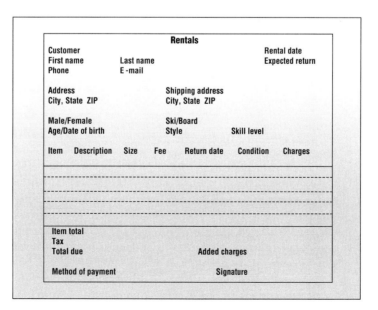

Renting ski equipment also raises the issue of reservations. On some holidays, all of the equipment is rented out before 10:00 A.M. Some long-term customers have suggested they would like to be able to reserve equipment. Currently, the rental managers sometimes set aside equipment if a valuable repeat customer calls in advance. This process works reasonably well, but the managers have talked about creating a system that is available to everyone. One of the drawbacks is that they are concerned that the general public might reserve items and then never show up, leaving equipment unused that could be rented to someone else.

Lab Exercise

The first step in any project is to identify some basic elements of the system. What are the goals? What is the scope? What tools will be needed? What are the benefits? What are the expected costs? How much development time will be needed? All of these questions are difficult to answer and rarely have a single value. Instead, you need to create a project plan. The plan will include a feasibility statement that describes the basic costs and potential benefits. As a real-world project, the plan would also include a list of developers and a statement of expected fees, so the owners can evaluate the decision to hire you.

Project Outline

As a first step in developing the project plan, you need to summarize the overall project. This summary should contain a brief description of the project, its goals, and initial lists of primary forms and reports. Ultimately, this summary would also include the scope and anticipated budget for the project.

Activity: Review the Case and Research the Industry

For the purposes of this lab, you will prepare a project proposal for developing the sales system needed by the All Powder Board and Ski Shop. The rental component will be left for another exercise. You should begin by reviewing the description of the company. You should also use the Internet to check out some of the manufacturers and some of the competitors. You need to be sure that you understand the key factors in the industry. Figure 1.5 provides a possible structure for your summary. You should review the case and enter the basic information requested.

FIGURE 1.5

Project Title: Sales System for Boards and Skis
Customer: All Powder Board and Ski Shop
Primary Contact: Katy
Goals:
Project Description:
Primary Forms:
Primary Reports:
Lead Developer:
Estimated Development Time:
Estimated Development Cost:
Date Prepared:

Project Plan

The project plan consists of a detailed breakdown of the steps needed to create the final system. A common approach is to follow the steps of the systems development life-cycle methodology: Initiation, Analysis, Design, Implementation, and Review. Some organizations have rigid descriptions of each of the steps involved in this process. Some organizations adopt a more flexible approach. Either way, this plan should outline the basic steps that need to be completed and an estimated schedule.

In the initial phase, it is also helpful to identify any potential risks to the project development. At various stages, what might go wrong? If you are aware of the potential problems, managers can monitor for them and can prepare solutions more quickly.

Activity: Create the Initial Project Plan

Project plans and schedules are often shown with Gantt charts to illustrate how the various steps depend on each other. If you have access to software such as Microsoft Project, it is relatively easy to create the project plan. Figure 1.6 shows the basic steps that the labs will follow in building the application. Ultimately, you would estimate the times required for each step. However, until you have read the rest of the book and worked with the databases, it is difficult to estimate the times needed for each step. For now, evaluate the steps and try to identify any dependencies between the tasks. For example, is it possible to create the forms without having the database tables and relationships? Assuming you have several people to help, reorganize the tasks so that as many tasks as possible can be done at the same time.

Feasibility

Feasibility studies are notoriously difficult. The concept is certainly simple: Identify the potential costs and potential benefits of a system and compare them. The problem is that benefits might not be quantifiable, so it is difficult

FIGURE 1.6

1. Define the project and obtain approval.
2. Analyze the user needs and identify all forms and reports.
3. System design
    a. Determine the tables and relationships needed.
    b. Create the tables and load basic data.
    c. Create queries needed for forms and reports.
    d. Build forms and reports.
    e. Create transaction elements.
    f. Define security and access controls.
4. Additional features
    a. Create data warehouse to analyze data as needed.
    b. Handle distributed database elements as needed.
5. System implementation
    a. Convert and load data.
    b. Train users.
    c. Load testing.
6. System review

FIGURE 1.7

Assumptions		Present value	Subtotal
Annual discount rate	0.03		
Project life/years	5		
Costs		Present value	Subtotal
One time			
DBMS software			
Hardware			
Development			
Data entry			
Training			
Ongoing			
Personnel			
Upgrades/annual			
Supplies			
Support			
Maintenance			
Benefits			
Cost savings			
Better inventory control			
Fewer clerks			
Strategic			
Increased sales			
Other?			
Net Present Value			

to attach meaningful numbers. Nonetheless, it is useful to at least write down the anticipated costs and expected benefits. Even if numbers are not available, at least managers can see a concise statement of the analysis.

Activity: Create the Feasibility Analysis

Figure 1.7 shows the basic elements of a feasibility study. You need to create a spreadsheet with these main categories. Use research to identify approximate costs of the various components. For example, assume that the shop will need to purchase a server to host the main database and two client computers for the sales staff. With Microsoft Access, several configurations are possible. Examine the software license to determine the number of copies you will need and the approximate cost. Other numbers, including benefits, can be estimated. Remember that annual costs and benefits should be discounted to compensate for the time value of money. Use the present value (PV) function in Excel. Although the benefits are relatively well-defined, they can still be difficult to estimate. For example, how will the system reduce the need for sales clerks? How many or how many hours? How much do clerks earn? Likewise, in terms of inventory control, how much money will be saved by not having to slash prices at the end of the season to clear the unsold inventory? You need to know or estimate the number and value of items typically left at the end of the season. In practice, the managers might have answers to some of these questions, but you will still have to do additional research. In this example, be sure that you spell out your assumptions.

The Database Management System

Activity: Explore the DBMS

Although Oracle is one of the most popular database systems, it can be somewhat difficult to install and maintain. Generally, the Oracle DBMS is installed on a server and the client software is installed on the individual workstations. However, it is possible to install the personal version of Oracle onto a single computer. If you are working in a classroom lab, an Oracle server should already be configured, and your machines should have the Oracle client software installed and tested. If you are working on your own computer, Figure 1.8 shows where you can obtain the Oracle software through two main programs: the academic initiative and the technology network. If your school does not participate in the OAI program, the technology network enables software developers to download the most recent software and the documentation, but it requires a relatively fast Internet connection. Most of the labs in this book can be completed using the enterprise 9i database and the developer suite (DS) of tools.

To access an Oracle database, the machine you are using must have an Oracle network configuration that describes how to reach the database. This configuration file defines a name for each Oracle database that it knows how to reach. To connect to an Oracle database, you need the database name, a user name, and a password.

As shown in the enterprise manager in Figure 1.9, the data for an Oracle database can be stored in several files called tablespaces. If you are running Oracle on your own computer, you can probably use the default Users tablespace for the projects in this book. However, for larger projects, you might need to add tablespaces. When your user account was created, either by you or a database administrator, Oracle probably created a new schema for you. You will have access to the items you create with the schema, but others should not be able to see your work, unless you grant them permission or they are system administrators. Schemas are useful for keeping projects separate, so you might want to create a second schema if you will also be

FIGURE 1.8

```
http://oai.oracle.com
    Oracle academic initiative-software
http://otn.oracle.com
    Oracle technology network-downloads
http://otn.oracle.com/documentation/content.html
    Oracle documentation—requires OTN
```

FIGURE 1.9

working on a final project. The system administrator can use the enterprise manager to create a new user. At a minimum, this user will need permission to create tables. If you are running Oracle on your own machine, give yourself DBA permissions.

To get a quick perspective of the various components of the DBMS, you need to build a simple database. One of the first things you have to understand with Oracle is that it is heavily reliant on SQL—which will be covered in greater detail in later chapters. Most administrators perform all tasks by writing SQL statements. However, the more recent versions of Oracle have added graphical tools to help with common tasks. These tools will be shown in this chapter, but it will also show the SQL statements so you have them available for future reference. Start the enterprise manager console for Oracle. Expand the databases tab and expand the main database you have been assigned to use. At this point, you will be asked to log in. Expand the schema section and expand your username. As you select the various icons (tables, indexes, views, and so on), you will see that your schema is mostly empty.

Relational databases consist of a collection of tables, so the first step is to create a new table. Figure 1.10 shows the definition of a customer table. Figure 1.11 shows how to specify the primary key column. Select the Constraints tab, enter a unique name for the constraint (PK_CUSTOMER), select the type as Primary, then select the column that makes up the primary key (CustomerID). If you click the Show SQL button, you will see the SQL statement that will generate the table. If you memorize the syntax of this

FIGURE 1.10

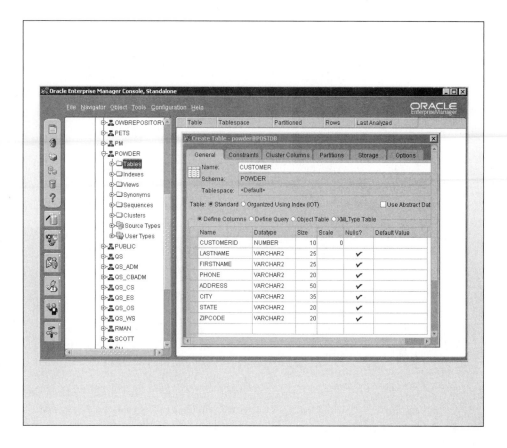

statement, you could have skipped the design screen and typed the statement directly. More importantly, you can copy this statement and put it into a text file that you can execute later if you ever need to re-create this table. When you have finished entering all of the fields, click the Create Table button.

FIGURE 1.11

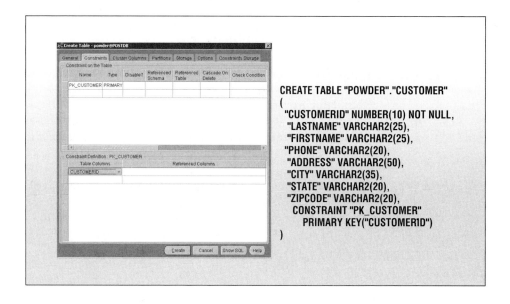

FIGURE 1.12

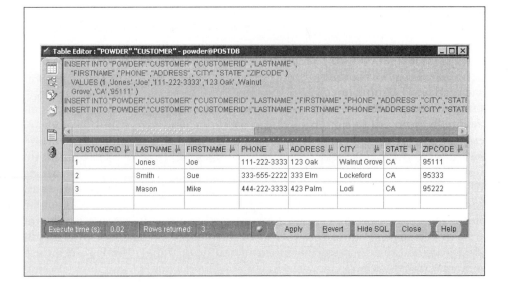

Within the figure:

Table Editor : "POWDER"."CUSTOMER" - powder@POSTDB

```
INSERT INTO "POWDER"."CUSTOMER" ("CUSTOMERID" ,"LASTNAME",
   "FIRSTNAME" ,"PHONE" ,"ADDRESS" ,"CITY" ,"STATE" ,"ZIPCODE" )
   VALUES (1 ,'Jones','Joe','111-222-3333','123 Oak' ,'Walnut
   Grove','CA','95111' )
INSERT INTO "POWDER"."CUSTOMER" ("CUSTOMERID" ,"LASTNAME","FIRSTNAME" ,"PHONE" ,"ADDRESS" ,"CITY" ,"STATE
INSERT INTO "POWDER"."CUSTOMER" ("CUSTOMERID" ,"LASTNAME","FIRSTNAME" ,"PHONE" ,"ADDRESS" ,"CITY" ,"STATE
```

CUSTOMERID	LASTNAME	FIRSTNAME	PHONE	ADDRESS	CITY	STATE	ZIPCODE
1	Jones	Joe	111-222-3333	123 Oak	Walnut Grove	CA	95111
2	Smith	Sue	333-555-2222	333 Elm	Lockeford	CA	95333
3	Mason	Mike	444-222-3333	423 Palm	Lodi	CA	95222

Execute time (s): 0.02   Rows returned: 3   Apply   Revert   Hide SQL   Close   Help

---

Action

Start the enterprise manager console.
Open the database and log in.
Find and open your schema.
Right-click on tables, select Create table.
Enter column names and data types.
Select the Constraint tab.
Enter the PK_CUSTOMER name.
Select the Customer table.
Select the CustomerID column.
Click the Create button.

Action

Right-click the table name.
Select View/Edit contents.
Enter sample data.
Click the Apply button.

Action

Start the forms builder.
Choose Tools/Data block wizard.
Use the Customer table.
Select all of the columns.
Use the default layout choices.
Choose all columns for the form.
Save the form.

Oracle also provides a table wizard that steps you through the process of creating one field at a time, but ultimately, it is faster to enter the columns on the main design screen. The next step is to open the table and enter some data for fake customers. Right-click on the table name and select the option to View/Edit contents. Again, you could use SQL to insert rows and you can click the Show SQL button to see the actual statement. However, when you first work with Oracle, it is easiest to enter the data directly using the table editor. Figure 1.12 shows some sample data you can use, or make up three rows of data on your own. Click the Apply button to save the data.

You can copy the data from Figure 1.10 or just make up your own. Access provides several tools in the table window to examine the data. You can sort by columns or even filter the rows to just see customers that meet some criteria. However, you will rarely give users direct access to tables. Instead, you will build forms and reports for managers to use. Close the Customer table.

In practice, you will rarely enter data directly into tables. Instead, you will build forms that users can run to enter and edit data. Oracle provides the form builder to help create forms. The form builder has a couple of wizards (data block and layout) to make the process easier. Start the forms builder and you will begin with a blank module and blank form. Choose the Tools/Data block wizard menu option. Follow the basic prompts to select the Customer table. Select all of the columns by moving them to the right-hand window. The data block retrieves the desired data from the database. When the data block is created, the layout wizard will start. Again, select all of the columns so they are displayed on the form. Stick with the default layout choices, but you can edit the labels to make them look

FIGURE 1.13

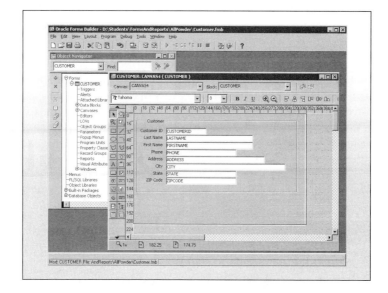

nicer. Finish the wizard and save the form, giving it the Customer.fmb name. Ideally, you should save the form in a folder on the server. Choose the Program/Compile Module option to compile the form. As shown in Figure 1.13, you can use the layout editor to change the size of the text boxes or the form itself, but it is not critical at this point. If you do make changes, be sure to save the form and recompile it.

To run the form, the database either needs the full 9iAS configuration, or the listener has to be started. You can test the form with Program/Run form. If you receive an error message regarding the listener, use the Windows menu option under the Forms Developer to Start OC4J Instance. As shown in Figure 1.14, Oracle 9i forms are processed through a Web browser, such as Internet Explorer. Once the forms have been developed and compiled, users simply open the forms through a website. There is an important catch: Every

FIGURE 1.14

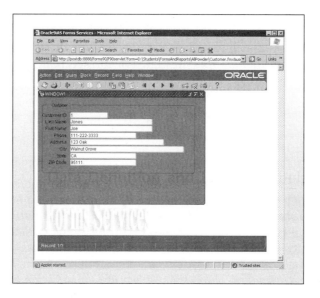

user's browser has to install an Oracle ActiveX component called JInitiator. The first time users try to open a form, they will be asked to install this special program.

Note that the form is initially empty. To load the data, you need to click the button in the middle of the toolbar to execute the query. Later, this step can be automated. Clicking the Forward and Back buttons will cause the form to scroll through the list of customers. Oracle also has a reports builder that produces totals and subtotals but you do not have enough data yet to justify a report. More complex database applications will be built following these same steps: Create the tables, build forms and reports, and tie them together so the user sees a seamless application.

Exercises

Many Charms

Madison and Samantha, friends of yours, have a small business selling charms for bracelets and necklaces. They buy some of the charms; others they make. So far, they have run the business as a hobby, selling primarily to friends and relatives. But they have recently established a website to display pictures and prices of some of the charms. You have agreed to build a database for them to track their inventory, customers, and sales. Any orders they receive through the website will be e-mailed, so the website does not have to be connected live to the database. The database is a relatively traditional sales system, but it is slightly complicated by the nature of the charms. Charms come in a variety of shapes, sizes, and materials. For example, customers who want a quarter-moon charm have a choice of 4 mm and 8 mm, and a choice of materials: silver, gold, gold plate, bronze, or painted ceramic. Charms are also offered in categories such as animals, hearts, birthdays, and so on. The duo also offers a variety of chains and pins to hold the charms. Eventually, they want to be able to track the sales by all of these categories, so they know which items are selling the most and which make the most profit. Costs and prices tend to fluctuate. If they purchase items in large bulk, the per-piece cost is lower, but they need to be sure they can sell the entire shipment. If an item sits around too long, they find that they have to significantly cut the price just to clear out the stock. Of course, gold charms are more expensive, making them more difficult to sell, and they are reluctant to tie up their money in high-priced merchandise.

1. Research similar sites on the Internet. Describe or sketch the major forms and reports that the company might use.
2. Create the initial proposal and feasibility study.

Standup Foods

Laura runs a catering company that focuses on Hollywood movie studios. Her chefs prepare hors d'oeuvres, sandwiches, and other items that are served to the cast and crew members of movies and various studios. To be fresh, the food is prepared each day in the main kitchens, and then assembled and displayed onsite. For some projects, the company vans deliver new food every few hours. To hold costs down, many of Laura's employees are part time—only a few chefs and managers are full-time employees. Some of Laura's clients call at the last minute, so she maintains a large list of potential workers who can perform a variety of tasks, from driving to food preparation and display, as well as cleanup. The chefs and managers evaluate workers after each job in terms of timeliness, appearance, friendliness, and the ability to take orders and accomplish tasks. Workers often perform many tasks at a given event. For instance, the driver might also be a server. But some tasks require specific certifications. Not all workers are licensed to drive, and only a few have been trained to perform some tasks such as cutting meats. Most of the employee ratings are somewhat informal at the moment, but she would like to computerize them to help her select the best workers for future jobs. At some point, she would like to offer bonuses or higher pay to workers who routinely perform well. Another challenge that Laura faces is that some clients are finicky about certain types of food. In particular, some movie clients have special preferences as well as some items that cause allergic reactions. The chefs currently keep these two lists in paper folders for some major performers and actors. But, to be safe, Laura wants to computerize those lists and, ultimately, computerize the recipe ingredients. Then, when a chef plans meals, the computer could check the list of main guests and their allergies against the recipe list to identify potential problems.

1. Research similar sites on the Internet. Describe or sketch the major forms and reports that the company might use.
2. Create the initial proposal and feasibility study.

EnviroSpeed

Brennan and Tyler are owners/managers of a consulting firm that specializes in environmental issues. In particular, the company's scientists are experts in cleanups for chemical spills. For example, if a tanker crashes and spills chemicals on a highway, the company can quickly evaluate the potential problems and identify the best method to clean up the spill and prevent problems. The company itself does not clean up the spill, but it has contacts with several crews around the globe that it can call if local emergency workers need additional help. The primary focus of the company is to provide expert knowledge in the time of a crisis. This task requires specialized scientists, good communication systems, and in-depth training and practice. Brennan wants to improve the existing information system to maintain a database of case histories. Then, if a similar problem arises in the future, the scientists can quickly search the database and identify secondary problems and examine which solutions and ideas were successful and which ones caused more problems. Tyler has explained that at a minimum, the database has to hold the contact information for all of the scientists and emergency crews. It must also list the specialties, training, and skill levels of each person in a variety of areas. In terms of actual situations, the database should track the identities and roles of the various people and the key time frames (when reported, response time, and so on). Scientists also need the ability to list all of the chemicals involved and details about the terrain (hills, water, soil composition). More subjective data must also be captured, including comments by the onsite team and a description of the problem and secondary factors. All proposed solutions should be entered into the database, along with comments regarding their strengths and weaknesses as well as the final selections and an evaluation of the result. It is important to track potential solutions that were discarded. Even if they did not apply to the original problem, they might be useful for a future event with different circumstances.

1. Research similar sites on the Internet. Describe or sketch the major forms and reports that the company might use.
2. Create the initial proposal and feasibility study.

Final Project

The main textbook has an appendix with several longer case studies. You should be able to work on one of these cases throughout the term. If you or your instructor picks one, perform the following tasks.

1. Research similar sites on the Internet. List the major forms and reports that the company might use.
2. Create the initial proposal and feasibility study.

Chapter

Database Design

Chapter Outline

Objectives

- Design the initial tables for the case.
- Create the design in the database design system.
- Determine the initial relationships for the case.
- Identify the data types needed for the attributes.

Database Design

You can design a database using paper and pencil. As you gain experience and become more skilled at the task, using pencil and paper will be relatively easy. However, when you are learning, using pencil and paper is tedious because you find that you often need to remove items from potential classes or even alter the entire diagram. As an alternative, you might consider going directly to the DBMS and defining the tables or classes off the top of your head. This approach will not work with Oracle because Oracle limits the changes you can make to tables—particularly after relationships have been built and data has been added.

A few computer-assisted software engineering (CASE) tools remain that can help you define classes in a graphical environment. They are relatively powerful, and many have the ability to generate the final tables based on the class diagram. However, they are also expensive, hard to install, and cumbersome to learn. But if you work for a company that has invested in these tools, they are an excellent way to define the database classes. Oracle 9i does have a designer to build entity-relationship diagrams. This system is useful because it will generate the tables from the diagrams. But it has limited advice and design checking facilities.

There is a better tool to learn database design. The database design system is an online expert system that enables students to create class diagrams graphically in a Java-enabled Web browser. The system makes it easy for you to create classes (entities) and build associations (relationships). More importantly, it provides immediate feedback on the design, which is the expert system part. The system runs on a custom Web server and diagrams are stored in a central database. This approach means that you can access your diagrams from almost any computer. Changes you make in class or in your instructor's office are saved and available when you return to a lab or your own computer. From an instructional perspective, the best part is that the system contains some complex rules to provide feedback on your diagram. The system recognizes most design errors and points them out with suggestions to improve the design. Your instructor can obtain the database design system for your class. If it is available, you should use it to get the benefit of the immediate feedback. If it is not available, you can draw the class diagrams with paper and pencil or with a graphics package such as Visio or even PowerPoint.

Oracle Data Types

As a database designer, your job is to define the database tables that efficiently store the organization's data and support the business rules. In this process, you will define the tables in terms of the data columns (attributes) and the table relationships (associations). You will also need to know what type of data will be stored in each column. Also, for some columns, you will want to identify specify constraints (such as salary cannot be negative).

Selecting the proper data type can sometimes be a difficult step. Any DBMS supports only a limited number of domains and you have to understand the capabilities and limitations of each type. You must also understand the underlying business data—both the values collected today and the potential values that may be collected in the future. For example, workers may

FIGURE 2.1

	Name	Data	Bytes
Text (characters)			
Fixed	CHAR or NCHAR	2000 bytes	Fixed
Variable	VARCHAR2	4000 bytes	Variable
National/Unicode	NVARCHAR2	4000 bytes	Variable
Memo	LONG	2 gigabytes	Variable
Numeric			
Byte (8 bits)	NUMBER(38)	38 digits	2-21
Integer (16 bits)	NUMBER(38)	38 digits	2-21
Long (32 bits)	NUMBER(38)	38 digits	2-21
(64 bits)	NUMBER(38)	38 digits	2-21
Fixed precision	NUMBER(p,s)	p: 1 . . . 38, s: -84 . . . 127	2-21
Float	NUMBER	38 digits	2-21
Double	NUMBER	38 digits	2-21
Currency	NUMBER(p,4)	38 digits	2-21
Yes/No	NA		
Date/Time	DATE, TIMESTAMP	1/1/-4712 to 12/31/9999 (sec)	7/11/13
Interval	INTERVAL YEAR/MONTH		
Image	LONG RAW or BLOB	2 gigabytes, 4 gigabytes	Variable

only use integer values to represent a quality rating. But, in the future, it is likely that the company will want to use fractional values as well. Although database types are becoming more standardized over time, each DBMS uses its own type names. Even more confusing, the actual values supported can be different even if the data type name is the same. The numeric data type is variable length in Oracle, because you can specify the number of significant digits. A full 38 digits requires 21 bytes of storage.

Figure 2.1 shows the main data types available in Oracle 9i. The types you will use most often are VARCHAR2, DATE, and NUMBER. When you need to store date or time values, be sure to use the DATE or TIMESTAMP type. It supports date arithmetic so users can subtract two dates to obtain the number of days between them. The LONG RAW and BLOB types can hold pictures or even spreadsheets or documents. Note that Oracle also supports the ANSI SQL keywords. In many cases, it is easier to use those instead of the Oracle types, but ultimately Oracle converts them into native types. For instance, SQL defines the INTEGER data type, which Oracle converts to NUMBER with a scale of zero.

Oracle essentially uses one numeric type for every type of number. This approach is relatively easy to use, but might not yield the most efficient use of storage space. On the other hand, storage space is cheap today, and no one really knows how many product item numbers the application will eventually need. So, using some extra storage space now is probably not a major problem. The issue of precision and scale is sometimes confusing. Precision represents the total number of significant digits supported in the value—regardless of any decimal points or size of the number. For example, a number with a precision of 5 digits would include 12345 as well as 12.345. If the scale is specified, it indicates a fixed number of decimal points and controls round off to that value. It is particularly useful for handling currency values.

The other confusing issue in modern databases is the use of Unicode or "national" character sets. The older VARCHAR2 data type assigns one character to one byte and can only handle ASCII codes or essentially English-language characters. If your database needs to store text in additional languages, it will have to use Unicode character sets that typically assign two bytes to any character or ideogram. In this case, use the NVARCHAR2 data type, but note that it cuts the maximum length of text in half. VARCHAR2 can handle strings up to 4,000 bytes. NVARCHAR2 can also handle 4,000 bytes, but that is only 2,000 Unicode characters.

Case: All Powder Board and Ski Shop

With any database project, the first step is to understand the various elements of the organization and the components that will become part of the database application. This knowledge is critical, because the database design must reflect the business rules. In an actual work environment, you can ask workers about the processes and underlying assumptions. With a written case, it can be more challenging to determine all of the necessary rules. On the other hand, real life is messier, and people often give inconsistent answers. It takes experience to learn how to talk with users to identify exactly which components are the most important, and how the pieces relate to each other. Cases avoid this design complication but generally require you to make assumptions on your own. Because the goal is to make reasonable assumptions, you should search the Internet or read a few articles on snowboards and skis before you tackle the database design.

Business Objects: First Guess

One of the first steps in designing the database is to identify the business objects. In many ways, this case is a fairly typical business problem, so you would expect to see many of the traditional business objects, such as Customer, Employee, and Sale. Because the store also rents equipment, there will be a Rental object similar to the Sale object. Figure 2.2 shows initial versions of these four classes. These objects are relatively standard, but some issues arise in this case. Notice that you must also begin to think about primary keys. In each of these four tables, the primary key is a new value that will be generated by the DBMS. In Oracle, you have to assign this column a NUMBER or INTEGER data type. Later, you can create a sequence that will generate the values needed. In terms of the design, it is useful to indicate that this key is internally generated by the DBMS, so the database design system refers to it as an AutoNumber data type. In most situations, the actual key values will be hidden from the users, and they will see only the relevant names.

Notice that several attributes are missing from these initial classes. The main reason is that it is important to ensure that the columns you include at this stage are correct. If there is any doubt about a column in a potential class, leave it out and think about it. A few other classes should be relatively obvious for this case. In particular, several support tables are used to provide lookup data for other tables. Ultimately, you will have to define all of the objects, identify the columns for each table, and specify the data type for each column.

FIGURE 2.2

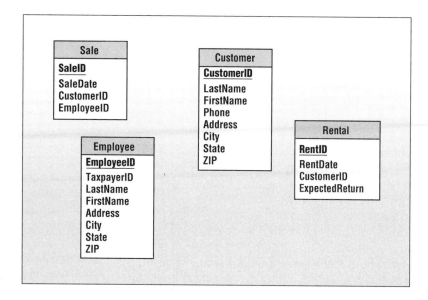

Relationships

Classes or entities are related to other classes. For example, notice that the Sale table contains a CustomerID property. Values in this column match entries in the Customer table, which is keyed by CustomerID. So, if you found a CustomerID value of 112 in the Sale table, you could look up the matching customer data by finding the row in the Customer table that has a primary key value of 112. This association also expresses several business rules. In particular, (1) each sale can be placed by only one customer, (2) a sale must be identified with a customer, (3) any given customer can participate in many sales, but (4) a customer might not have bought anything yet.

Relationships are displayed on the diagram by drawing connecting lines between the two tables involved. The business rules are shown as annotations at the end of each connection. Each side of the connection displays minimum and maximum values. Figure 2.3 shows the association between the Sale and Customer tables. Notice that the annotations match the four business rules described in the previous paragraph. The 1 . . . 1 notation on the Customer side represents rules 1 and 2. At a minimum, each sale requires

FIGURE 2.3

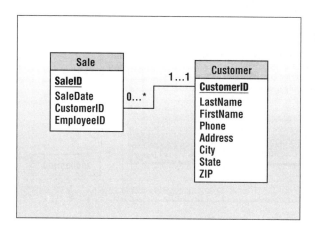

at least one customer, and at a maximum, a sale can have no more than one customer. Likewise, the 0 . . . * annotation represents rules 3 and 4. A customer can participate in zero to many sales. There is no maximum (*), so a customer can participate in any number of sales, and the zero means that a customer might not have bought anything yet. As a database designer, your job is to identify the entities and relationships needed for this case.

Lab Exercise

Database Design System

The database design system is designed as an instructional tool, so your instructor should have already registered to obtain an instructor account. The instructor also chooses and schedules assignments for the class. You will need a class code to register for a class, so be sure you get the correct admission code from your instructor. You will also need a set of numbers to create a new student account on the system. Check with your instructor to obtain these numbers. With the two sets of numbers, and the class admission code, you are ready to create your personal account.

Activity: Getting Started

Use your browser to navigate to the database design website and select the link as a new student who has two key numbers. Figure 2.4 shows the form you need to fill out. First, enter the key numbers that you have. Next, create a username and password that you will remember. You must choose a username that is different from all others. Be sure that you enter your name, e-mail address, and Student ID number correctly. Your instructor will use the name and ID number to correctly identify you so you receive credit for working on assignments. Note that your ID and password are encrypted on the website database to protect them. Your e-mail address is important so the system can send you the username and password in case

Action

Browser: http://time-post.com/dbdesign
New student who has two key numbers.

FIGURE 2.4

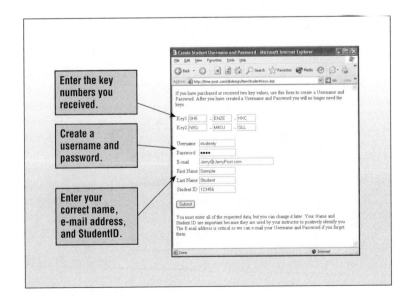

FIGURE 2.5

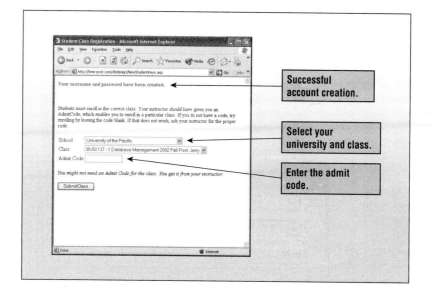

you forget what you selected. When you have entered the data, click the Submit button. If you have an error in the key codes, or if your username has already been selected by someone else, you will receive a message and be asked to correct the items. Note that the key codes can only be used once and can be discarded after the account has been created.

Once you have successfully created the new account, you must register for the specific class. As shown in Figure 2.5, you simply choose your university and your correct class. Enter the admission code provided by the instructor and click the button to register for the class. If you do not have the proper code and are unable to register, you can get the code and return later. From the main page, enter your username and password to log in. If necessary, once you are logged in, you can click the link at the bottom of the main design page to register for a class.

All Powder Design

Activity: Create Tables and Columns

When you have created an account, registered for a class, and logged into the system, you are ready to begin designing the database. Figure 2.6 shows the main elements of the system with the beginning of the

Action
File/Open, choose All Powder case.
Right-click/Add Table.
Right-click header/Rename table.
Drag columns from right onto table.
Right-click name/set data type.

solution. When you begin, the various windows will be empty. You must first open a problem using the File/Open menu choice and select the Workbook case. When the problem loads, the right-hand window will display a list of available columns. Initially, it will probably not include the key columns. You will add those in a minute.

You create a table (class/entity) by clicking the right mouse button on the main screen where you want the table located. Then select the Add Table option. Rename the table by right-clicking the table heading, typing "Sale" as the new name, and pressing the Enter key.

Now you get to add columns to the table. All columns are added to a table by dragging them from the right-hand window and dropping them onto the desired table. In the case of the Sale table, you will need to generate a new

FIGURE 2.6

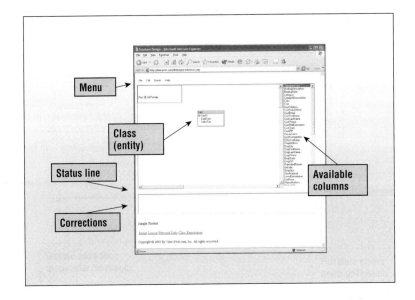

primary key column (SaleID). To create a generated key column, drag-and-drop the top label for Generate Key. Then, rename the newly created column. You rename columns by right-clicking the name either in the table or in the right-hand window. Be careful: Do not give two columns the same name, even if they are in different tables. You will not be able to tell them apart in the main list of the right-hand window. Now you can add some of the other columns needed in the Sale table. Look through the right-hand window to find the SaleDate and SalesTax entries. You can simplify your search if you sort the list by right-clicking on it and selecting Sort. Drag the desired column onto the Sale table. Once a column is in the table, you can change the order by dragging and dropping it higher or lower in the list.

At this point, you should set the data types of the columns in the table. The default type is Text, so in many cases you will not have to change it. However, you should choose Date/Time for the SaleDate, and Currency for the SalesTax column. Right-click on the column name within the table and the current data type is displayed at the bottom of the pop-up menu. Move the cursor to that item and a complete list of data type choices pops up. Choose the desired data type by highlighting it and clicking the left button. Be sure to save your work every few minutes in case you lose the Internet connection or the server times out.

Activity: Create Relationships

Associations or relationships are a key element of database design. In a relational database, columns in one table are connected to columns in other tables through common data. In the case, the Sale table needs to connect to a Customer table. Eventually, both tables will contain a CustomerID column. First, you have to create the Customer table, so right-click on the design screen, add a new table, and rename it. Again, to ensure that each customer is assigned a guaranteed unique identifier, add a Generate Key column to it. Rename this new column as the CustomerID. It is critical that you understand that this key value will be generated for each new customer added to the table. This value can only be generated in this table. You would never create another generated key column and call it CustomerID. So, how do you get CustomerID into the Sale table? Scroll the right-hand window to the bottom and notice that CustomerID has been added to the list of available columns. You could also sort the list and find it alphabetically. You can now drag this new column into the Sale table. Set its data type to Integer32 (Long). Before attempting to build the relationship, add the other customer properties to the Customer table by dragging them from the right-hand window. You can double-click the table heading to automatically resize the table design box to fit the columns it contains. Set the appropriate data types.

Now that you have both the Sale and Customer tables, and they both have a CustomerID column, you can build an association or relationship between them. Figure 2.7 shows how to create this relationship in the design system. Click on the CustomerID column in the Customer table and drag it to the Sale table. Release the mouse button to drop the cursor onto the CustomerID column in the Sale table. The relationship window then asks you to specify the minimum and maximum values for each side of the relationship. These values specify the business rules, and are often the most difficult items to identify. In the sale case, the typical assumptions are that exactly one customer can place an order, and a customer can place from zero to many orders. So, on the Sale side of the window, select the Optional and Many buttons. On the Customer side, choose the One option for both Min and Max values.

Remember that relationships generally involve at least one side in a primary key, but it is not a requirement. Also, the column names do not have to be identical. However, the data types do have to match, and the relationship has to be logical. For example, it would never make sense to connect an ItemID to a CustomerID, because that relationship would imply that a customer can also be an item and vice versa. Finally, notice that the cascade boxes are selected as the default. You should almost always leave these checked. In the database, cascade on delete means that if you delete a particular customer,

Action
Add Customer and Sale tables.
Add GenerateKey to Customer table. Rename it CustomerID.
Drag new CustomerID from right side into Sale table.
Drag CustomerID from Customer and drop it on CustomerID in Sale table.
Fill out relationship box.

FIGURE 2.7

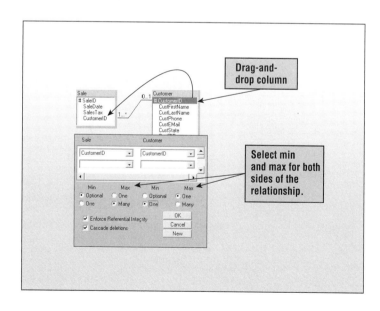

all of the orders placed by that customer will also be deleted. If you do not specify the cascade, then you could end up with orders that contain a CustomerID, which has no matching customer data. After you close the relationship window with the OK button, you might have to refresh the display screen by right-clicking the design window and selecting Refresh.

Activity: Evaluate the Design

One of the most powerful aspects of the database design system is that it contains an expert system to help analyze your design for errors. You can quickly obtain comments by selecting the Grade/Grade and Mark option on the menu. At this point, you only have two tables partially created, so the most important comment you should receive is that overall, you are missing several tables. The system might also point out that you are missing columns from the Sales table, because you have not yet added the salesperson (employee) and the shipping information.

To illustrate the power of the system, you will add a new table (Item), and then build a new relationship that is incorrect. Add a new table for Inventory, and add the SKU column (a common retail abbreviation for stock-keeping unit) used to identify individual products. Right-click the SKU column in the Inventory table and set it as a key. Add the Size and QOH columns to the Inventory table. Set their data types to Single and Integer16 respectively. Now add the SKU column to the Sale table as an intentional error. Create a relationship from Inventory to Sale using the SKU columns.

Choose the Grade/Grade and Mark menu option to save the changes and obtain comments on the design. Again, the design is not finished, so focus on the other error messages. In particular, find the message "Does SKU in table Sale really depend on SaleID?" and double-click it. Figure 2.8 shows the resulting diagnostic screen. The SKU column in the Sale table is highlighted as a potential problem. Indeed, it is an issue, because placing SKU into the Sale table as shown would mean that for each Sale, only one item (SKU) can be sold. Notice that SKU is not part of the primary key. You might

FIGURE 2.8

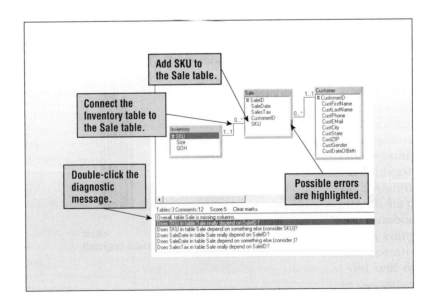

consider setting the SKU as a key column in the Sale table to solve the problem. But that would cause even more problems. For instance, the SaleDate depends only on the SaleID and not on the SKU. If you leave SaleDate in the table with both SaleID and SKU set as keys, you would be declaring that items within a single sale can be sold on different dates.

If you set SKU as a key and resubmit the problem for grading, it will return several messages. One of them will be the question "Does SaleDate in table Sales really depend on SKU?" Notice that sometimes a table has many errors, so you must carefully review the entire table to make sure you fix the primary problems first. The Grade menu also contains an option to generate a separate HTML file that lists all errors by table. This listing is easier to print.

> **Action**
>
> Choose Grade/Grade and Mark.
> Double-click messages in window.
> Fix errors by removing columns and adding new tables.

Primary keys are one of the most difficult things for students to understand when they first start designing databases. In particular, generated keys are tricky. In terms of the database design system, primary keys are critical because they are used to identify the tables. If you make major mistakes in the primary keys, the system will give confusing feedback because it cannot correctly identify your tables. For this reason, it is always best to begin with one or two tables, test them, and then slowly add more tables and relationships.

You still need to fix the problem with the Inventory and Sale table association. In a broad sense, it seems that there should be some type of connection between Inventory item and Sale to indicate which items were purchased by the customer. But placing the SKU attribute into the Sale entity appears to be a bad idea. The reason is straightforward. If there is an association between Inventory and Sale, it must be many-to-many. That is, a Sale can include many items (SKUs), and an Inventory item (SKU) can be sold many times. Relational databases do not handle many-to-many relationships directly. Instead, you must create an intermediary or junction table.

Figure 2.9 shows the creation of the intermediary table. It contains the key columns from both the Inventory (SKU) and Sale (SaleID) tables. Both

FIGURE 2.9

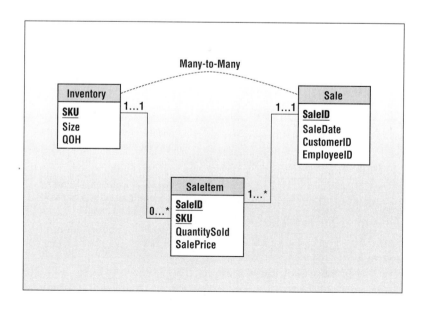

columns are keyed in the new SaleItem table. Examining the keys within the SaleItem tables reveals that each sale can contain many items, and each item can appear on many sales. This is exactly the many-to-many relationship needed. The additional columns of QuantitySold and SalePrice indicate the number of items being purchased and any discounts applied—for an individual item on a specific sale. The dashed many-to-many line is never created; it is simply used here to show the goal of the two relationships.

The new SaleItem table corresponds to the repeating lines of items that you would see listed on a paper sale form. Examining the two new relationships reveals how the table works. Reading from the Sale to the SaleItem table, each sale can contain from one to many items, and in reverse, each SaleItem line (SaleID and SKU) refers to exactly one sale. Essentially the same association exists from Inventory to SaleItem. However, since items might not have been sold, each item can appear on zero to many sales lines, and a given sales line refers to exactly one item. All many-to-many relationships must be split and joined with a junction table that contains the keys from both of the original tables.

Activity: Fix Inventory Design

Return to the database design system and delete the association between Inventory and Sale. Then delete the SKU column from the Sale table. Now you can create the SaleItem table. Simply drag the two keys into the table from the right-hand window—do not attempt to re-create them with a generate key. Finally, build the two new relationships in the Figure 2.9 example.

Action
Create the SaleItem table.
Create the ItemModel table.
Include the proper columns.
Set the keys.
Set the data types.
Grade/Grade and Mark.

If you grade this version, you will see that the detail issues have been corrected. However, some design issues still exist in terms of handling inventory. The inventory for a ski shop is somewhat more complicated than for a typical retail store. In particular, snowboards and skis are sold in varying lengths to match the individual customer. Figure 2.10 shows the two

FIGURE 2.10

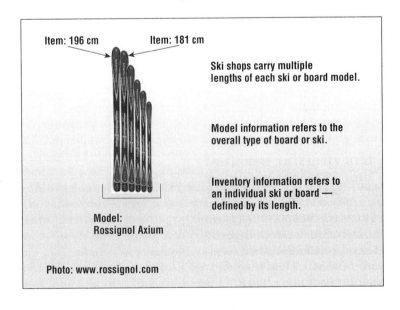

Item: 196 cm   Item: 181 cm

Ski shops carry multiple lengths of each ski or board model.

Model information refers to the overall type of board or ski.

Inventory information refers to an individual ski or board — defined by its length.

Model: Rossignol Axium

Photo: www.rossignol.com

FIGURE 2.11

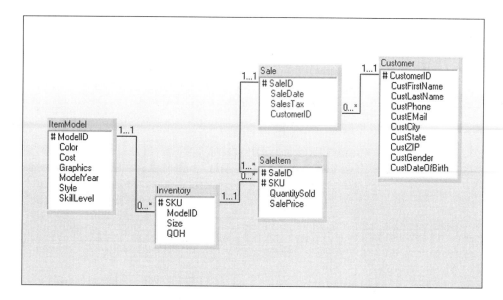

concepts. A manufacturer produces a model line that exhibits certain characteristics such as width, flexibility, and side cut. For a model type, several different lengths are available. From the perspective of the All Powder store, the database has to keep information on each model, but the actual inventory must refer to a specific item or length within the model type. Each item will receive a different SKU. For example, SKU 1173 might refer to a Rossignol Axium ski that is 196 cm in length, while SKU 1174 references a Rossignol Axium ski of 181 cm.

The catch is that it would waste considerable space to repeat all of the model data for every possible size of ski or board. Consequently, it is important to create two entities to handle the details: ItemModel and Inventory. Figure 2.11 shows the basic tables and the resulting relationships. Observe that each model results in many inventory items (multiple sizes of boards or skis), but each item can be only one model type. At this point, you should be able to add more attributes and more tables to the design, but the completion of the design will be left to the next chapter.

Exercises

Crystal Tigers

Crystal Tigers is a service club with about 150 members. The club primarily sponsors events such as community pancake breakfasts, local concerts, and sporting competitions. The club successfully uses the events to raise money for various charitable organizations. The club needs a database to help track the roles of the various members—both in terms of positions within the organization and their work at the events. The following form represents the basic data that needs to be collected.

Last name, First name Phone, Cell phone Address City, State ZIP code		Year	Position/Title	Comment

	Member Activities for Event			
Event title Start date End date Charity Charity contact Phone Amount raised	Date	Hours Activity	Comment	

Analyze the form and create the main classes and associations needed to maintain the data for this organization.

Capitol Artists

Capitol Artists is a partnership among several commercial artists that work on freelance and contract jobs for various clients. Some jobs are contracted at a fixed price, but complex jobs require billing clients for the number of hours involved in the project. To help the artists track the time spent on each project, the firm wants you to build an easy-to-use database. On a given day, the artist should be able to select the time slot, and choose a category and a job. All jobs are given internal numbers, and each job has only one client. But it is helpful to list the client information on the form once the job has been selected. The artist then enters a short task description, the billing rate, and any out-of-pocket expenses. The billing rate is somewhat flexible and depends on the client, the job, the task, and the artist. For example, the company can charge higher rates for an artist's creative work time but lower rates for copying papers. The following form contains the basic information desired.

Employee Last name, First name Date							
Time	Category	Client	Job #	Task description	Hours	Rate	Expenses
8:00 AM	Meeting	Name+Phone	1173				
8:30 AM							
9:00 AM							
9:30 AM							
. . .							

Analyze the form and create the main classes and associations needed to maintain the data for this organization.

Offshore Speed

The Offshore Speed company sells parts and components for high-performance boats. Some of the customers modify the boats for racing; others simply want faster boats for informal races. The engine parts tend to be highly specialized, and new variations are released each year by manufacturers. Compatibility of parts is always a major issue, but most are tested by the manufacturers with data available from their websites. Customers tend to order parts through the store, but sometimes they will buy off-the-shelf components. The store also keeps many spare parts in stock because customers tend to break them often, and the profit margins are good. The store also has arrangements with other firms that can help customers redesign and upgrade interiors and cabins, for example, new upholstery for seats and complete systems for beds and sinks for cabins. Lately, the store has been successful selling and installing high-end GPS and communication systems. The form below is used to place custom orders for the clients. Discounts are given to customers based on several subjective factors that will not be entered into the database.

Customer					Employee		
Last name, First name							
Phone, E-mail					Sale date		
Address					Estimated receive date		
City, State, ZIP							
Boat: Brand, Year, # Engines, length							
Engine 1: Brand, Year, Out drive, Year							
Engine 2: Brand, Year, Out drive, Year							
Manuf.	Mfg part no.	Category	Description	Quantity	List price	Extended	
					Subtotal		
					Tax		
					Discount		
					Total Due		

Analyze the form and create the main classes and associations needed to maintain the data for this organization.

Final Project

The main textbook has an appendix with several longer case studies. You should be able to work on one of these cases throughout the term. If you or your instructor picks one, perform the following task.

Analyze the forms and create the main classes and associations needed to maintain the data for this organization.

Chapter 3

Data Normalization

Chapter Outline

Objectives

- Understand how to use generated keys (sequences).
- Create tables and specify data types.
- Create relationships and specify cascades.
- Establish column constraints and default values.
- Create tables using SQL.
- Estimate the data volume for the database.

FIGURE 3.1

```
OrderIDCustomerID
CustomerOrder(OrderID, CustomerID, . . .)
```

Database Design

The main objective of database design is to define the tables, relationships, and constraints that describe the underlying business rules and efficiently store the data. The normalization rules are critical to properly identifying the columns that belong in each table. The first step is to make sure the keys are correct. A key uniquely identifies the rows in the table. If multiple columns are part of the key, it indicates a many-to-many relationship between the key columns. Note that if a base table contains a generated key column, it is the only column that may be keyed.

If you are uncertain about which columns should be keyed, write them down separately and evaluate the business rules between the two objects. Figure 3.1 shows a typical situation with orders and customers. First ask yourself, For a given order, can there ever be more than one customer? If the answer is "yes" based on the business rules, then you would mark the CustomerID column as key. But most businesses have a rule that each order is placed by only one customer, so CustomerID should not be keyed. Second, reverse the question and ask yourself; For a given customer, can there be more than one order? Obviously, most businesses want customers to place repeat orders, so the answer is "yes." So you mark the OrderID as key. Since only OrderID is keyed, both columns belong in the CustomerOrder table.

Once the keys are correct, you need to check each nonkey column to ensure that it follows the three main normalization rules. First, each column must contain atomic or nonrepeating data, for example, a single phone number, but not multiple values of phone numbers. Second and third, each nonkey column must depend on the whole key and nothing but the key. You need to examine each potential table, determine that the keys are correct, and then check each column to ensure that it depends on the whole key and nothing but the key. If there is a problem, you generally need to split the table. Remember that any time you make a change to the keys in a table, you have to reevaluate all of the columns in that table.

Generated Keys: Sequences

Key columns play a critical role in a relational database. The key values are used as a proxy for the rest of the data. For instance, once you know the CustomerID, the database can quickly retrieve the rest of the customer data. That is why you only need to place the CustomerID column in the CustomerOrder table. However, the database requires key values to be unique. Guaranteeing that key values are never repeated can be a challenging business problem. In some cases, businesses have separate methods to create key values. For instance, the marketing department might have a process to assign identifier numbers to customers and products. But the process must ensure that these values are never duplicated. In many situations, it is easier to have the database generate the key values automatically. In particular, orders often require keys that are generated quickly and accurately.

Oracle has a sophisticated sequence process to generate new key values. You assign a NUMBER type to the primary key in a table where you want the key value created. This data type does not actually create the number. To create numbers, you need to define a sequence that will generate the numbers on demand. The sequence generator is relatively flexible and you can specify a starting value and an increment. The final step is to create a database trigger that automatically gets a newly generated key value and places it into the primary key column. This step is a little trickier since database triggers are covered in a later lab. However, sequences really should be set up when you define the table so that you remember to do it. One of the activities in this lab will show you how to set up an automatically generated key value; you can copy the process for your other projects.

For now, you must carefully identify the key columns that might need generated values. For instance, the CustomerID column in the Customer table, or the OrderID in the Order table might be assigned a generated value. But the CustomerID column in the Order table would never be a generated key. It would be given the same numeric data type, although the actual key generation can take place only in the original (Customer) table. Make sure you understand the difference. The CustomerID is the only column that is a primary key in the Customer table, and it is the source table for customers. Consequently, it is acceptable to generate key values for CustomerID in the Customer table. On the other hand, the CustomerID is a placeholder in the Order table—it represents the customer placing the order. The customer is not created in the Order table, so the CustomerID value cannot be generated in the Order table. The CustomerID must already exist in the Customer table before it can be assigned to a row in the Order table.

Case: All Powder Board and Ski Shop

When you first approach a database design problem, you will often experience one of two perspectives: the project seems immensely complicated, or the project seems too easy. Usually, both perspectives are wrong. Even a difficult project can be handled if you divide it into small enough pieces, and few projects are as easy as they first appear. The main issue is to correctly identify the business rules. And there always seem to be complications with some of the rules. For the All Powder case, consider the issue of customer skill level. Whether a customer is renting or buying a board or skis, the salespeople need to match the person to the proper board or ski based on the customer's skill level. In terms of business decisions, managers need to identify the types of customers to plan for the models and inventory decisions for next season.

As shown in Figure 3.2, consider what happens if you try to place the Style (downhill, half pipe, and so on) and SkillLevel directly into the Customer table. The problem is that the business rules state that each customer can have one skill level in many styles, and each style can apply to more than one customer. For example, customer Jones could be an expert downhill skier, but only a beginner in half-pipe snowboard. However, customer Sanchez is an expert at half pipe, but has never tried any type of skiing. If you place Style and SkillLevel in the Customer table, you might try keying

FIGURE 3.2

Consider what happens if you (incorrectly) try to place Style and SkillLevel in the Customer table:

```
CustomerID, LastName, ... Style, SkillLevel
CustomerID, LastName, ... Style, SkillLevel
```

Business rule: Each customer can have one skill in many styles.
Business rule: Each style can apply to more than one customer.
Need a table with both attributes as keys.

```
CustomerID, LastName, ... Style, SkillLevel
```

But you cannot include LastName, FirstName, and so on, because then you would have to reenter that data for each customer skill.

only CustomerID. But that action would state that each customer participates in only one style, with one skill level. On the other hand, if you key just the Style column, you would be indicating that each style can be performed by only one person. The only solution is to key both the CustomerID and the Style columns. Then, each customer can participate in many styles (with one skill rating per customer per style), and each style can apply to many people (with possibly different skill ratings). But you cannot leave the Style and SkillLevel columns in the main Customer table along with columns such as LastName. It is clear that a customer's last name does not change for each different style. A customer's last name depends only on the CustomerID, so you need to split the tables.

Figure 3.3 shows the resulting design. The Customer table is keyed only by CustomerID and contains attributes that describe each customer. The Style and SkillLevel tables are used as lookup tables to ensure that clerks select from the defined list of choices. Without them, the database would

FIGURE 3.3

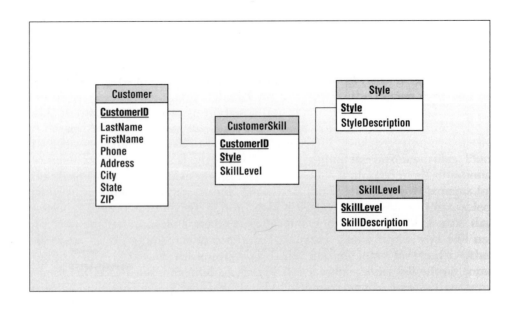

quickly become a mess because everyone would use different spellings and abbreviations for the entries. The CustomerSkill table contains the CustomerID and Style as key columns to support the business rules.

Lab Exercise

All Powder Board and Ski Database Creation

You should use the database design system to refine your table definitions. The system is designed to check the main design rules and ensure that your tables meet the requirements of good database design. However, if you make different assumptions about the underlying business rules, you can create slightly different tables than those recommended by the design system.

Activity: Create Tables

Once you have determined the overall database design, you have to select between the two methods for creating tables in Oracle. The enterprise manager console contains a visual editor that makes it easy to enter column names and select the data types. However, ultimately, the editor converts your choices into an SQL statement that actually creates the table. For some things, the designer is easy to use, but ultimately, you will want to learn the SQL syntax. For now, begin with the designer, and use the Show SQL button to see the statement that it creates. You should copy this statement and paste it into a text file so that you can build up a complete list of all of the tables. This way, if you ever need to re-create the tables, you simply have to execute the text file as a set of SQL statements.

Action
Create Customer table with enterprise manager.
Enter column names.
Select data types.
Assign the primary key.
Create the table.

Figure 3.4 shows the basic elements of the table design screen. Note that if you still have the Customer table created in Chapter 1, you can either edit that table or simply drop it and start over. As you enter the column (field) names, you select the data type from a drop-down list. For text data you should

FIGURE 3.4

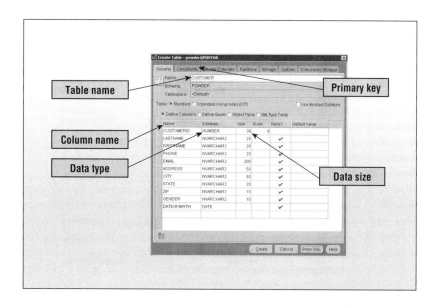

FIGURE 3.5

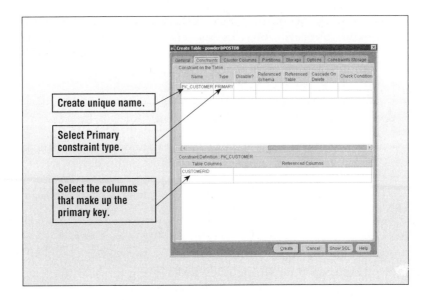

generally use NVARCHAR2 instead of the older VARCHAR2. You never know when someone will want to store names or other data using a different language alphabet. Some data types have size limits. For example, you should specify the maximum number of characters expected in a text column. Oracle will efficiently store the data even if it takes less than the specified number of characters, but it will not allow anyone to enter a value with more than the number entered. Oracle will allow up to 2,000 characters for the NVARCHAR2 data type, but try to be somewhat conservative because Oracle uses those values to set default format widths. One aspect you need to be careful about is that the design editor assumes that all columns are required—do not allow missing (null) values. In general, this assumption is fine for key values, but there will be many times when a clerk will not immediately have a value for a column. In particular, you probably will not have data of birth for all customers. Make sure you check the box to allow nulls for many of the fields.

Primary keys are a little tricky in Oracle, since they are entered as constraints on the table. Figure 3.5 shows the process. Begin by selecting the Constraint tab. Each constraint must have a unique name within the schema. A good way to choose unique names is to begin with a two-letter abbreviation of the constraint type followed by the name of the table. In this case, PK_Customer is the name of the primary key constraint for the Customer table. Choose "Primary" as the type of constraint; the other types will be explained later. The only elements in a primary key constraint are the names of the columns involved, so select those in the lower half of the form. The Customer table has only one key column (CustomerID).

Although Oracle handles all numerical data with the NUMBER data type, you must still be careful about selecting the size and scale of the number. In particular, you have to make a decision about decimal places. If the column will contain only integer values, you enter a zero for the scale since there are no digits to the right of the decimal point. If the column will hold currency data, you will usually specify a scale of 2, but you could use additional digits if you want to examine round-off issues. To get floating point numbers, enter zero for both the size and scale values.

In the All Power case, most skis and boards are measured in centimeters, so the numbers are not overly large. However, some manufacturers might choose to use fractional lengths, so the single-precision floating point is appropriate. This step is sometimes difficult for beginners to catch. If you forget to choose the single-or double-precision subtype, you will not be able to enter fractional values (with decimal points). If you ever encounter that problem, simply return to the Design view and set the proper size and scale values.

Activity: Create Constraints and Default Values

In many cases, you will want the database to enforce the business rules. Placing the rules in the database means that they will be enforced in all situations, without relying on other programs. Figure 3.6 shows the primary elements for setting a condition to ensure gender data is entered consistently. In the constraint section, create a unique name for the constraint and select the CHECK type of constraint. The only other step is to enter the condition to be tested against each row. Almost any SQL condition can be used and they will be explained in detail in Chapter 4. In this example, you want people to enter data from a fixed list of items (female, male, and unidentified). You could probably get by without the "unidentified" option by using null values for that purpose, but it is a litter easier for users if you specify it as a possibility. The condition that enforces this constraint is UPPER(Gender) IN ('FEMALE', 'MALE', 'UNIDENTIFIED'). The UPPER function converts whatever text is entered into all uppercase characters because the comparison is case sensitive. The three acceptable items are entered in the list with single quotes around each word or phrase and separated by commas. You could also make basic numeric comparisons, such as Salary >= 0.

After you have entered the check condition, click the Apply button. If you receive a message indicating there is a syntax error in the condition, modify it until it is correct. Once the constraint has been accepted, you cannot modify it. However, you can delete it and start over. Enter some sample data, including some invalid items, to ensure that the constraint works correctly. Notice that the error message is not very useful to the average user, but it does work.

Action
Select the Constraints tab.
Enter unique name: CK_CUSTGENDER.
Select CHECK as the type.
Enter check condition:
Upper(Gender) IN ('FEMALE', 'MALE', 'UNIDENTIFIED').
Click the Apply button.
Test the constraint with sample data.

FIGURE 3.6

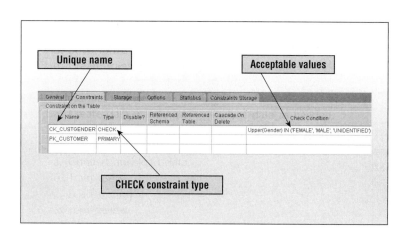

Notice that it is also easy to specify default values. These are values that you want entered whenever the user does not provide a value for the specified column. The user can override the default value and enter something else, but it is often convenient to display a commonly used value to save time for users entering data. For example, a SaleDate can be set to the SYSDATE function so that the current date is automatically entered. You can create default values for your tables, but they will not work the way you expect in the enterprise manager editor. That tool does not display the default values and instead enters blank values. Later, when you use SQL, you will see that you do not have to specify a value for a column assigned a default value.

Activity: Create Tables with SQL

It is relatively easy to create tables in Oracle with the design screen in the enterprise manager. However, if you click the Show SQL button, you will see that the table is actually being created in SQL. The design screen simply takes your choices and converts them into the proper SQL syntax. Eventually, you will find several advantages to simply creating the tables in SQL yourself. For starters, all you need is a simple system to execute SQL commands instead of the visually oriented design screen. You can quickly build and execute SQL commands and send them across the Internet when you are thousands of miles away from the main database machine. Also, some options are easier to control by entering them directly into the SQL—instead of trying to figure out how to get the designer to understand what you want. But probably the most important reason for using plain SQL is that you can create and store the statements in a simple text file. Whenever you need to rebuild the tables, you simply execute the file and all of the tables will be created. Figure 3.7 shows the SQL statement that creates the Customer table with the primary key and gender constraints. Notice that the syntax for the columns is straightforward. Simply list the column name followed by its data type. The columns are separated by commas. If the column names are reserved words or contain special characters you must put double quotes (" ") around the name.

FIGURE 3.7

```
CREATE TABLE Customer
(
  CustomerID       NUMBER(12),
  LastName         NVARCHAR2(25),
  FirstName        NVARCHAR2(25),
  Phone            NVARCHAR2(25),
  Email            NVARCHAR2(120),
  Address          NVARCHAR2(50),
  City             NVARCHAR2(50),
  State            NVARCHAR2(25),
  ZIP              NVARCHAR2(15),
  Gender           NVARCHAR2(15),
  DateOfBirth      DATE,
  CONSTRAINT pk_Customer PRIMARY KEY (CustomerID),
  CONSTRAINT ck_CustGender
    CHECK (Upper(Gender) IN ('FEMALE', 'MALE', 'UNIDENTIFIED'))
);
```

FIGURE 3.8

```
CREATE TABLE ProductCategory
(
  Category              NVARCHAR2(50),
  CategoryDescription   NVARCHAR2(250),
    CONSTRAINT pk_ProductCategory PRIMARY KEY (Category)
);
```

The primary key constraint is straightforward. It is identified with the CONSTRAINT keyword followed by the name of the constraint (pk_Customer) and the type of constraint (PRIMARY KEY). The key columns are then listed in parentheses. If there are multiple columns, they are separated with commas. The check constraint on the gender column is similar. Some people prefer to write it directly beneath the Gender column, but it is equally easy to read if all check constraints are listed at the end of the definition. Again, it is straightforward: begin with the CONSTRAINT keyword and its unique name. Add the CHECK keyword and follow it by the condition to be evaluated. Check constraints are used to specify one type of business rules and to ensure that the database retains consistent data.

> **Action**
>
> Start the Windows Wordpad program.
> Type the **CREATE TABLE** commands.
> Save the file as ProductCategory.sql.
> Start the Oracle SQL Plus program.
> Log in as the All Powder developer.
> Enter the command to execute your file:
> @<directory location>
> ProductCategory.sql.

For practice, you should create the ProductCategory table shown in Figure 3.8 using the SQL statements. The most powerful aspect of using SQL is that you can have a file of commands that you can execute on a different machine to create the tables. To illustrate the process, start a text editor (Wordpad) and type in the commands to create the ProductCategory table. You do not have to worry about tab spacing, but the alignment does make the command easier to read in the file. You do have to be extremely careful about commas and parentheses. Also, notice that you must include the semicolon at the end of the command. Save the file as "ProductCategory.sql."

Now, start the Oracle SQL Plus program that executes SQL commands. You should find a link to it under the Application Development folder in the start menu, but you should also consider placing a shortcut on your desktop—you will use it often. Once you log in you will see a mostly blank screen with an SQL> prompt. You could just type in the commands at this point, but the editor is a little cumbersome and it does not automatically save the commands. To run the text file with the SQL command, you simply enter an at sign (@) followed by the name of the file. However, you will have to specify the full pathname of the file. For example, if you saved the file on the C drive in a Temp folder, the command would be: @C:\Temp\ProductCategory.sql. The command will execute in a couple of seconds and it will tell you that the table has been created. However, if you receive any error messages, return to the text file and make sure the commas and parentheses are correct.

If you want to remove the table, simply type DROP TABLE ProductCategory; at the prompt and the table will be removed. When you are done, type EXIT and the SQL Plus program will close.

There is one more critical step in creating Oracle tables. You have to tell Oracle to build indexes and analyze the data patterns so that it can efficiently create queries. The details of using indexes and improving Oracle performance are covered in other labs. However, without this step, Oracle

FIGURE 3.9

```
ANALYZE TABLE ProductCategory COMPUTE STATISTICS;
```

performance is relatively slow, so you should run one additional command after creating a table. This command should be run from SQL and you can easily include it in the SQL file to create the table. Figure 3.9 shows the Analyze Table command for the ProductCategory table. Each table should have a similar command.

Relationships

Activity: Define Relationships

Relationships in Oracle and SQL can be somewhat difficult to see, since there is no visual representation. In the database design system class diagram or an entity-relationship diagram, relationships are shown as a line between two tables. Figure 3.10 shows a typical relationship between the Department and Employee tables. Employees are assigned to a department, but the department comes from a list in the Department table. In this example, the Department column in the Employee table is a foreign key because it refers to a primary key in a second table. The Department table is the reference table because it supplies the data to the Employee table.

Relationships are created in Oracle by defining foreign key constraints. In this example, any department value entered into the Employee table must already exist in the Department table. Any other value would be invalid and an error message will be presented to the user. Creating a foreign key constraint has the same requirement: You must first define the reference table before you can create the foreign key relationship. In this case, you must first create the Department table. At a minimum, the Department table should have a Department column as the primary key. You might also consider adding a Description column in case the names of the departments need a longer explanation. You can create this table with the designer or with SQL. Just remember that it must be created before the Employee table is defined!

You can build a foreign key constraint in the enterprise manager design screen when you create the Employee table. First, enter the columns and data types for the Employee table. Then create the primary key constraint

FIGURE 3.10

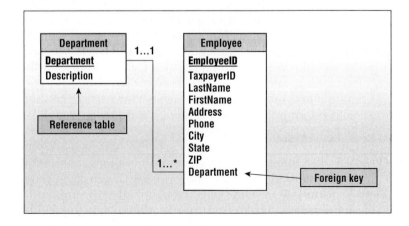

FIGURE 3.11

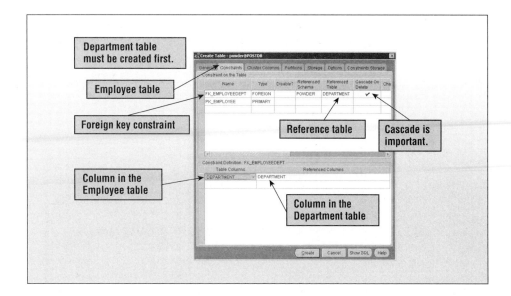

to define the EmployeeID as the primary key column. Figure 3.11 shows the elements needed to create the foreign key relationship from the Employee table to the Department table. As usual, enter a unique name for the constraint (FK_EmployeeDept) and set the type as a foreign key. To select the reference table, you must first select the schema; then you can select the Department table from the list.

Action
Create the Department table.
Be sure the Department column is keyed.
Create the Employee table.
Set EmployeeID as a primary key constraint.
Create a new foreign key constraint.
Name it FK_EmployeeDept.
Select the current schema.
Select the Department table as a reference.
Check the Cascade On Delete option.
Select Department as the Employee table column.
Select Department as the Department table column.
Create or Alter the table.

Be sure that you check the Cascade Delete option. With this option enabled, if anyone deletes a department from the Department table, the DBMS will automatically remove all employees in that department. Why? To ensure consistency of the data. If the department no longer exists, then you cannot say that employees belong to that department. Cascade deletions save you an enormous amount of grief in the long run because they keep the data accurate. However, deleting one row of data in a high-level table could result in the deletion of huge chunks of the database. Later, you will learn how to assign security permissions to the tables so that only a few people will be allowed to delete departments.

The next step is to switch to the lower half of the form and select the Department column in the Employee table and the Department column in the Department table to show exactly how the tables are related. Click the Create or Alter button to establish the foreign key constraint.

You can also create foreign key relationships within SQL. If you click the Show SQL button in the table designer, you can see the syntax. Foreign key relationships are the main reason that it is often easier to create tables within a text file first and then execute the text file. Remember that the tables must be created in a specific order. In this example, the Department table has to be defined before the Employee table. You could go back in the designer and alter a table to set a new relationship, but it is much safer to define everything at one time. With a text file, you save the entire database structure and

FIGURE 3.12

```
CREATE TABLE Department
(
  Department       NVARCHAR2(50),
  Description      NVARCHAR2(150),
    CONSTRAINT pk_Department PRIMARY KEY (Department)
);
CREATE TABLE Employee
(
  EmployeeID       NUMBER(12),
  TaxpayerID       NVARCHAR2(50),
  LastName         NVARCHAR2(25),
  FirstName        NVARCHAR2(25),
  Address          NVARCHAR2(50),
  Phone            NVARCHAR2(25),
  City             NVARCHAR2(50),
  State            NVARCHAR2(15),
  ZIP              NVARCHAR2(15),
  Department       NVARCHAR2(50)
    DEFAULT 'Sales',
  CONSTRAINT pk_Employee PRIMARY KEY (EmployeeID),
  CONSTRAINT fk_DepartmentEmployee FOREIGN KEY (Department)
    REFERENCES Department(Department)
    ON DELETE CASCADE
);
```

re-create it almost instantly. Figure 3.12 shows the SQL to create the Department and Employee tables. The foreign key constraint is straightforward, but you have to enter the keywords in the specified order. You begin with the CONSTRAINT keyword followed by the name of the constraint as usual. The FOREIGN KEY phrase specifies the type of constraint, and it is followed by the name of the column (or columns) in the Employee table that is affected by the constraint. The keyword REFERENCES is followed by the name of the reference table (Department), and the column referred to is listed in parentheses. Note the use of the ON DELETE CASCADE command to set the Cascade option. One table can have several relationships with other tables. You simply list each one as a new foreign key constraint.

Figure 3.12 also shows how to specify a default value for the Department column. In this case, employees will be assigned to the Sales department if no other value is entered. Of course, you should make sure that the Sales department is listed in the Department table.

At this point, you should create all of the All Powder tables in Oracle. You can use the table designer to help you get started, but you should look at the SQL and copy it into a text file. Then, if anything goes wrong or you need to make substantial changes to the design, you can drop all of the existing tables and start over. Make any necessary changes to the text file, then return to SQL Plus and execute the file to rebuild all of the tables.

Activity: Estimate the Database Size

At some point, you need to estimate the size of the database project. Of course, any estimate at this early stage will be very rough. Your goal is not to be perfect, but to be able to categorize the overall project size. The

FIGURE 3.13

CustomerID	NUMBER(12)	8
LastName	NVARCHAR(50)	30
FirstName	NVARCHAR(50)	20
Phone	NVARCHAR(50)	24
Email	NVARCHAR(150)	100
Address	NVARCHAR(50)	50
State	NVARCHAR(50)	4
ZIP	NVARCHAR(15)	20
Gender	NVARCHAR(15)	20
DateOfBirth	Date	7
Average bytes per customer		283
Customers per week (winter)		*200
Weeks (winter)		*25
Bytes added per year		1,415,000

information will help you identify the basic category of database server and perhaps narrow your choice of tools. In particular, it will help you determine how much disk space you need to purchase, and whether you will need more servers and faster processors. Note that with Oracle, the database administrator has to set aside table space files to hold the data, so it helps to have some idea of the storage requirements early in the process.

To estimate the database size, you begin by estimating the size of each data table. You must already know which columns belong to each table. Figure 3.13 shows the process for the Customer table. Some of the column size estimates are straightforward. Look back to Chapter 2 for a reminder that a long integer uses 4 bytes of storage in Access. The text columns are a little trickier. For instance, although the database will allow up to 50 characters of text for the last name, almost no names will actually be that long. Instead, you need to estimate the average length of customer last names. You could use existing data, or perhaps a sample from a phone book. Perhaps an average last name is 15 characters long. But the DBMS stores text in Unicode format, which requires 2 physical bytes of storage for each character, so the average storage space needed for a last name is 30 bytes. Use a similar process to estimate the number of bytes needed to store an average row of customer data.

Action
Create a spreadsheet.
Enter table names as rows.
Add columns for: Bytes, Rows, Totals.
Calculate the bytes per table row.
Estimate the number of rows.
Compute the table and overall totals.

Next, you need to estimate how many new customers will arrive each year. In a real case, you could look at past records or talk with the expert users. Here, assume it is about 200 per week, but there are only 25 weeks of the ski season; so there are about 5,000 new customers a year. Multiplying the estimated number of customers by the size of an average row yields the initial data size of the Customer table to be about 1 million bytes.

You need to follow a similar process for all of the tables in the case. Figure 3.14 lists some of the basic assumptions you can use. You should build a spreadsheet that lists each table, the average number of bytes per row, the estimated number of rows, and the total estimated size for the table. There is still some flexibility in the final number, but your estimate should be around 5 to 6 megabytes. Remember that this is data for only one year.

FIGURE 3.14

> 200 customers per week for 25 weeks
> 2 skills per customer
> 2 rentals per customer per year
> 3 items per rental
> 20 percent of customers buy items
> 4 items per sale
> 100 manufacturers
> 20 models per manufacturer
> 5 items (sizes) per model

Also, additional space will be required for indexes, overhead, queries, forms, and reports. But even if the final number is closer to 20 megabytes, Oracle can easily handle this database on a PC-based server.

Exercises

Many Charms

Samantha and Madison want you to build the database for their charms sales. They emphasized that the system has to be easy to use. They also pointed out that a key element of their business is tracking all of the products and the various suppliers, and monitoring the costs so they can set their prices accurately. They are also concerned about monitoring how quickly items sell. They figure they will need to start with at least 200 basic charms initially, but most charms come in two sizes, along with the different metals. When asked, they are uncertain how many customers they will have, but would like to get at least 50 sales a week. Although some of the sales might be small, they hope to build a solid list of clients who return for new purchases on a monthly basis. To encourage return customers, they are thinking about offering some type of frequent-buyer program, where, after purchasing a specified number of charms, customers receive discounts or maybe a free charm.

1. Define the final tables needed for this case.
2. Create the database.
3. Estimate the size of the database for one year of operation.

Standup Foods

Laura's business has been established for several years. Many of her clients are old customers, and she has a couple of thousand in her files—although some have gone out of business. Her business has grown considerably based on referrals from existing clients. She gets so many good comments and referrals, she is thinking that she needs to track which customers pass her name on to others so she can call them or send thank-you gifts. But her more immediate concern is tracking employees. Over the course of a year, she has a relatively high turnover in some positions. Other employees have been with her for years. In total, she probably deals with 400 to 500 employees a year. Employees are rated after each job, and typically employees work 15 to 20 jobs a year for her. On average, employees tend to have three tasks per event. For instance, a driver will also be a server, and probably a busboy or dishwasher. They are evaluated on 10 items for each task they perform, as well as an overall rating. Client food preferences are somewhat complex, so Laura wants the ability to add free-form comments to cover extreme cases. But some common elements arise, such as allergies to nuts, so she wants to keep itemized lists as well—both for desired items and forbidden items. Some clients are easygoing, but this is Hollywood, so many have long lists of items—often ranging to 50 or even 100 items.

1. Define the final tables needed for this case.
2. Create the database.
3. Estimate the size of the database for one year of operation.

EnviroSpeed

For good or bad, Tyler and Brennan have been busy. Their firm has been averaging 4 to 5 cleanups a week. While there are not many permanent employees (fewer than 100), they have close associations with about 200 experts in various areas. All of these people need access to the environmental documents and other information. Additionally, about 400 crews around the world are called in to work on various problems. The crews consist of 10 to 20 people. Initially, experts are the ones contributing the most information. Sometimes an expert will contribute hundreds of pages of documents and comments. Once an incident is opened, most of the new data and the searches come from the emergency crews. Time schedules, environmental factors, and comments can arrive quickly from all of the crew members. Some of the notes are on paper and saved until the emergency is over, when clerks enter the basic data. A typical incident can generate dozens of pages of notes and schedules from each crew member. Although there are hundreds of possible chemicals, the firm has found that only about 50 major chemicals are typically involved in critical incidents. One important aspect of this case is the need for experts and crew members to search through documentation based on keywords. For example, crews will need to search for certain chemicals, possibly in combination with other chemicals, and often include the type of problem, such as water or road spill. Brennan estimates a typical document needs to include at least 20 keywords to identify the exact purpose of the document.

1. Define the final tables needed for this case.
2. Create the database.
3. Estimate the size of the database for one year of operation.

Final Project

The main textbook has an appendix with several longer case studies. You should be able to work on one of these cases throughout the term. If you or your instructor picks one, perform the following tasks.

1. Finalize your database design.
2. Create the tables in the DBMS.
3. Estimate the amount of data that might be generated for one year.

Chapter

Data Queries

Chapter Outline

Objectives
Database Queries
Case: All Powder Board and Ski Shop
Lab Exercise
  *All Powder Board and Ski Data
  Computations and Subtotals*
Exercises
Final Project

Objectives

- Create or import sample data into a database.
- Create basic queries to answer common business questions.
- Use joins to create multitable queries.
- Use queries to perform simple calculations.
- Answer business questions involving totals and subtotals.

Database Queries

Relational databases are designed to efficiently store data. Efficiency results in splitting the data into many tables, interconnected by the data. Consequently, you need a good query system to retrieve data. SQL is a powerful standard designed to perform several tasks in retrieving and manipulating data in relational database systems. Most modern systems implement some version of SQL. The catch is that the standard continues to evolve, and it takes time for the DBMS vendors to catch up. Also, vendors tend to include proprietary extensions to provide additional features. At one time, Oracle included a visually oriented QBE system, but as of 9i, it no longer exists as a stand-alone system. So you really need to learn and understand the straight-text SQL. The logic of SQL is the same as for QBE, but it can be cumbersome because you have to type more text. Also, the JOIN statements are a little more confusing in SQL.

Oracle has three related methods to enter SQL commands: (1) SQL Plus, (2) SQL Plus Worksheet, and (3) command-line sqlplus. In general, you will find the SQL Plus Worksheet easier to use for most queries because it displays the results in a separate window and the SQL is relatively easy to edit. However, SQL Worksheet does not support running-text files (with the @file.sql command), so in real life you will end up using SQL Plus. The command-line version is particularly useful if you need to connect to the database across the Internet or if you need to build a batch file to process SQL commands. If you use SQL Plus, you must remember to enter the semicolon (;) to signify the end of the SQL command. You should also use the semicolon in SQL Plus Worksheet, but you have to click the Execute button to run the commands.

There is one other important issue you need to know about Oracle SQL. You often need to issue a COMMIT command to ensure that your changes are written to the database. It is part of the transaction processing system that is explained in more detail in Chapter 7.

This chapter focuses on the data retrieval aspects of queries. SQL can also be used for data definition (e.g., CREATE TABLE) and for data manipulation (e.g., UPDATE and DELETE). These features and more complex queries are covered in Chapter 5. Once you learn the foundations of queries presented in this chapter, the other topics are easier to understand.

In any database, when you are writing queries, it helps to have a copy of the class (relationship) diagram handy. One of the more difficult aspects to creating a query is to find which tables hold the data you need. This problem is one of the reasons it is so important to label your tables and columns carefully when you create the database. Managers need to be able to identify the tables and columns that match the business questions. With dozens or even hundreds of tables with confusing or abbreviated names, it can be difficult to find the correct data.

Case: All Powder Board and Ski Shop

Before you can build queries, you need data in the tables. Even with a small number of tables, it is time-consuming to create reasonable data. You have to match the foreign keys across the relationships. For instance, it is straightforward to create basic customer data, although it would take a while to type in data for a thousand customers. Then, when you want sales data, you have to select CustomerID values from the existing list. You also have to create ski and board models, generate data for items with appropriate attributes, and then choose the proper ID values for the sales and rentals. In a typical business project, you can test the database with a few dozen examples, and then wait for the business to generate real data to analyze. In a class setting, it is better to use sample data. For that reason, sample data is available for the tables in the All Powder case. The one catch is that your tables might not contain exactly the same columns. So you might have to edit the data slightly in Excel before you import it into your database. This data was randomly generated with specially built generators. The business interpretations might not be useful, but the dataset is consistent.

Lab Exercise

All Powder Board and Ski Data

At this point, the main tables of your database should be similar to those in Figure 4.1, although several supporting tables have been removed from the figure. The Manufacturer, Customer, Sale, and SaleItem tables are common to most business databases. The Rental and RentItem tables simply mirror the sale aspects. The Inventory and ItemModel tables arose because of the characteristics of the board and ski products.

FIGURE 4.1

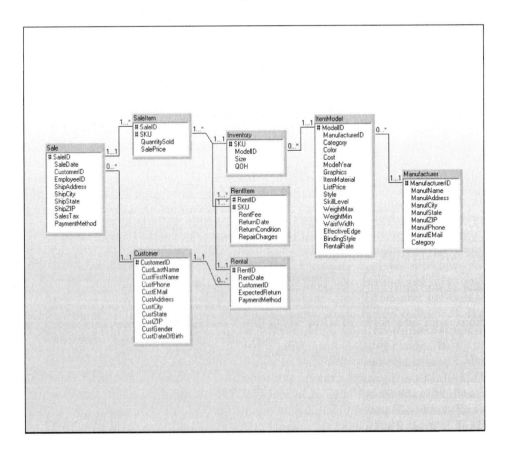

To save time and effort, sample data files are provided on the main text-book CD for each of these tables, plus the common supporting tables. Unfortunately, Oracle 9i does not have an easy-to-use system for importing data. However, Oracle 9i now supports external tables. The files for each of these tables are stored in the standard comma-separated values (CSV) format. Oracle can open these flat files and read data from them as external tables. The syntax for defining these tables is a little tricky—particularly when dates are involved. Rather than force you to enter all of the commands by hand, you can run an SQL file that will create the internal Oracle tables, define the external data tables, and transfer the data from the files into the main Oracle tables. There are two complications: (1) The internal tables created by the SQL script might conflict with tables you have already created, and (2) You need to edit the main script file to enter the directory location of the CSV data files.

Activity: Import Data

To begin, you should copy all of the files in the BuildAllPowder folder (including the subfolder) to a folder on the computer running Oracle SQL Plus. To simplify the process, the best approach is to start with a clean schema. Notably, you should delete any tables that might conflict with the new tables. The easiest way to delete the tables is to run the included SQL script file DropAll-PowderTablesOracle.sql. Your other option is to check the names in that file and see if any conflict with tables that you already have, then rename your tables.

Action
Copy files from BuildAllPowder.
Drop or rename conflicting tables.
Set the directory name to point to the CSV files in BuildAllPowderOracle.sql.
Start SQL Plus (not the worksheet).
@@BuildAllPowderOracle.sql.

The second required step is to edit the BuildAllPowderOracle.sql file in Wordpad. This file contains a line (line number 10) that lists the directory that holds the CSV files. You have to open the file using a simple text editor (Wordpad), and change the directory so that it matches the location on the server that holds the CSV files. Make sure the directory is delimited by single quotes (' ') and be sure to include the full pathname including the drive letter. Save the file.

The rest of the installation is relatively automatic. Start SQL Plus and tell it to run the build file by entering the command @<pathname>Build-AllPowderOracle.sql, where <pathname> is the directory holding the file, for example, @d:\myfiles\BuildAllPowder\BuildAllPowderOracle.sql.

After a minute or two, the tables should be created, the data copied, and the tables analyzed to improve performance. You should not receive any error messages. If you do see errors, they are probably due to an incorrect directory name. As you can see in Figure 4.2, after the SQL script has completed with no errors, the tables and indexes that were created will be displayed in the enterprise manager console.

If you ever need to transfer files and the database structure to a different computer, this approach is a useful solution. As long as you can export the data as a CSV file, you can use a similar set of scripts to transfer the data. At some point you should examine the SQL files to see how the transfer is accomplished. But it is best to wait until after the next couple of labs.

Activity: Create Basic Queries

Creating a query requires that you translate a business question into a format the query system can process. Sometimes this step is straightforward;

FIGURE 4.2

at other times it is difficult. It helps if you format your query in terms of the four main questions: (1) What do you want to see? (2) What do you know or what are the constraints? (3) What tables hold the data? (4) How are the tables connected? In Oracle, these questions are all entered using SQL text commands. As shown in Figure 4.3, SQL Plus Worksheet provides the easiest editor for creating and modifying SQL commands. You enter SQL statements separated by commas in the top half of the screen. When you click the Execute button, the results of the query and any messages show up in the bottom window of the form. You can remove all text from a window by clicking on the window and selecting the Edit/Clear All menu option.

As you work through the queries in this lab, you will want to keep two things handy: (1) the list of tables in the database and (2) the syntax chart for SQL statements.

FIGURE 4.3

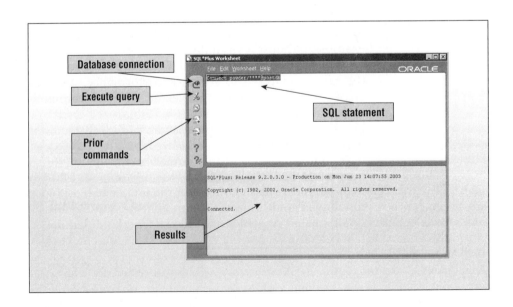

FIGURE 4.4

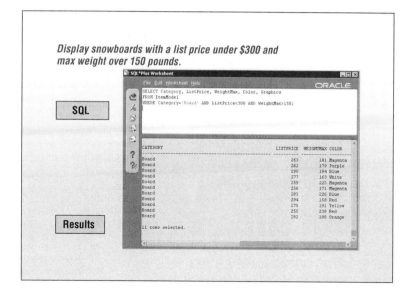

Display snowboards with a list price under $300 and max weight over 150 pounds.

SQL

```
SELECT Category, ListPrice, WeightMax, Color, Graphics
FROM ItemModel
WHERE Category='Board' AND ListPrice<300 AND WeightMax>150;
```

Results

CATEGORY	LISTPRICE	WEIGHTMAX	COLOR
Board	263	161	Magenta
Board	262	179	Purple
Board	290	194	Blue
Board	277	163	White
Board	259	223	Magenta
Board	256	171	Magenta
Board	283	226	Blue
Board	294	158	Red
Board	270	191	Yellow
Board	255	239	Red
Board	292	188	Orange

11 rows selected.

Action
Clear the windows.
Enter SELECT . . . FROM . . . WHERE.
Type the select columns: Category, ListPrice, WeightMax, Color, and Graphics.
Enter conditions: Category='Board' AND ListPrice<300 AND WeightMax>150.
Enter ItemModel on the FROM line.
Run the query.

Begin with a straightforward query: Display the snowboards with a list price under $300 for riders over 150 pounds. The potential buyer wants to know what color and graphics are available for boards that meet those conditions. The most difficult step in this query is to identify the table and columns that match the conditions. For example, snowboards are identified by the Category column in the ItemModel table. If you examine the data, you will see a "Board" entry for each item that is a snowboard. The list price, maximum weight, color, and graphics columns are also in the ItemModel table.

Figure 4.4 shows the basic query and the results. To create the query, first enter the main three SQL keywords on separate lines: SELECT, FROM, and WHERE. Now you can build the query simply by filling in the blanks after those keywords. Generally, determining what you want to see (SELECT) is straightforward, so enter the column names on that row: Category, ListPrice, WeightMax, Color, and Graphics. Next, enter the criteria given for the problem on the WHERE line: Category='Board' AND ListPrice<300 AND WeightMax>150. Note that text qualifiers (Board) have to be enclosed in single quote marks (' '). Also remember to put the semicolon (;) at the end of the statement. Finally, check the column names in the SELECT and WHERE statements and see which tables they fall in. In this case, all of them are in the ItemModel table, so simply enter that table name on the FROM line. Run the query to see the 11 boards that meet the conditions.

Action
Add format statements above the SELECT command.
Column Category Format A12;
Column ListPrice Format $9999.00;
Execute the query.

Notice that the columns do not fit on the screen very well. Of course, you can stretch the window so that more of the output is visible, but there will be limits when you are dealing with multiple columns. You can scroll the window horizontally to see the rest, but sometimes, it is useful to reformat the column widths so more data fits into one window without scrolling.

FIGURE 4.5

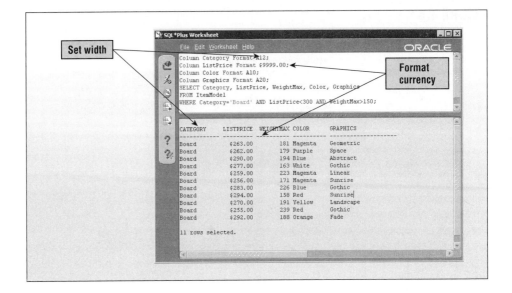

Before the SELECT statement, you can specify a column width using the COLUMN command. For example, Column Category Format A12; specifies a 12-character width for the Category column. Figure 4.5 shows that you can use similar commands to format numeric data and prices. Just remember to set the format statements above the SELECT query. You can find more details about the types of formats in the Oracle documentation. If you do not set the column widths, the alphanumeric columns will default to the maximum width specified in the table declaration. Often, this number is extremely wide and the output is nearly impossible to read. You will often want to set column formats to make the results easier to read.

Activity: Create and Test Multiple Boolean Conditions

Action
Clear any existing SQL and results.
Enter the keywords SELECT, FROM, WHERE.
SELECT Category, Color, ItemMaterial, Style, ListPrice.
Enter ItemModel as the table on the FROM line.
Enter conditions: Category='Ski' And Style='Jump' And ItemMaterial='Composite'.
Run the query to ensure it works.
Add the conditions for Color='Yellow' and ListPrice<300.
Test the query.
Add the conditions for Color='Red' and ListPrice<400.
Add the correct parentheses.
Run the query and test it.

Interpreting business questions can sometimes be difficult because of the ambiguity of natural languages. It is one of the reasons SQL remains so important. SQL requires you to specify exactly what you want to see and to write the conditions mathematically. Of course, these conditions can become relatively long when the business question is complex. Consider a customer who wants skis for jumping. She wants them made from composite materials, and the main color can be red or yellow. She does not want to spend more than $300, but if they are red, she is willing to pay up to $400.

Begin with a new query, and again recognize that all of the attributes are in the ItemModel table. Looking through the data, the first three conditions are straightforward: the Category is Ski, the ItemMaterial is Composite, and the Style is Jump. The colors appear to be straightforward, except that the choice is connected with Or. Whenever a query contains both And and Or conditions, you must be careful, so start with basic conditions

FIGURE 4.6

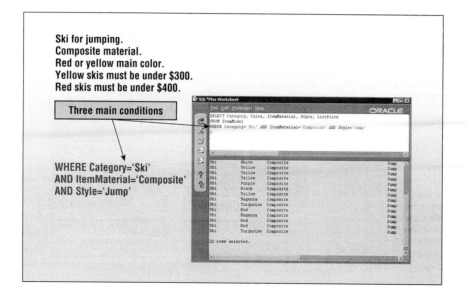

and check the results as you go. Figure 4.6 shows the initial query with the three main conditions that must always hold (ski, jump, and composite).

Now you can think about how to add the other two aspects of the question. Yellow skis are required to cost less than $300, so what happens if you add both conditions to the query? Figure 4.7 shows the query and the results. Since all of the conditions are on the same Criteria row, all five must be true at the same time. So, the query returns only yellow skis.

To see the red skis, you have to add the option of Red as a color, but you also have to establish the higher acceptable price for red skis. The solution is to use parentheses. Anytime you encounter a query that contains both And and Or connectors, you will have to use parentheses to specify how the conditions are grouped. Remember from algebra that conditions inside the innermost parentheses are evaluated first. The key in this example is to group

FIGURE 4.7

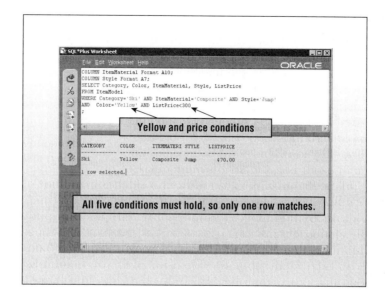

FIGURE 4.8

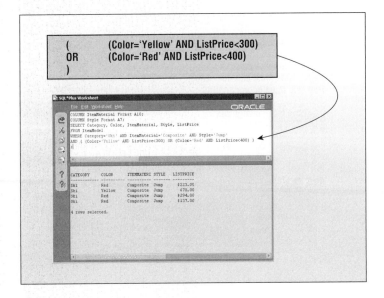

the color yellow with its price condition and group the color red with its price condition. As shown in Figure 4.8, you also need to put parentheses around both of these new groups. If you leave out these last major grouping parentheses, the query will return yellow jumping skis or any red ski less than $400. The final query shows that four skis match the conditions. Check them carefully to ensure that all conditions are met. Even if all of the skis in the result are acceptable, how do you know if the query found all of the matches? This question highlights one of the difficulties of any query language. The only way you know if the query is right is if you carefully build it step-by-step and test the individual steps. In this example, the first query was straightforward and ignored color and price constraints. It returned 20 matches, so the four matches returned by the final query seems like a reasonable number. In this case, the two sets are small enough that you can check the results by hand.

Activity: Use Multiple Tables in a Query

Relational databases require the tables to be carefully designed so that the DBMS can efficiently store large amounts of data. This process entails placing data into multiple tables. Consequently, a key feature of SQL is its ability to join the tables to make it easy to retrieve data from many tables with one query. Oracle 9i supports the SQL standard for joining tables. As it is the easiest to understand, it will be used here. The older Oracle syntax is shown at the end of this section because you will still see many queries in Oracle that use it.

To understand the join process, create a new query using just the Sale table. The objective is to find all of the sales in May that were made with a cash payment. Figure 4.9 shows the initial query. Note the use of the Between clause to specify the month of May. Also observe the date format carefully. It is generally easiest to use the standard Oracle date format (dd-Mon-yyyy). If you want to use a different format, you need to use the TO_DATE function to specify the conversion method. For example, each date could be replaced with TO_DATE('01/05/2004', 'mm/dd/yyyy').

FIGURE 4.9

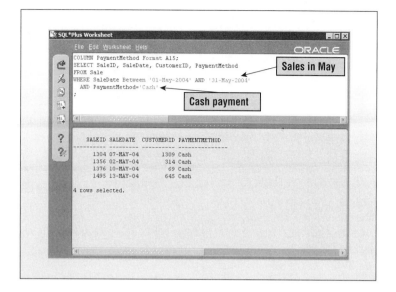

Action

Start with a blank query.
Add SELECT, FROM, WHERE.
Set SaleID, SaleDate, CustomerID, and PaymentMethod.
Use only the Sale table.
Set the SaleDate between 01-May-2004 AND 31-May-2004.
Set PaymentMethod to Cash.
Run the query to test it.

Action

Add the INNER JOIN line after FROM.
Add the Customer table.
Add the join condition: ON Sale.CustomerID = Customer.CustomerID.
Change to Sale.CustomerID on the SELECT statement.
Add Customer LastName and FirstName to the SELECT statement.
Run the query to test it.

Observe that the query returns the CustomerID. But no one is going to memorize CustomerID numbers. Instead, you need to look up the matching customer names. If you look at the relationship diagram (part of it is shown in Figure 4.1), you find that the CustomerID and matching names are stored in the Customer table. Now you could take each of the ID values returned by the Sale query and create a new query on the Customer table and manually enter the values to find the names. However, the table JOIN command is much easier and more powerful to use.

In the SQL query, add the INNER JOIN line that adds the Customer table and specifies how it is connected to the Sale table: INNER JOIN Customer ON Sale.CustomerID = Customer.CustomerID. You will also have to add the table prefix to the CustomerID column in the SELECT statement: Sale.CustomerID. Finally, add the Customer LastName and FirstName columns to the SELECT phrase.

Figure 4.10 shows the basic query design. Once the tables are joined correctly, you can add any column to the other clauses. In this case, place the Customer Last-Name and FirstName columns in the SELECT clause. Run the query to see that the DBMS automatically looks up the names that match the ID values. If you want to double-check the lookup, you can add the CustomerID column from the Customer table and see that it matches the CustomerID values from the Sale table. Just be sure to specify the table name (Customer.CustomerID).

To see the power of the SQL joins, consider a slightly more challenging business question: Which customers bought Atomic skis in January or February? Note that Atomic is the name of a ski manufacturer. Before leaping into the SQL, it is best to think about the query and look at the

FIGURE 4.10

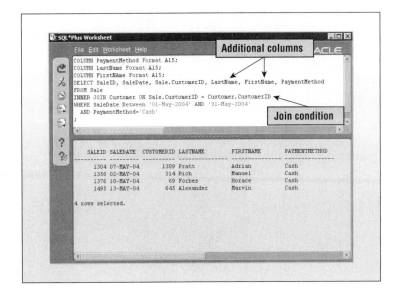

relationship screen for a minute. As shown in Figure 4.11, begin with what you want to see: the names of the customers. These are in the Customer table. Now, what facts do you know? In this case, you are given the name of the manufacturer, the ItemModel.Category, and the range for the SaleDate. You should also begin writing down the tables you need to provide these facts: Customer, Sale, ItemModel, and Manufacturer so far. When you examine the relationships for the database, you will see that these four tables are not enough—they do not connect together. You will also need the SaleItem and Inventory tables.

Figure 4.12 shows the final query in Design view. Notice the large number of tables involved. But, you need to verify that each connection is correct for the specific problem. Once the tables have been selected and joined, you can quickly place the columns you need on the query grid, and then enter the desired conditions. Running the query reveals the two people who meet the desired conditions. The join statements are the key to creating this query. Begin with one table, then add each new table after an INNER JOIN command. Be sure to specify the table links using a collection of ON

FIGURE 4.11

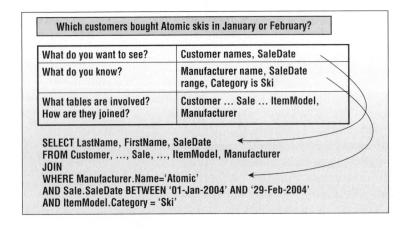

FIGURE 4.12

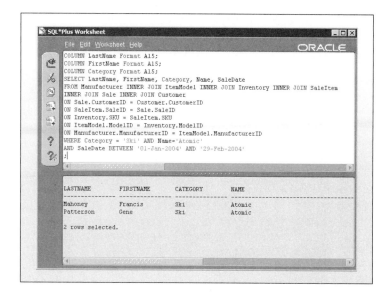

conditions. Once the tables and links have been defined, you can use columns from any of the tables. Just remember that if a column by the same name exists in more than one table, you refer to that column with its full Table.Column name.

Older Oracle queries are based on the older SQL syntax. Join conditions represent one of the greatest differences in this syntax. To see the difference, the Sale/Customer query will be rebuilt. Figure 4.13 shows the difference. Begin the query with the SELECT, FROM, and WHERE clauses. Enter the columns to be displayed, then the date condition in the WHERE clause. List the Sale and Customer tables in the FROM clause separated by a comma. Finally, add the join condition (Sale.CustomerID = Customer.CustomerID) to the WHERE clause. There are no INNER JOIN or ON statements. When you run the query, you should receive the same results as earlier.

FIGURE 4.13

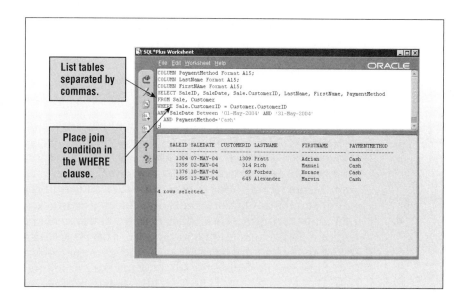

FIGURE 4.14

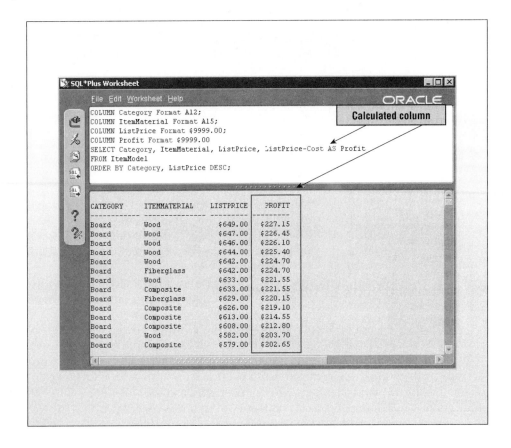

Computations and Subtotals

Activity: Compute Values with Queries

In general, it does not make sense to store some columns in the database. In particular, the DBMS query system has the ability to perform common calculations. Figure 4.14 shows how the query system can easily calculate the profit margin for each item. In this case, the table holds the item's list price and the acquisition cost. The profit is simply the difference between the list price and the cost. In the SELECT clause you enter the calculation and give it a name using the AS keyword: ListPrice-Cost AS Profit. Notice that the query is sorted by Category and ListPrice. Simply add an ORDER BY clause at the end of the command with the columns you want sorted. The DESC option specifies a descending order.

Action
Create a new query using only the ItemModel table.
In the SELECT row, add a new pseudo column to compute ListPrice-Cost As Profit.
Add the ORDER BY line to sort by Category and List Price descending.
Run the query.

Calculations written in this form are always performed on data on the same row. It does not calculate across rows. You can use the standard mathematical operators (add, subtract, divide, and multiply). You can also use several standard functions built into Access. Figure 4.15 shows some of the commonly used functions. Most are straightforward, but the date functions require a little explanation and practice. The TO_CHAR function enables you to specify detailed formats for date and numeric columns.

To illustrate the power of some of the date functions, create a new query using the Sale table and display the SaleID and SaleDate columns. Now, as

FIGURE 4.15

Lower	To lowercase
Length	Length/number of characters
Substr	Get substring
Trim	Remove leading and trailing spaces
Upper	To uppercase
SYSDATE	Current date
ADD_MONTHS	Add days, months, years to a date
MONTHS_BETWEEN	Subtract two dates
TO_CHAR	Highly detailed formatting
TO_DATE	Format dates
SYSDATE	Current date and time
Abs	Absolute value
Cos	Cosine, all common trig functions
Floor	Integer, drop decimal values
Round	Round-off

shown in Figure 4.16, add a new column TO_CHAR(SaleDate,'yyyy-mm') AS SaleMonth. Be sure to enter the quoted format correctly—it controls the way the date will be converted to character format and displayed. In this case, it will display the four-digit year, followed by a two-digit number for the month. You often want to format months in this way to ensure that they sort correctly. The TO_CHAR function has many options, and you can consult the Oracle Help documentation for details. Search for TO_CHAR or Format Models in the **SQL Reference** book.

SQL automatically performs data arithmetic with days. Adding or subtracting a number from a date results in a new date that is different by the specified number of days. Figure 4.17 shows how easy it is to add 30 days to a SaleDate to produce a common billing late date. Notice that the date arithmetic is correct in that it automatically handles months, years, and even

FIGURE 4.16

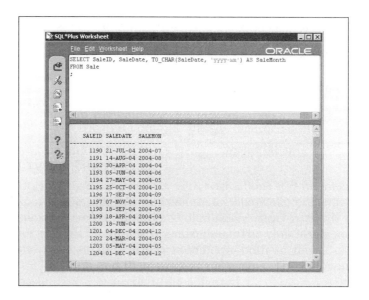

FIGURE 4.17

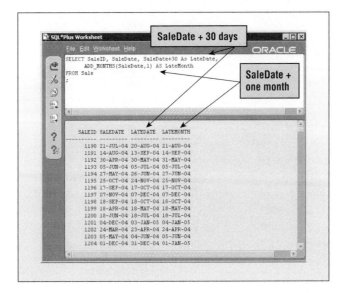

Action

Create a new query.
Use only the Sale table.
SELECT SaleID and SaleDate.
Add 30 days to the SaleDate to get LateDate.
Use ADD_MONTHS to add one month to the SaleDate to get SaleMonth.
Run the query.

leap years. If you want to add or subtract in increments other than days, you need to use Oracle's ADD_MONTHS function. To subtract dates in terms of months, use the MONTHS_BETWEEN function. Both the day and month arithmetic can use fractional values. For example, you could add 1.5 months to a date. You will often see fractional values if you subtract a date from today's date, which is given by SYSDATE. Since SYSDATE also includes the time of day, you will get noninteger results. If you only want the integer portion, you can use the Floor or Round functions. The Floor function truncates fractional values by throwing away all digits to the right of the decimal point. The Round funtion performs standard rounding to the specified decimal place.

Activity: Calculate Totals and Subtotals

Business managers often need to compute totals across rows of data. SQL provides several aggregation functions to perform these tasks. The most commonly used functions are Sum, Average, and Count. Of the three, the Count function can be the most confusing. Just remember that it simply counts the number of rows, while Sum adds up the numbers within a row. The challenge is to identify when you need to use Count instead of Sum.

The Sum function is straightforward. For example, how much sales tax does the company owe to the state of California? Begin by creating a new query based on the Sale table, because it has the ShipState and SalesTax columns. As a criterion for ShipState, enter the CA abbreviation for California. Ignoring totals for the moment, run the query, and you should see two columns: each row will have CA in the state, and a value for the SalesTax. To compute the total, return to SQL. Remove the SaleState from the SELECT statement and add the Sum function

Action

Create a new query.
Add the Sale table.
SELECT ShipState and SalesTax
WHERE ShipState = 'CA'.
Run the query.
Verify the correct states are displayed.
Remove ShipState from SELECT.
SELECT Sum(SalesTax) AS SumOfSalesTax.
Run the query.

FIGURE 4.18

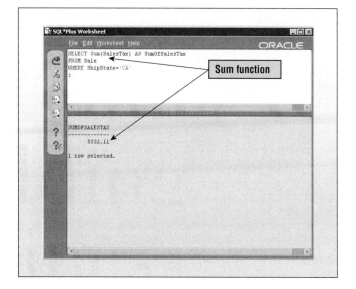

around the SalesTax: Sum(SalesTax) AS SumOfSalesTax. Figure 4.18 shows the total you should receive when you run the query. Why was it important to run the query first without the total? Because the total shows you only one number. How do you know the number is correct? You should always run a straight retrieval to ensure that the correct rows are being selected before you perform calculations on them. Of course, most aggregation queries will also use multiple tables—which makes it even more important that you check the detail rows first.

To understand some of the power of SQL, what if you want to see the total tax owed to each state? Of course, it would be possible to edit the CA condition and replace it with each state, but there is an easier way. As shown in Figure 4.19, start a new query the same way as the last one. Use the Sale table and select the ShipState and SalesTax columns, but do not specify any

FIGURE 4.19

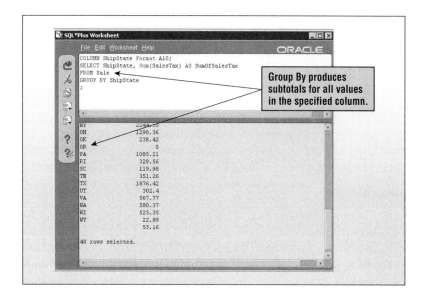

Action
Create a new query.
Use the Sale table.
Select columns: ShipState and Sum(SalesTax) AS SumOfSalesTax.
Add a row at the bottom: GROUP BY ShipState.
Run the query.

limiting conditions. Use the Sum function to total the SalesTax column and be sure to set the alias name. Do not include a WHERE statement. The tricky part is the next line: Add a GROUP BY clause at the end of the command. Tell it to compute the totals for each state with GROUP BY ShipState. When you run the query, you will get a list of all of the states with sales followed by the total sales tax collected for that state. Of course, you could compute the average or count the number of items in a group just as easily. In fact, you can compute multiple functions at the same time, just by including multiple copies of the desired column and selecting a different aggregation function.

For practice, you should compute the total value of sales to customers in Colorado (the state code is CO). Create a new query and add the Sale and SaleItem tables. Use the ShipState column from the Sale table. To compute the total value of the actual sale is slightly trickier. You need to multiply the QuantitySold by the SalePrice from the SaleItem table then compute its sum. To be safe, first do the multiplication and check your progress. Create the formula on the SELECT row with the command: QuantitySold * SalePrice AS SaleTotal. To select the state, enter 'CO' as the criteria in the WHERE clause. Run the query and check the results to see if they make sense. You might want to list the QuantitySold and SalePrice separately, and then use a calculator or spreadsheet to verify some of the calculations. Returning to the SQL, you need to compute the total. As shown in Figure 4.20, simply add the Sum function and place the parentheses around the multiplied values.

There is one more trick you need to learn before finishing this lab. You need to be able to save a query so that you can use it in other queries or reports. In Oracle, a saved query is called a View. Figure 4.21 shows how to save a query as a view. Using the query you just finished, simply add one line at the top, CREATE VIEW ColoradoSales AS, and run this query. You now have a view called ColoradoSales that performs the SELECT statement. To

FIGURE 4.20

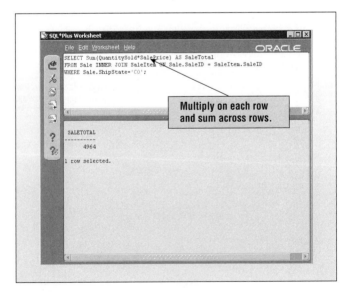

FIGURE 4.21

```
CREATE VIEW ColoradoSales AS
SELECT Sum(QuantitySold*SalePrice) AS SaleTotal
FROM Sale INNER JOIN SaleItem ON Sale.SaleID = SaleItem.SaleID
WHERE ShipState='CO'
```

test it, clear the SQL window and create the simple query: SELECT * FROM ColoradoSales. Run this query and it will execute the stored query to compute and display the total sales in Colorado. You could use the enterprise manager to delete this new view, or simply issue the SQL Drop command: Drop View ColoradoSales.

Exercises

Crystal Tigers

Enter sample data for the Crystal Tigers service club database. You can make up data, but remember that it has to be consistent. You might want to share data with other students so that everyone has a larger database to work with. Then create queries to provide the following business information.

1. List all of the members who have been president of the organization.
2. List the charities for which the club has raised more than $1,000.
3. Pick an event and list all of the members who worked at that event.
4. Count the number of events and the amount of money raised for each charity.
5. List the total number of service hours provided in the latest year.
6. List the number of service hours provided by each member.
7. List the members who have held the most number of officer positions.

Capitol Artists

Enter sample data for the Capitol Artists business. You can create random data, but remember that it has to be consistent. You might want to share data with other students so that everyone has a larger database to work with. Then create queries to provide the following business information.

1. Pick a date and an employee and list all of the tasks by that person on that date.
2. List all of the tasks performed for a specific job (e.g., Job #1173).
3. List all of the client jobs that had active tasks on a specific date.
4. Count the number meetings held regarding one client (pick any client).
5. List the employees who have attended the most number of meetings.
6. Pick a job and compute the amount of money billed (hours * rate).
7. List the clients in order beginning with who has provided the greatest revenue (billing + expenses).

Offshore Speed

Enter sample data for the Offshore Speed company. You can create random data, but remember that it has to be consistent. You might want to share data with other students so that everyone has a larger database to work with.

Then create queries to provide the following business information. If you have not created data that matches these questions, either add more data or change the query to match your data. For instance, if you do not have any sales of propellers, pick a category of item that you have sold several times.

1. Pick a month and list all of the customers who purchased propellers (Category).
2. List all of the parts sold on a particular day.
3. What is the most expensive steering wheel we have sold?
4. List the manufacturers sorted by the number of parts we sell from each one.
5. List the employees to identify the best salespeople in terms of value.
6. List the brands of boat for which we sell the most oil pumps (Description).
7. For a given order, compute the total value of the order and the sales tax, assuming a 6 percent tax rate.

Final Project

The main textbook has an appendix with several longer case studies. You should be able to work on one of these cases throughout the term. If you or your instructor picks one, perform the following tasks.

1. Create a few rows of sample data for all of the tables.
2. Identify at least five business questions that manager would commonly ask and provide the queries to answer those questions. At least two of the questions should involve subtotals or averages.
3. Exchange three business questions with other students in your class and write the queries for the questions you receive.

Chapter

Advanced Queries and Subqueries

Chapter Outline

Objectives

Advanced Database Queries

Case: All Powder Board and Ski Shop

Lab Exercise

All Powder Board and Ski Data
SQL Data Definition and Data
Manipulation

Exercises

Final Project

Objectives

- Create more complex SELECT queries using subqueries.
- Understand the role of INNER and LEFT joins.
- Create theta joins using inequalities to match categories.
- Use a UNION statement to merge rows of data.
- Use DDL to CREATE and DROP tables.
- Use DML to INSERT, UPDATE, and DELETE data.

Advanced Database Queries

SQL is a powerful language. For many queries, you will not need the full power of SQL, but some seemingly innocent business questions can be tricky to answer. In these cases, you need some additional capabilities. Some of these capabilities can be challenging to understand, but if you follow the examples carefully, you should be able to use the ideas to create similar queries in the future.

Subqueries are one of the more interesting features of SQL. A subquery is a query that calls a second query to obtain additional data. Instead of looking up a second set of numbers yourself, you can add a second query to do the work automatically.

Joins offer other powerful options. Joins are commonly used as a lookup link between tables, making it easy for you to build a query that uses data from multiple tables. However, joins have several options to help you answer even more complex questions. It is especially important that you understand the difference between inner and outer joins.

One of the strengths of SQL is that it operates on sets of data. Instead of thinking in terms of individual rows, you can concentrate on collections of rows that meet specified conditions. SQL offers some interesting set-operation commands that provide detailed control over rows of data. For example, the UNION statement combines rows of data from multiple SELECT statements.

Advanced queries generally rely exclusively on text-based SQL. Even if you have a visual QBE system available, it is much safer to use straight text to create difficult queries. One of the most dangerous aspects of any query is that the system will almost always return some type of data. You need to make sure the system is returning the correct data by ensuring that the query is actually asking for exactly what you think it is asking. Most of the data definition statements (such as CREATE TABLE, INSERT, DELETE, and UPDATE) will often be stored in text files that can be run as separate batches later to accomplish some larger task. Just remember to test all of them first.

Case: All Powder Board and Ski Shop

As the queries become more complex, it is better to work from a common set of data. Figure 5.1 shows the primary tables for the All Powder Board and Ski Shop. Your tables and sample data should be very close to these tables. Note that several supporting tables are not displayed in this diagram, but you will also need those in your database. As explained in Chapter 4, you can import the sample data to these tables. If you add more data, your query results may be slightly different from the ones shown in this chapter. While the query is more important than the actual results, the results are useful to help you decide if you have constructed the query properly.

One of the greatest challenges with any database query is that most queries return values, but they might not be answers to the question you thought you were asking. You must learn to carefully build the queries and test each intermediate step so that you can be sure the final result is an accurate answer to the question being asked.

FIGURE 5.1

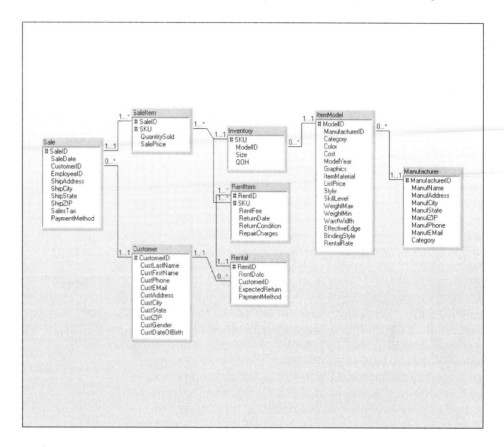

Lab Exercise

All Powder Board and Ski Data

Subqueries are used to create a second (or more) query to look up additional data that can be used in the primary query. The value is often used within a WHERE clause to make comparisons in more depth. For example, Katy, the manager, wants to identify the best customers of the shop. In particular, she would like to know which customers have placed the most sales. You could just give her the complete list of customers and the sales made by each. However, eventually this list would be too long. Instead, she wants a list that displays the customers whose total purchases are larger than the average number of purchases per customer. Although the business question is reasonable, this question is slightly tricky because you have to build the query in pieces.

Activity: Create a Subquery

The first step in the query is to recognize that you need to compute total sales by customer. The phrase "by customer" is an indication that you need to compute subtotals using the GROUP BY clause. Figure 5.2 shows the initial query that computes these subtotals. Of course, it lists the sales for every customer, and Katy only wants

Action
Create a new query.
Tables: Customer, Sale, SaleItem.
Columns: CustomerID, LastName, FirstName, Sum(QuantitySold*SalePrice) AS SalesValue.
Group By the other columns.
Run the query.
Save as a view CustomerSales.
Create new query.
Table: CustomerSales query
SELECT Avg(SalesValue) ...
Run the query.

FIGURE 5.2

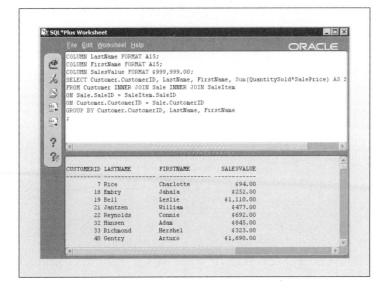

the sales of greater than average amount. But this query is an important step and needs to be saved as CustomerSales.

The next step is to use this first query to compute the average amount of sales for customers. This computation is straightforward. You simply build a new query using CustomerSales as the only table, and calculate the average of the sales column. Figure 5.3 shows the basic query and the result based on the current data. Notice that the SQL is straightforward. In this case, the SQL is critical for the next step. It is not necessary to save this query, but you might want to leave the SQL window open for the final step.

The last step is to create a new query that answers the overall question to determine which customers spend more than average. The new query will also be based on the CustomerSales query created in the first step, so just add that query. This time, select the LastName, FirstName, and SalesValue columns. If

FIGURE 5.3

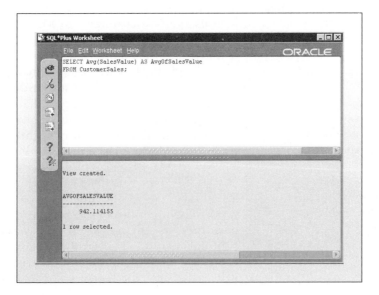

FIGURE 5.4

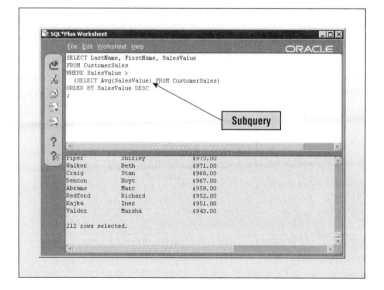

Action
Create a new query.
Table: CustomerSales query.
Columns: LastName, FirstName, SalesValue.
Criteria for SalesValue >(SELECT Avg(SalesValue) FROM CustomerSales).

you ran the query at this point, you would get the same results as in the first query. Instead, you want to add a criterion to only display the customers with a SalesValue greater than the average. The simple approach is to enter the value 942.11 as a condition in the query. Although this approach works this time, it does not work very well over time. It would require the owner to run the average query first, then copy the value into the Design view of the main query. It makes more sense to automate the entire process. So instead of entering the actual number as the condition, you need to enter the subquery calculation. You can write the complete SQL statement, but it must be contained within parentheses. Figure 5.4 shows the final query that you can give to Katy. Notice that it is sorted in descending order by SalesValue so the customers with the largest total purchases are listed at the top. Also, always remember to put the subquery inside parentheses—otherwise the query will not run at all. If you want to save some typing and reduce errors, you should create the subquery first in a separate query to test it. When it is correct, you can copy the SQL statement and paste it into the WHERE clause for the final query. Again, remember to add the parentheses around the subquery.

Activity: Build Outer Joins

Action
Create a new query.
Tables: Rental and Sale.
Columns: RentDate, SaleDate, and CustomerID from both tables.
Join the tables on CustomerID.
Run the query.
Add a join between the tables on RentDate=SaleDate.
Run the query.

Joining tables is one of the more complex issues in SQL. Up to this point, the joins have been simple equality joins designed to show how a column in one table links to data stored in a related table. It is important that you understand the effect of this join. Jim, the sales manager, and David, the rental manager, want to know if customers who rent equipment also purchase items for sale. As with many questions, there are several different ways to build this query. Figure 5.5 shows the effect of an inner join. Build a new query and add the Rental and Sale tables. Join these tables through CustomerID by dragging and

FIGURE 5.5

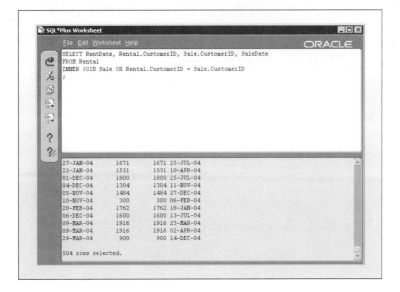

dropping the CustomerID from one table onto the column in the other table. When you display both CustomerID values in the query and run it, you can see that they are the same. The effect of this join is that the results show the customers (ID only) who participated in a sale and a rental—at anytime.

If you want to know which customers made a purchase on the same day as the rental, you could add a condition that RentDate equals SaleDate. Or you could add a second join that connects RentDate and SaleDate. Figure 5.6 shows the query with the second join condition. Notice the use of the AND in the join statement. This query demonstrates the effect of the inner join. In many respects, it is equivalent to a WHERE clause. The inner join restricts the rows that you will see by forcing values to be equal.

On the other hand, perhaps Jim would like to see a list of all of the customers who participated in sales, and then check to see which of those have rented

FIGURE 5.6

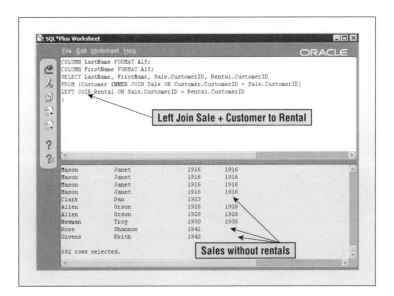

FIGURE 5.7

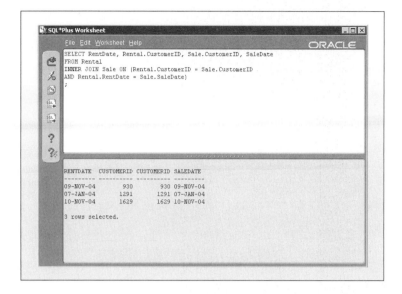

items. You need to build a new query. This time include the Customer table so their names can be displayed. Then add the Sale and Rental tables. Delete the join from Customer to Rental. That join would force all of the CustomerIDs to be equal, which is not what Jim wants. Then connect Rental to Sale by CustomerID, but this time, double-click the resulting line to modify the join properties. Figure 5.7 shows the basic query. Select the option to display all of the values from the Sale table and only the matching values from the Rental table. As shown in the SQL, this option sets up a LEFT JOIN, which displays all values in the Sale table (the left table in the SQL query list), even if the customer never rented items. If you have problems running the query, you might have to remove the Customer table from the query. Sometimes Access cannot figure out how to establish left joins when more than two tables are in the query. In these cases, you build the left join with only two tables, save the query, then create a second query based on the saved query and any other tables needed.

Action
Create a new query.
FROM (Customer INNER JOIN Sale ON Customer.CustomerID= Sale.CustomerID) LEFT JOIN Rental ON Sale.CustomerID = Rental.CustomerID. Columns: LastName, FirstName, and CustomerID from Sale and Rental. Run the query.

Figure 5.7 also shows some of the results from running the query. Notice that several of the rows show missing values for the Rental.CustomerID. These are the customers who purchased items but have never participated in a rental. If you want to see only this list of people, you can add the condition that Rental.CustomerID Is Null. Observe that the full list from the main query might not include all of the customers. To review your knowledge of joins, you should be able to identify the customers that might not be in this list. Looking at the design, notice that there is still an inner join between the Customer and Sale tables. Consequently, customers who have not participated in sales at all will not be displayed in this list. If you truly wanted a list of all customers, you would have to use a left join from the Customer to the Sale table. However, you will probably have to do one of the joins at a time, save the query, and then do the second join.

Recall the question of listing the customers who have purchased items but have not rented anything. With the left join, it is straightforward to get this

FIGURE 5.8

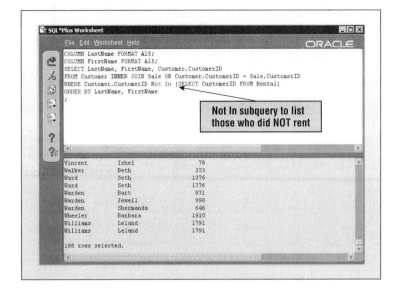

list by adding the Is Null condition. But you must be very careful when creating this query. If you forget to specify the left join and stick with the standard inner join, the query will indicate that no customers match that condition. The reason is because an inner join automatically leaves out the customers you are searching for. This question can also be answered with a subquery. Figure 5.8 shows the subquery approach. Start a new query and add the Customer and Sale tables. Sort the columns by LastName and FirstName. Then add the condition CustomerID Not In (SELECT CustomerID FROM Rental). As always, remember to put the subquery in parentheses. This query will retrieve all Customers who have participated in sales but have not rented any items. You should compare the results from this version to the left join version to ensure that both queries return the same results. Most systems support either method to answer the question, but there can sometimes be performance differences between the two approaches. Access seems to be faster using left join, but you would have to time large sets of data to measure the difference.

Action

Create a new query.
Tables: Customer and Sale.
Columns: LastName, FirstName, and CustomerID.
WHERE CustomerID Not In (SELECT CustomerID FROM Rental).
Run the query.

Activity: Create Complex Joins

Jim, the sales manager, is concerned about excess inventory. He wants to be able to monitor the status of quantity on hand (QOH) for all inventory items. He is particularly concerned about identifying which models are selling quickly versus models that have large numbers of items sitting around. Remember that models are product lines from the manufacturers, while individual items are specific sizes within a model group. He wants the totals for the model. To see if there is a problem, construct a new query that totals the quantity on hand and sorts it in descending order by ModelID. Figure 5.9 shows the total quantity on hand for the various models. Save the query as ModelsOnHand.

Action

Create a new query.
Table: Inventory.
Columns: ModelID and Sum(QuantityOnHand).
Sort by the Sum descending.
Run the query.
Save it as ModelsOnHand.
Create a new table: SalesCategory.
Columns: CategoryID, CategoryName, LowLimit, HighLimit.
Enter data from Figure 5.10.

FIGURE 5.9

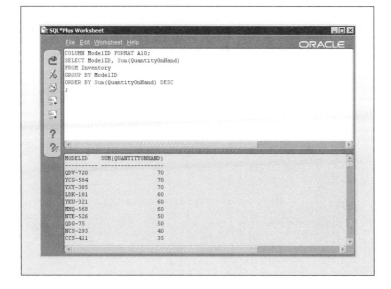

But Jim does not want to wade through the entire query every day. Instead, he is proposing a categorical system, where items with more than a certain QOH will be called slow sellers, and items with minimal QOH will be hot sellers. He also wants a few categories in between. While you have the tools to build this query, there is one catch: he wants the ability to fine-tune the numbers on the ranges for each category. The solution is to create a new table that defines the category and the upper and lower limits for each category: SalesCategory(CategoryID, CategoryName, LowLimit, HighLimit). If the QOH for a model is greater than or equal to the LowLimit and less than the HighLimit, it falls into the specified category. The CategoryID ensures a unique key and could be used to sort the rows if necessary. Figure 5.10 shows the initial categories.

Using the categories in a query requires slightly tricky join conditions. You need to use inequality (theta) joins. Begin with a new query based on

FIGURE 5.10

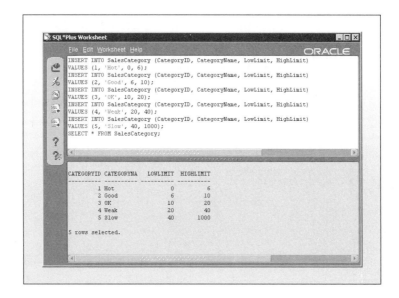

FIGURE 5.11

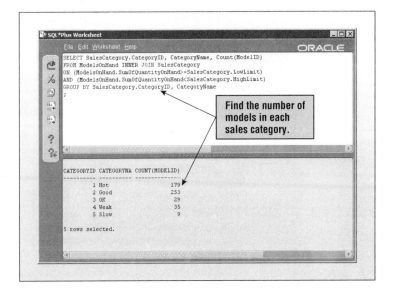

Action

Create a new query.
Columns: ModelID,
SumOfQuantityOnHand, CategoryID,
and CategoryName.
Tables: ModelsOnHand and
SalesCategory.
Add the inequality join.
Run the query.

the ModelsOnHand query and the SalesCategory table. Display the ModelID and SumOfQuantityOnHand along with the CategoryName. But, do not attempt to join the tables in Design view. Instead, switch to SQL view and modify the FROM clause to match the Figure 5.11 inequality join statement. Access can handle inequality joins but cannot display or edit them in Design view. Figure 5.12 also shows the sample result from the query. Save the query as ModelSales so Jim can perform some additional analysis on the data.

Jim might create a new, simpler query that counts the number of models that fall within each of the categories. Figure 5.11 shows the basic query. It is built using the results of the previous query. This query hides the

FIGURE 5.12

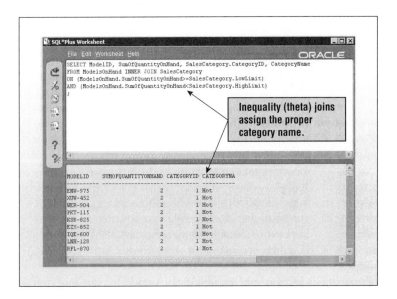

complicated details and Jim needs to see only the simple data results. The final aggregation query uses the CategoryID to sort the results logically; otherwise, they would be sorted alphabetically by the category name. Fortunately, most of the models appear to be in the categories indicating that they sell relatively quickly. However, the category definitions might not be accurate, but Jim can quickly alter the range numbers and rerun the query to see the results.

Activity: Combine Data Rows with UNION

You need to understand the role of the UNION command. It is designed to combine rows from multiple queries. Read that sentence carefully. It says combine rows not columns. If you have two queries that retrieve similar columns of data, the UNION statement will combine the results into one set of data. To illustrate the process, consider a request that Katy made to see a single list of customers who purchased items in January or in March. You could build this query using simple WHERE conditions, but if you want to list people twice if they bought items both in January and in March, the UNION query is easier.

Action
Create a new query.
Columns: CustomerID, LastName, FirstName, and SaleDate.
Tables: Customer and Sale.
Set January sale date in WHERE.
Copy the entire statement.
Add the word Union.
Paste the SELECT statement and change the date condition and name to March.
Run the query.

As shown in Figure 5.13, create a new query using the Customer and Sale tables. Display the CustomerID, LastName, and FirstName columns. Add the SaleDate column, but uncheck the box to display the date. Add the condition to select sales only in January. If you run the query at this point, you will see a list of customers who bought items in January. To get the March customers, copy the entire statement without the semicolon. Add the word "UNION" after the existing query, then below that, paste a copy of the query. Now modify the dates in this copy to indicate March instead of January. Finally, in the first (January) SELECT statement, add a computed column to display "Jan" As SaleMonth. Do the same thing for the second SELECT statement, but display "Mar" for March. This column will identify each row

FIGURE 5.13

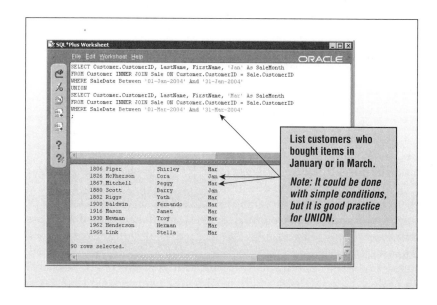

to indicate the month for the sale. Run the query, and you will see a combination of rows from both queries. If you want to sort the data by Customer or by date, first you will have to save the query, then you can build a second query based on the first and sort the columns as needed.

SQL Data Definition and Data Manipulation

Activity: Create Tables

Although it is possible to create and delete tables in Oracle using the enterprise manager, you will often have to create a table using the data definition language (DDL) CREATE TABLE command. For example, after working with the database for a while, you realize that it would be useful to have a separate table that lists salespeople and other contacts at the manufacturers. Each person has a direct phone number and an e-mail address. To practice building tables, Figure 5.14 shows the CREATE TABLE command for the new Contacts table. Essentially, you list each desired column along with its data type. Since Oracle supports the ANSI standard data types, it is often more convenient to specify INTEGER for numeric data types instead of NUMBER; but either version will work.

Enter the SQL code in either SQL Plus or SQL Plus Worksheet. Run the query and you should receive the "Table created" message. If not, check your typing carefully. You should create the primary key constraint to indicate the ContactID is the sole primary key column. For other tables, if you need multiple columns, simply create a comma-separated list. The foreign key constraint is similar, but you must also specify the table and column that is referenced by the foreign key. Be sure to specify the ON DELETE CASCADE option for the foreign key. If rows are deleted in the master table (Manufacturer), then any contacts in this table associated with that manufacturer will also be deleted automatically.

Generally, with Oracle it is easier to create tables with SQL. It is particularly useful to create a text file that contains several CREATE statements that will generate the database automatically. First, you want to test each statement individually and make sure it contains the correct statement. Then cut and paste the command into a separate text file. This file can be given to

Action
Create a new query. Enter the CREATE TABLE command. Run the query.

FIGURE 5.14

```
CREATE TABLE Contacts
(
    ContactID          INTEGER,
    ManufacturerID     INTEGER,
    LastName           NVARCHAR2(25),
    FirstName          NVARCHAR2(25),
    Phone              NVARCHAR2 (15),
    Email              NVARCHAR2 (120),
      CONSTRAINT pk_Contacts PRIMARY KEY (ContactID),
      CONSTRAINT fk_ContactsManufacturer FOREIGN KEY
      (ManufacturerID)
        REFERENCES Manufacturer(ManufacturerID)
        ON DELETE CASCADE
)
;
```

FIGURE 5.15

```
CREATE  TABLE  MyTemp
(
    ID        INTEGER,
    LName    NVARCHAR2(25),
    FName    NVARCHAR2(25),
    CONSTRAINT  pk_MyTemp
             PRIMARY  KEY  (ID)
)
;
```

others to create the database on a different system. The CREATE TABLE command is also useful for creating temporary tables. Figure 5.15 shows the table that you need to create.

The SQL ALTER TABLE command can also be used to add new columns to an existing table. However, you rarely need this command if you work from a good design. You can also use the Enterprise Manager console to add columns to a table—and it will show you the full syntax of the SQL command. For example, to add a TempCost column to the ItemModel table, the command would be ALTER TABLE ItemModel ADD (TempCost NUMBER(38,4)).

Activity: Insert, Update, and Delete Data

SQL also provides data manipulation language (DML) commands to insert, update, and delete rows of data. Consider the INSERT command first. The simple version of the command shown in Figure 5.16 inserts a single row into one table. Notice that you specify the table columns in the first list and the corresponding values in the second list. By listing the column names, you choose to enter the data in any order and to skip columns. Of course, you will rarely enter data this way, but occasionally it comes in handy. More importantly, the SQL statement can be generated using programming code with complex routines to extract data from one source, clean it up, and transfer it to the desired table. Notice that you must include the CustomerID column at this point. Chapter 7 will explain how to create a sequence number so this value can be generated automatically.

A second version of the INSERT command is more useful because of its power. You use it to transfer large blocks of data from one table into a second table. Note that the second table must already exist. The example in Figure 5.17 copies some data from the Customer table and transfers it to the temporary MyTemp table you created in the previous section. Again, you list the columns for the new table that will hold the data, then write a SELECT statement that retrieves matching data for those columns. Be sure to issue a COMMIT command after any INSERT command to ensure changes are saved to the table.

You should keep in mind that the SELECT statement can be as complex as you wish. It can include calculations, multiple tables, complex WHERE conditions, and subqueries. For complex queries, you should first build the SELECT

FIGURE 5.16

```
INSERT  INTO  Customer  (CustomerID,  LastName,
  FirstName,  City,  Gender)
VALUES  (4000,'Jones',  'Jack',  'Nowhere',  'Male');
```

FIGURE 5.17

```
INSERT INTO MyTemp (ID, LName, FName)
    SELECT CustomerID, LastName, FirstName
    FROM Customer
    WHERE City='Sacramento'
;
```

Action
Create a new query.
Type the INSERT command: INSERT INTO Customer (CustomerID, LastName, FirstName, City, Gender) VALUES (4000, 'Jones', 'Jack', 'Nowhere', 'Male');
Run the query.

statement on its own and test it to ensure that it retrieves exactly the data you want. Then switch to the SQL view and add the INSERT INTO line at the top. The ability to perform calculations has another benefit. You can add a constant to the SELECT statement that will be inserted as data into the second table. For example, you might write SELECT ID, Name, "West" to insert a region name into a new table. The INSERT INTO command is useful when you need to expand a database or add new tables. You can quickly copy selected rows and columns of data into a new table.

The UPDATE command is used to change individual values for specified rows. It is a powerful command that affects many rows. You must always be cautious when using this command because it can quickly change thousands of rows of data. To illustrate the power of the command, consider that the manufacturers have announced that costs will increase by 4 percent for the 2005 snowboards. The ItemModel table contains an estimate of the Cost for each model, so you need to increase this number by 4 percent, but only for the boards.

To be safe, begin by creating a query that displays the Cost data for the 2004 boards. You should run the query to ensure that it returns exactly the data that you want to update. Next, as shown in Figure 5.18, edit the query so that it uses the UPDATE command instead of SELECT. The Round function is used to ensure that the final Cost

Action
Create a new query.
Columns: Category, ModelYear, and Rounc(Cost*1.04,2).
Table: ItemModel.
Criteria: Category='Board' And ModelYear=2004.
Run the query.
Change the first two lines to.
UPDATE ItemModel
SET Cost = Round(Cost*1.04,2).
Run the query.

FIGURE 5.18

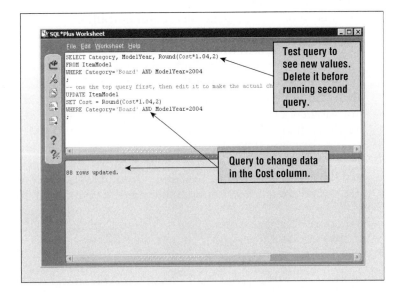

value is rounded off to cents instead of extended fractions. Be sure you run the SELECT query first to ensure the correct rows are selected by the WHERE clause. Then edit the query by adding the UPDATE statement. In practice, do not try to run both queries at the same time. They are shown here only so you can compare the two. After you run an UPDATE query, you should issue a COMMIT command to make sure the changes are recorded to the table.

Notice that the SQL statement is straightforward. It is also easy to change multiple columns at one time. Just separate the column assignments with commas. For example, SET Cost = Round(Cost * 1.04,2), ModelYear = 2005.

The DELETE command is similar to the INSERT and UPDATE commands, but it is more dangerous. It is designed to delete many rows of data at a time. Keep in mind that because of the relationships, when you delete a row from one table, it can trigger cascade deletes on additional tables. For the most part, these deletes are permanent. If you are not careful, you could wipe out a large chunk of your data with one DELETE command. To minimize the impact of these problems, you should always make backup copies of your database—particularly before you attempt major delete operations. If your system has an Oracle Management server installed, you can use the backup wizard in the Enterprise Manager console to make a backup copy of the schema.

To be particularly safe, this example is just going to delete data from the temporary table that was created in the previous section. Create a new query using the MyTemp table. As shown in Figure 5.19, to see the rows you are going to delete, display the ID, LName, and FName columns and set a condition to show only rows with an ID > 100. Run the query to verify that it returns only one row. Now, edit the query and replace the entire SELECT row with the DELETE command. Run the query. If only one row is deleted, issue the COMMIT command to make the deletions permanent. Your other option is to issue a ROLLBACK command to restore everything to the last point where you executed a commit.

Action
Create a new SELECT query.
Columns: ID, LName, FName.
Table: MyTemp.
Criteria: ID>100.
Test the query.
Change the SELECT row to DELETE.
Run the query.
Run a commit; command.

FIGURE 5.19

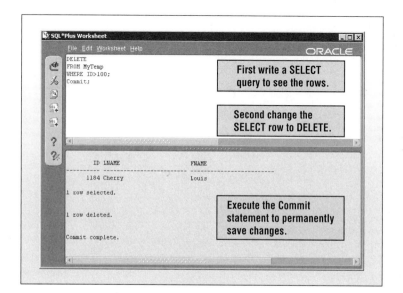

FIGURE 5.20

```
DROP TABLE MyTemp;
```

In practice, it is best to stick with simple WHERE clauses when possible. However, it can be complex and can include subqueries. Particularly in the complex cases, you should first build a SELECT statement using the same WHERE clause to ensure that you are deleting exactly the rows you want to delete. Then convert the query into a Delete Query, or delete the SELECT statement and replace it with the DELETE command.

The DROP TABLE command is even more dangerous. It removes the entire table and all of its data. Generally, you should only use it for temporary tables. As shown in Figure 5.20, the syntax is straightforward; just make sure you enter the correct table name. Again, it would be wise to make a backup copy of your database before removing tables.

The main aspect to remember about these commands is that they operate on sets of rows that you control with the WHERE clause. The WHERE clause can be complex and can include subqueries with detailed SELECT commands. All of the power of the SELECT command is available to you to control inserting, updating, and deleting rows of data.

Activity: Create Parameter Queries

Parameter queries are useful when you need to create a complex query that a manager runs on a regular basis but needs to change some of the constraints. For instance, you often use parameters to set starting and ending dates so the manager can easily select a range of data without having to know anything about building queries. The example in Figure 5.21 shows a query that displays the total rental income by Category for a specified range of dates. This query has fixed dates for the first quarter. The objective is to replace those fixed dates with parameters that can be entered quickly by the manager—preferably without having to see or edit the query.

Action
Create a new query.
Columns: Category, Sum(RentFee).
Tables: Rental, RentItem, Inventory, and ItemModel GROUP BY Category.
Test the query.

In Oracle, parameterized SELECT queries are somewhat complicated. They require the use of variables, which means you need to create a small package to hold the variable definitions and the procedure that executes the query. These topics are explored in more detail in Chapter 7, but it is worth typing in this example to see how they work.

To create the package and procedure, enter the commands in Figure 5.22 by typing them in. The commands are also stored as a text file on the student CD so you can cut and paste them to save some typing. The package

FIGURE 5.21

```
SELECT Category, Sum(RentFee) AS SumOfRentFee
  FROM Rental INNER JOIN RentItem INNER JOIN Inventory
  INNER JOIN ItemModel
  ON Inventory.ModelID=ItemModel.ModelID
  ON RentItem.SKU=Inventory.SKU
  ON Rental.RentID=RentItem.RentID
  WHERE RentDate Between '01-Jan-2004' And '31-Mar-2004'
  GROUP BY Category;
```

FIGURE 5.22

```
CREATE PACKAGE pckCategoryFees AS
  TYPE typeCategoryFees IS RECORD
  (Category            NVARCHAR2(15),
   SumOfRentFees       NUMBER(8,2)
   );
   TYPE typeCursorFees IS REF CURSOR RETURN typeCategoryFees;
   PROCEDURE GetCategoryFees
   (dateStart          IN DATE,
    dateEnd            IN DATE,
    cvFees             IN OUT typeCursorFees
    );
END;
/

CREATE PACKAGE BODY pckCategoryFees AS
  PROCEDURE GetCategoryFees
  (dateStart           IN DATE,
   dateEnd             IN DATE,
   cvFees              IN OUT typeCursorFees
   ) IS
    BEGIN
    OPEN cvFees FOR
      SELECT Category, Sum(RentFee) AS SumOfRentFee
      FROM Rental INNER JOIN RentItem INNER JOIN Inventory
           INNER JOIN ItemModel
      ON Inventory.ModelID=ItemModel.ModelID
      ON RentItem.SKU=Inventory.SKU
      ON Rental.RentID=RentItem.RentID
      WHERE RentDate Between dateStart And dateEnd
      GROUP BY Category;
    END;
END;
```

defines a record and a cursor that are used to return the selected values. It also contains the definition of the procedure. The package body contains the actual procedure. Notice that it is passed a starting and ending date and returns the matching rows of data. The heart of the procedure is the query that you already created. The only difference is that the two dates are specified as parameters. The package and procedure only have to be created one time.

Once the package is defined, the manager only needs to issue a couple of simple commands to enter new dates and obtain the total rental fees by category. Figure 5.23 shows the commands. Some of them are the common formatting commands. You would probably want to save these commands in a file so the manager can cut and paste them, and then edit the two dates to simplify the process.

You can build complex queries and insert parameters to request specific data from the person running the query. Although it requires several steps, query parameters are a useful method to quickly build queries that users can control without having to alter the query.

Action
Create a new query.
Copy or paste the code to create the package and procedure.
Run the package creation code.
Enter the five commands to execute the parameter query.
Run the query.
Change the dates to Oct–Dec.
Run the query.

FIGURE 5.23

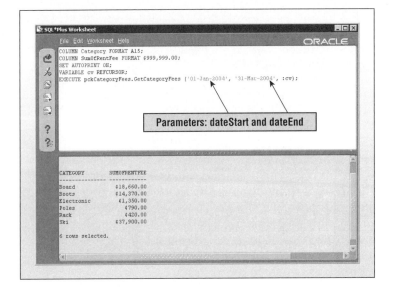

Exercises

Many Charms

You will need to create some additional sample data for each table. Madison and Samantha know that they will want certain information on a weekly basis, but they will not be able to build complex queries to retrieve the data. You will have to build a few queries for them that they can run when they want to see the results or need to change prices. Some of the queries should be parameter queries so they can easily select the values they need to control the results. *Note:* You will have to modify the queries slightly to match the data that you have entered.

1. Which of the customers who ordered bracelets have not ordered necklaces?
2. Which customers bought more gold charms than silver ones?
3. Which categories generated the most profit over a parameterized time period?
4. Are expensive charms more profitable than mid-priced or low-priced charms? *Hint:* Create categories based on the prices.
5. Create a parameterized query to enable Samantha to increase prices of a certain category of charms by a given percentage.
6. Create a new table with SQL and copy into it all of the customers who have not purchased items within the last three months.
7. Delete customers from the new table in the prior exercise who have spent more than $100 in the past year.

Standup Foods

You will need to create some additional sample data for each table. Laura knows she will want certain information on a weekly basis, but she will not be able to build complex queries to retrieve the data. You will have to build a few queries for her that can be run to display results or change prices. Some of the queries should be parameter queries so Laura can easily select the values she needs to control the results. *Note:* You will have to modify the queries slightly to match the data that you have entered.

1. Identify the employees who have below-average overall job evaluations.
2. Identify the main menu items that have not been served to a particular director or other celebrity (pick one from your list who wants something different).
3. Which customers have not yet referred her business to other clients?
4. Create a category table to segment the employee ratings (excellent, good, average, weak). Use the table to identify the employees with excellent evaluations as both server and dishwasher.
5. Create a temporary table and copy into it information about employees who have worked as drivers but have not driven within the last month.
6. Delete from the temporary table in the previous question the drivers whose average evaluations are less than 6 (on the 10-point scale).
7. Write a parameterized query that enables Laura to increase the base wage rate of employees by specifying a category, a minimum overall average evaluation, and the percentage increase.

EnviroSpeed

You will need to create some additional sample data for each table. Brennan and Tyler know that they will want certain information on a weekly basis, but they will not be able to build complex queries to retrieve the data. You will have to build a few queries for them that they can run when they want to see the results or need to change prices. Some of the queries should be parameter queries so they can easily select the values they need to control the results. *Note:* You will have to modify the queries slightly to match the data that you have entered.

1. List the experts who have worked with two or more crews in the same month.
2. Which experts have not contributed any documents within the last three months?
3. List the crews that are more than 25 percent larger than the average crew.
4. Create a table to categorize the expensiveness of cleanups. For example, spills that cost more than $1 million to clean up are expensive; spills that cost $500,000 to $1 million are merely costly; and so on. Create a query to apply these categories to the actual spills.
5. Write a query that retrieves documents based on a list of keywords entered by a user. The keywords might appear anywhere in the document, and the final query should sort the list based on the number of matches.
6. Write a parameterized query to update a severity value for an incident by allowing the user to enter a chemical name and a point-wise increase in severity.
7. Write a query to copy the data on experts to a new table who have participated in a total of at least three incidents in the last year.

Final Project

The main textbook has an appendix with several longer case studies. You should be able to work on one of these cases throughout the term. If you or your instructor picks one, perform the following tasks. You will have to create sample data for each of the tables.

1. Identify and create at least two parameter queries that would be useful to managers. Share the business question (not the query) with other students and solve their queries.
2. Identify a business question to list items greater (or less) than average. Write the query to return the results.
3. Create a temporary table and write a query to copy some rows of data from one table into the new table.
4. Write a delete query to remove a few rows of data from the temporary table.
5. Write an update query using parameters to change the value of one of the numeric columns in a table based on a percentage and conditions entered by the user.

Chapter

Forms, Reports, and Applications

Objectives

- Create forms (main, grid, and subforms) that make it easy for users to enter data.
- Create reports to display and summarize data.
- Build applications that connect forms and reports.
- Add toolbars and menus to forms.
- Add Help files to the database application.

Applications

The main purpose of the DBMS is to store data efficiently and provide queries to retrieve data to answer business questions. But from the perspective of businesses, the true value of the DBMS lies in the applications that can be built on top of the database. Oracle provides tools to help you build forms and reports. Once the database is designed, you can use the wizards to quickly build common business applications.

Forms are used to make it easier for users to enter data. You would never want users to enter data directly into the tables. For example, look again at the Sale table (see page 69). It contains mostly ID numbers, and you cannot expect workers to memorize thousands of ID numbers. Instead, you build forms to match the processes and styles of the business. Likewise, you rarely ask managers to build queries themselves. Instead, you create reports that display details and subtotals within a layout that is easy to read. You can even include charts to make it easy to compare values or examine trends over time.

A finished application contains all of the forms and reports needed to solve a particular problem. It also needs finishing touches such as menus and other navigation links between forms. Additionally, you usually have to create Help files to provide assistance to users when they first learn the system.

Note that Oracle 9i represents a substantial change in direction for Oracle forms and reports. Although the tools are similar to the earlier versions, the way that users interact with the forms has changed. In particular, forms and reports are now designed to be viewed in a Web browser. Although this approach has some significant advantages in a distributed environment, it requires that users install the Oracle ActiveX JInitator component on their machines. For internal applications where users work on employer-owned machines, this requirement is not an issue. Even for workers who choose to work from home, it is relatively painless to install the component. However, you would not be able to use this approach on a publicly accessible website since most users would not install the necessary component because of potential security issues. If you have older forms and reports not designed to run as Web pages, you can still install the older Forms and Reports developer version 6. The techniques for building forms and reports with the two methods are similar, so it is not too difficult to convert the files.

Case: All Powder Board and Ski Shop

The primary application at All Powder Board and Ski Shop is the need to track sales and rentals. Of course, these applications also require you to build forms and reports for inventory items and customers as well. Eventually, you will have forms that store data into each of the tables in the relationship diagram. However, before you leap to the forms wizard, make sure you understand the three major form types shown in Figure 6.1: main form, grid form, and main with subform. A main form shows one row of data at a time, such as a form to edit basic information about one customer. A gird form appears similar to the Table view in that it shows several rows at one time. Main and subforms combine the two: The main form shows one row of data from one

FIGURE 6.1

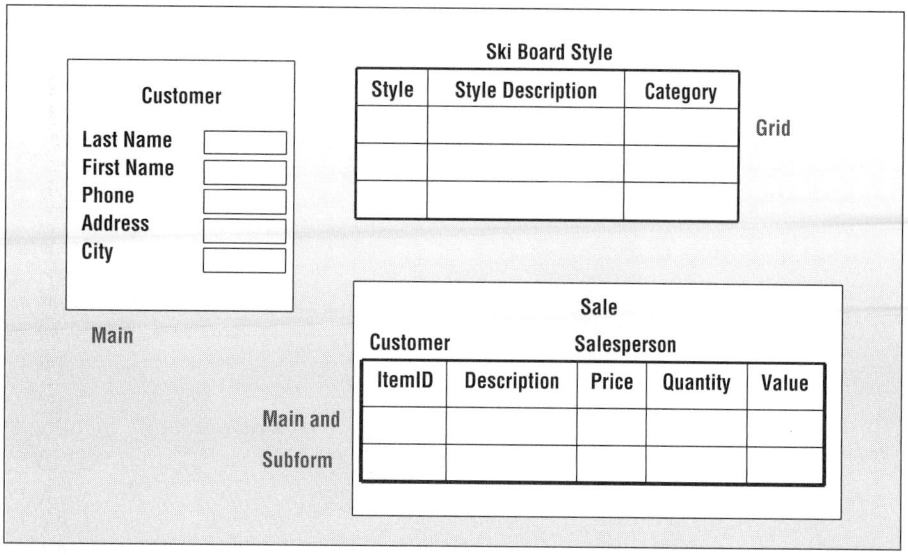

table, and the grid subform shows matching rows from a related table. The classic business example is the Sale form and SaleItem grid, where the main form shows data from one sale, and the grid shows the repeating items purchased and stored in the SaleItem table. At this point, your responsibility is to examine the business operations and determine the best type of form to handle each operation.

Lab Exercise

All Powder Board and Ski Shop Forms

Many of the forms in an application are straightforward main forms. Users want to see data for one row—such as one customer or one employee. You generally create main forms when you need more control over the layout.

Activity: Create Basic Main Forms

Figure 6.2 shows a simple version of the form to edit customer data. In its simplest layout, the main form contains labels and text boxes for each column in the table. You can enter any text into the label to help tell the user what data is to be entered into each text box. The data on the form is bound to the database table. Changes made to the data in the text boxes are automatically written to the database table. However, these changes are written only at certain times—such as when the user moves to a new row. The importance of the main form is that you have considerable control over the layout and presentation of the items. You can change the image of the form by setting the properties for the form or the controls to control descriptors such as size, position, and color. You can add new controls to display images or include buttons to delete or find records.

Creating a main form is straightforward using the wizard. To build the Customer form, create a new form using the Tools/Data Block Wizard menu

FIGURE 6.2

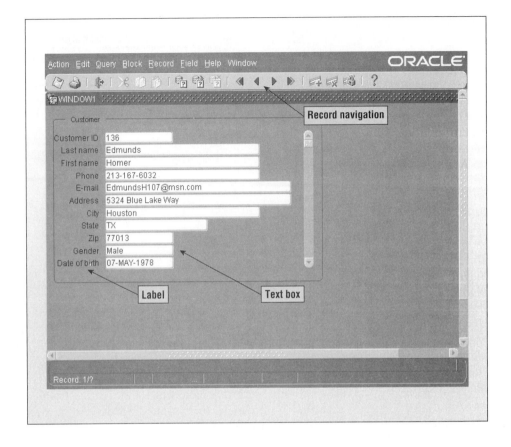

option. Figure 6.3 shows the most important step of the wizard—choosing the tables and fields. For this form, select the Customer table. Use the Browse button and you will be asked to log in and then given a list of the existing tables. Select all of the columns and move them to the right-hand side with the double-arrow button (>>). Stick with the default choices for other options, but you can provide a name (Customer) if asked.

When this data block wizard is finished, it will start the layout wizard by default. Again, select all of the columns to place them on the screen—or canvas in Oracle's terms. As shown in Figure 6.4, you should set the labels and the width of the text boxes for each column. The widths are measured in points, with 72 points per inch. Hence, a text box width of 216 points specifies 3 inches. A common font of 8 points should yield 5 to 6 characters per inch for around 40 characters in that text box. In practice, standard text characters are slightly narrower than that, so users will usually see more characters in the box. You can always change these values later, but it is easy to set them here—and the default values are generally too wide.

Stick with most of the default options, provide names (Customer) if asked. In the example, the only option chosen is to click the box to display the record-selector scroll bar. When the wizard is finished, save the form. You should create a folder to hold all of the forms for the application and save this form as Customer.fmb in that folder. To run the form, it must be

FIGURE 6.3

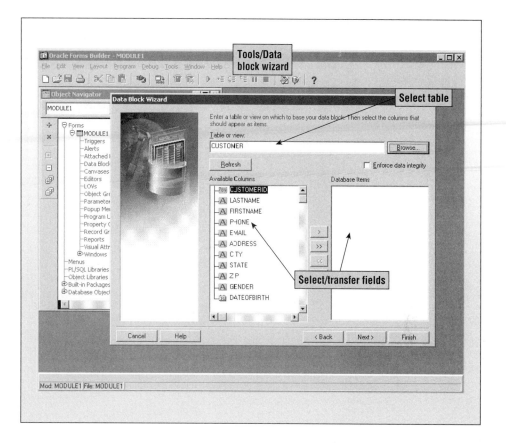

Action
Start the form builder.
Select Tools/Data Block Wizard.
Choose the Customer table.
Select all columns.
Stick with default options.
Run the Layout Wizard.
Choose all columns.
Clean up the prompts.
Enter smaller values for the widths.
Select the option to show the scroll bar.
Save the form design.
Run program: Start OC4J Instance.
Run the form to test it.
Click the Execute Query button.

accessible to a server that is running either the application server (Oracle 9iAS) or the OC4J listener. The developer server does not install the complete application server, so you will probably have to use the Windows start menu to run the Start OC4J Instance in the Oracle Developer Suite/Forms Developer menu. Now you can run the form to test it by clicking the Run Form button in the Forms Builder toolbar. After the browser loads, click the Execute Query button. The form shown in Figure 6.2 should be similar to your form.

The wizard does a decent job at displaying the data for the form, but invariably you will want to modify the design of the form. Sometimes you simply need to change the layout, formatting, and colors. Other times you want to add buttons to open additional forms or reports or to add or delete data rows. As shown in Figure 6.5 you can use properties to set the details of the form and its controls. Right-click a control, or right-click an entry in the object navigator to set the various properties or to define trigger event actions. The property box shows you which properties can be set for each item and helps you select the appropriate values. The toolbox contains additional controls that you can place on the form. If the designer is closed, select the Layout Editor from the Tools menu.

FIGURE 6.4

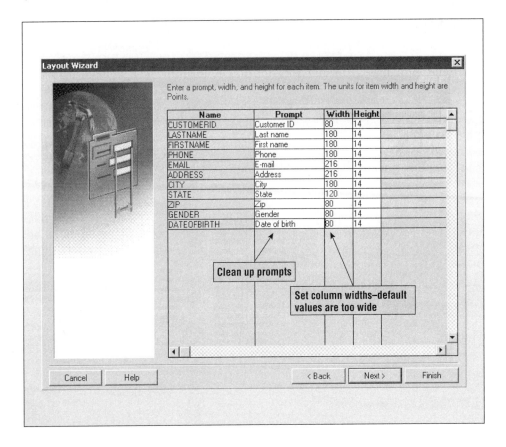

Oracle forms are somewhat complex and can have many different sections. On the form itself, a section is called a canvas and it holds the labels, text, and drawings. The data for a form comes from a data block that is responsible for retrieving and storing data in the database. It acts as a buffer between the items displayed on a form and the database. Generally, items in one data block are displayed in one canvas, but you are not required to follow this rule. Figure 6.6 shows the basic structure of an Oracle form.

The association from the database to the data block is shown in its properties. Likewise, the tie from a data block item to the text box on a form's canvas is listed in its properties. Figure 6.7 shows the basic sets of data properties for the data block and a text box on the canvas. In this example, the Data Source is the Customer table, and the Column Name is the LastName. The Data Source is a table or query that retrieves all of the columns that can be displayed and edited on the form. Almost always, you will want to use a table instead of a stored view or procedure. Stored views are rarely updatable in Oracle, and you would have to write your own update, insert, and delete procedures to process the form. If you scroll down the property list for the item (LastName), you will see the canvas and position entries that specify where the item is displayed on the form.

One of the first things you will notice when you run the form is that it is annoying to have to click the Execute Query button every time the form starts. The form should be able to run this query automatically and save the

FIGURE 6.5

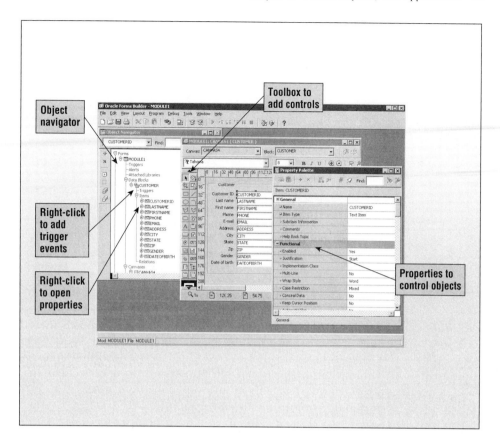

user a step. Figure 6.8 shows how to add an event trigger to the form so that the query is executed whenever the form opens. The form (and the individual controls) each experience several events as they are used. You can attach code to any of these events that will perform specific tasks. Chapter 7 explains the code in more detail. For now, you simply have to choose the correct event and add one statement. Right-click on the Triggers option for the Customer form and select the Smart Triggers option. In the resulting list, choose the WHEN-NEW-FORM-INSTANCE. Enter the code statement

FIGURE 6.6

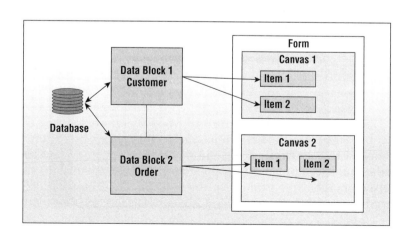

FIGURE 6.7

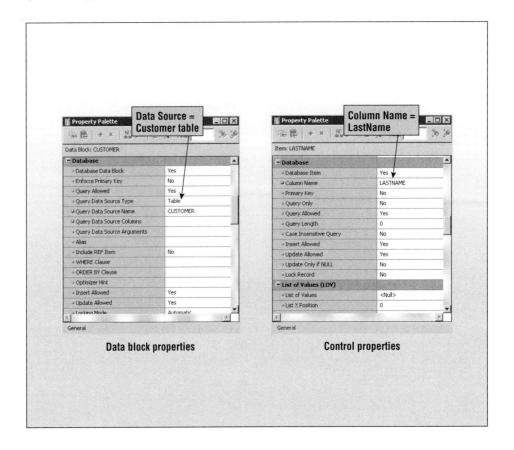

Data block properties

Control properties

Action
Right-click the Trigger option for the Customer form.
Select Smart Trigger.
Choose WHEN-NEW-FORM-INSTANCE.
Enter code line: Execute_query;
Close and save everything.
Run the form.

Execute_query; Be sure to include the semicolon (;) at the end. Click the Compile button to make sure you typed the code correctly, then close the box. Run the form and you will see that the user no longer has to click the button to execute the underlying query and retrieve the first row of data.

One more option should be added to the form. Notice the gender text box. Remember there is a check constraint on the table so users can enter only one of three values: Female, Male, or Unidentified. But, looking at the form, how does the user know those are the only three legitimate values? To improve usability and reduce errors, you need to add a list of values so the user can select from a fixed list of entries. Oracle has a list of values (LOV) wizard to assist in creating and displaying the list of options. However, since you want a fixed list of values (as opposed to selecting them from a table), you first need to create the list as a record group. Figure 6.9 shows the process of creating a static list of items. Find the record group list in the object navigator and select Edit/Create from the menu. Be sure to choose the static group option for this example. Enter the column name (Gender) in the top of the box, and enter the three values in the rows at the bottom. Close and save the record group, then rename it rgGender. If necessary, you can right-click the group and use its properties to change the values later.

FIGURE 6.8

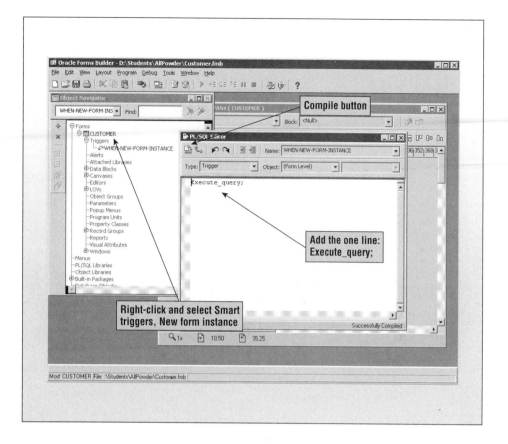

Action
Right-click the record group and create a new one.
Select a static group and add the three values (Female, Male, and Unidentified).
Save and rename the group.
Choose Tools/LOV wizard.
Select the new (existing) record group.
Choose the Gender column.
Click the Look Up button and select Gender as the return value column.
In the Gender box, add the WHEN-NEW-ITEM-INSTANCE trigger with the code List_Values;
Save everything and run the form.

The next step is to use the LOV wizard to create the list box and associate it with the Gender text box. Use Tools/LOV wizard to start the wizard and choose the existing group. Figure 6.10 shows the main form that appears after you select the Gender column. You need to select the "return value" to associate this list with the appropriate text box and column. The easiest method is to click the Look Up button and choose the Gender column from the list. Save everything and run the form. It will look exactly the same as it did before, but with one small difference. When you enter the Gender text box, you should see a note at the bottom that it has a list of values associated with it. To see the list and select from it, press the Ctrl+L keys, or select Edit/Display list from the Main Form menu.

Of course, forcing users to press an obscure key combination is somewhat distracting. Again, you can eliminate the problem by writing one line of code to tell the form to display the list automatically whenever users enter the Gender text box. Add the appropriate trigger by right-clicking the trigger option for the Gender text box and creating new trigger code for the WHEN-NEW-ITEM-INSTANCE event. Add the statement List_Values; to the code and compile it. Save everything and rerun the form. Use the Tab key or mouse to move into the Gender text box. The list of values box should pop up and allow you to select one of the three items.

FIGURE 6.9

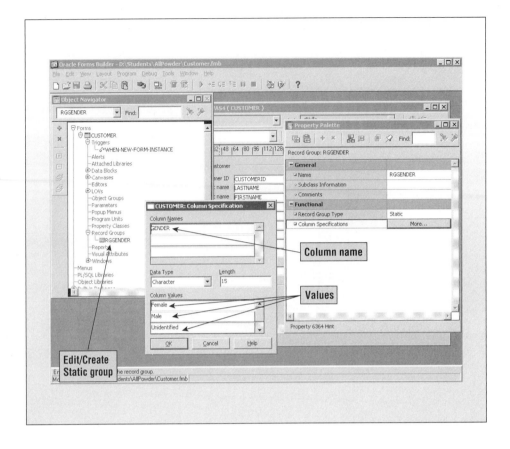

Activity: Create Grid Forms

Grid forms are another simple type of form. They are used when a table has a limited number of columns and rows. The columns should all fit on one screen—users find it difficult to edit data if they have to scroll horizontally. The number of rows should be limited because the grid form has few methods for searching, and users should not be forced to scroll through thousands of rows to change one piece of data. Figure 6.11 shows an initial grid form for the SkiBoardStyle table. Notice that the data in this table is generally used only to provide consistent values to other tables. This form will generally be used only by an administrator once in a while to modify or add a style. The data all fit on one screen, making it easy to find the items to be altered, and to compare the various entries across the rows. In practice, you will use grid forms for similar tasks aimed at administration. Think hard before you use one of these forms for general users. Although you have some control over the form design, your options are limited, so users need to know what they are doing.

You create a grid form in much the same way as a main form. Start the Data Block wizard, select the table, and choose the columns you want on the form. When you get to the Layout wizard, be sure to set the column widths judiciously so they display the relevant data but the columns fit on one screen. The important step after entering the sizes is to select the Tabular option to get the grid form. As shown in Figure 6.12, you will then be asked to specify the number of rows to display for the grid and the spacing

FIGURE 6.10

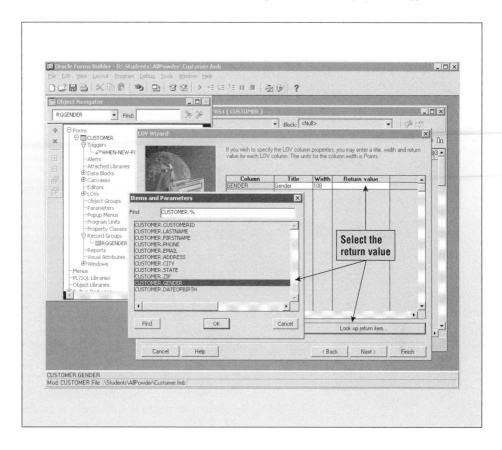

between each row. You can change these values later using the property palette.

Look closely at the data in Figure 6.11 and you will see that the Category data actually comes from a second table: ProductCategory. Of course, you

FIGURE 6.11

FIGURE 6.12

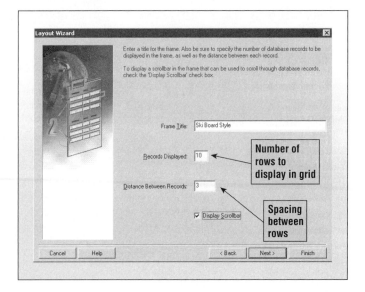

Action
Start a new form with Tools/Data Block wizard.
Base it on the table: SkiBoardStyle.
Select all three columns.
Choose defaults and run the Layout wizard.
Choose all three columns again.
Set the column widths (144, 216, 72).
Choose Tabular (not Form).
Enter a frame title, number of records (10), and space between records (2).
Save the form as SkiBoardStyle.fmb.
Run it.

should also build a grid form to enable administrators to update this table as well. However, at this point, you need to make it easier for people to enter data into the Category column of the main SkiBoardStyle table. If users have to retype the data for every row, they might abbreviate or misspell the entries—leading to inconsistent data that is difficult to search. Instead, you want to create a combo box on the form that makes it easy for users to select the desired category.

As shown in Figure 6.13, the Design view is straightforward. Although the multiple rows are displayed, you set properties for the individual columns and these properties apply to all of the rows. The next step is to add a list of values (LOV) to the Category column so users can select the items from a list. This list of items is actually stored in another table (ProductCategory), which becomes the source for the LOV.

To create the LOV, use Tools/LOV wizard to start the wizard. Choose a new record group and build a new SQL query by clicking the button. Choose the ProductCategory table as the source of the rows and select both the Category and CategoryDescription columns. Use the button to check the SQL syntax and go to the next screen when the query works correctly. Place both columns in the LOV, but reset the display widths to 72 and 144, respectively. Figure 6.14 shows the step where you associate the LOV Category value with the Category column in the underlying SkiBoardStyle table. First click the Return Item column for the Category row, then use the button to look up the return item. Select the Category column in the SkiBoardStyle table to match the Category column in the ProductCategory list. When users pop up the list of values, it will be filled with the list of items from the ProductCategory table. When they select one of the items, the key value (Category column) will be transferred to the foreign key column (Category)

FIGURE 6.13

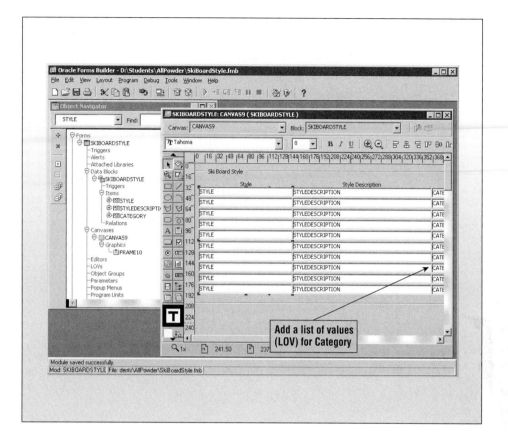

Action
Start the Tools/LOV wizard.
In a new record group, build an SQL query using the ProductCategory table. Select both columns, close the designer. Check the SQL syntax.
Put both columns into the LOV and set their widths (72 and 144).
Click the return item column in the Category row and click the Return Item button.
Select the SkiBoardStyle.Category column.
Finish the wizard by accepting the default values.
Save the form and run it.

in the underlying SkiBoardStyle table. Using the object navigator, you should rename the LOV and record groups that were created by the wizard. In a large project, it is difficult to keep track of these items unless you assign them meaningful names.

As shown in Figure 6.15, when you run the form, the rows appear similar to the original version. However, when the cursor is in the Category column, you can click Ctrl-L to open the LOV box. Selecting an item in the box will transfer the key value into the main table.

Just as it is with the main form, it is cumbersome to require the user to click the Execute Query button and to use Ctrl-L to open the list of values box. Again, you can create a couple of simple lines of code to automate these steps. In the object navigator right-click the trigger section directly beneath the form name. Choose smart triggers and select the WHEN-NEW-FORM-INSTANCE event. Add the line Execute_query; and remember the semicolon at the end. Compile the code to check it. Similarly, in the main data block, find the Category item and for the smart trigger, select the WHEN-NEW-ITEM-INSTANCE event and add the command List_values; to it. Compile it, save the form, and run the form to test it. Note that there are times you might not want to automatically open an LOV whenever a user enters the box. Sometimes the LOV takes

FIGURE 6.14

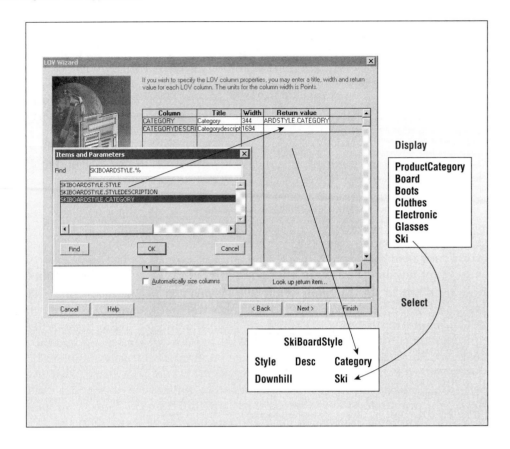

time to load and it slows down data entry. In these cases, you might simply leave a note for the users so they can decide to open the LOV box only when necessary.

Activity: Create Main Forms and Subforms

Now that you understand the main forms and grid forms, it is time to combine them into a main form and subform. Remember where this process began: with business forms—particularly the Sale form. A typical business sale form has data for the sale (SaleID, SaleDate) and customer (name, address, and so on). It also has a section of repeating data to hold the specific items being purchased by the customer. This repeating section was split into the SaleItem table, with some elements placed in the Inventory and ItemModel tables. The purpose of the main and subform is to recombine these tables. Keep in mind that each form can be associated directly with only one table. In this case, the Sale form will be based on the Sale table, and the subform will be based on the SaleItem table. Additional data from the other tables can be displayed on the forms, but only the primary keys from those two tables will be used.

The Data Block wizard is again used to start the forms by creating a Sale form. Begin by selecting all of the columns from the Sale table. Essentially, you will build the form for the sale first, then add the subform for the SaleItem table. Then you will compute a Value column as price times quantity and total it. Finally, you can add elements from the Customer table and

FIGURE 6.15

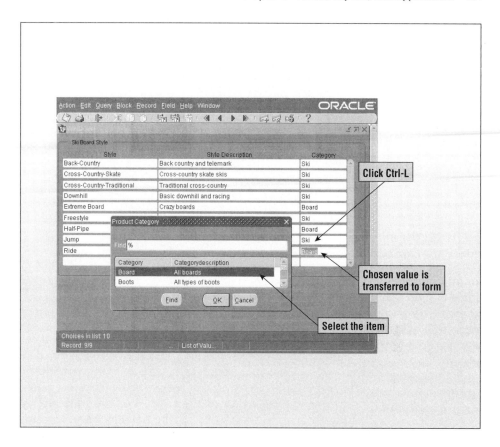

Action
Create the Sale form with the wizard.
Set property ORDER BY to SaleDate.
Format the SalesTax to $990.00.
Rearrange the items to the top of the form.
Use the Data Block Wizard to add the SaleItem table with all of its columns.
Create the relationship to Sale.
In the Layout Wizard, choose tabular and do not include the SaleID column.
Choose 5 rows and display the scroll bar.
Save and run the form.

other features that make the Sale form easier to use. The Sale form is essentially a simple main form at this point, so follow the default values. Then rearrange the items to the top of the form so there will be room at the bottom for the repeating rows of the SaleItem subform. You probably want to set the frame property for Update Layout to Manually. You should also set the ORDER BY property of the data block to SaleDate, SaleID so users can scroll through sales sequentially. While you are at it, set the justification and format for the Sales Tax field. Save the form and run it to test it. Figure 6.16 shows an initial layout for the main form, but the layout can be improved later.

The next step is to add the SaleItem subform. Start the Data Block wizard again and select the SaleItem table. Choose all columns in the SaleItem table for the data block. As shown in Figure 6.17, the next step is to create a relationship between the Sale and SaleItem data blocks. This relationship reflects the table join between the Sale and SaleItem tables. The Sale table is a master table, with the SaleItem table providing details, or multiple rows, for each sale. When the Layout wizard runs, include all of the columns, except the SaleID. Most importantly, be sure to select the tabular style and select five rows to be displayed with a scroll bar.

FIGURE 6.16

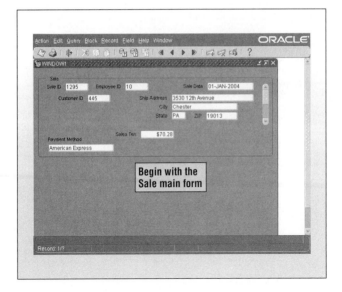

Figure 6.18 shows the Design screen at this point with both the Sale and SaleItem data blocks. Notice that all five rows are displayed in the subform so you can see the layout as it will appear when the form is run. Although there are multiple rows, you assign properties just once for each column and they are applied to all of the rows. For example, you should set the format and justification properties for the SalePrice and QuantitySold columns. Note that when the form runs, the tab order for the main form is determined by the listing order of the items within the object navigator. For example, because CustomerID appears above EmployeeID in the Sale block, users pressing the Tab key will be brought to the CustomerID field before the EmployeeID field. You should correct this order now so that it creates a logical data entry sequence for users that matches your form layout.

FIGURE 6.17

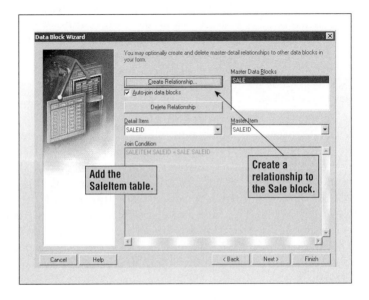

FIGURE 6.18

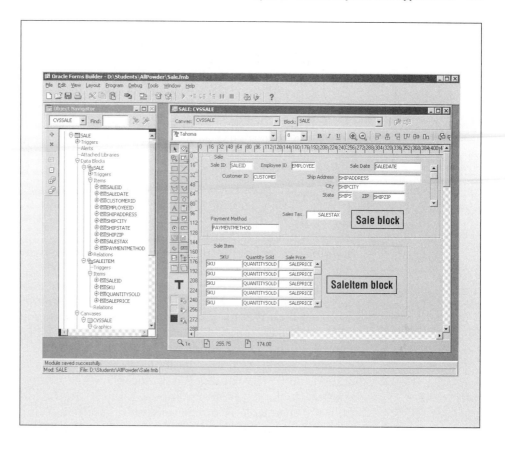

Figure 6.19 shows this initial form when it is run. Notice that the subform (SaleItem) is automatically linked to the main (Sale) form. The entire SaleItem table holds data for all sales. Yet the form displays only those items that were purchased on the Sale being displayed in the main form. They are linked by SaleID. You could have displayed SaleID on the subform to verify

FIGURE 6.19

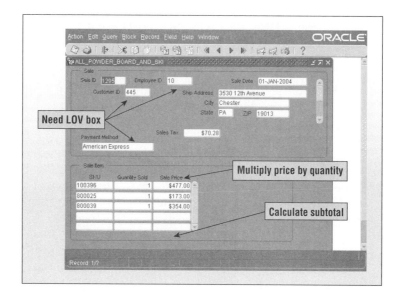

this link, but users would wonder why the same value was repeated on every row. The form works—you can enter some data and click the Save button to test it. However, it is somewhat difficult to use since it relies on ID numbers and does not display totals.

Action

Use the LOV wizard to create lists for the employee, customer, payment method, and SKU .
The SKU will use columns from the Inventory and Item model tables.
Add a button for the CustomerID that opens the LOV box.

To improve the form, begin adding the LOV boxes for EmployeeID, CustomerID, and PaymentMethod. While you are at it, you should create an LOV for the SKU. In most cases, the sales clerks will simply enter the SKU that is printed on each item, but once in a while they might want to look up an item or check a price. The initial process is the same as the one you used with the main form. Use the LOV wizard (four times) and choose the table that contains the data from which you want to select. Be sure you add an ORDER BY clause to the query that you build and check the syntax to make sure the query will run. Also, remember to set the return value to the Primary Key column. Finally, since there will be four LOV lists, you should rename the LOV and the record group within the object navigator so you can find the correct items later. For the SKU, you should include data from both the Inventory and ItemModel tables. You will have to join the tables within the query builder. Notice that the builder uses the older join syntax by defining the condition within the WHERE clause.

The sales clerks should rarely have trouble with the employee, payment method, and SKU values. When necessary, they can click the Ctrl-L combination to look up an unknown value. On the other hand, they will probably need to look up customers quite often. You could trigger this list automatically using the WHEN-NEW-ITEM-INSTANCE trigger. To demonstrate another approach, add a small button next to the CustomerID box that the user can click to bring up the LOV box.

First, click the Sale data block in the object navigator to ensure the button is assigned to the correct data block. Then use the toolbox to place a small button just to the right of the CustomerID box. Use the property palette to assign a better name (btnCustomerLOV) and a simple label (v). A lowercase v looks similar to the arrows used in most interfaces. If you have time, you could find or create an image of an arrow instead. Create a smart trigger for the WHEN-BUTTON-PRESSED event and add two lines of code:

```
Go_Item('CustomerID');
List_Values;
```

The next step is a little more complicated. You need to create a column on the subform that multiplies price by quantity and displays the result. You also need to compute the subtotal and display it on the main form. Both of these computations require adding a text box to the subform. Because the text box tends to have a different format than the existing columns, the easiest way to create these two new columns is to copy the existing SalePrice column. Click on the column, use Ctrl-C to copy it and Ctrl-V to paste the copy. Drag the copy to the right and set the properties. Figure 6.20 lists the main properties that need to be set. Be careful with the formula that does the multiplication. You must include the leading colon for both of the variable names. You can probably get by without setting the last four database properties listed, as long as you set the Database Item property to No.

FIGURE 6.20

```
Name: Value
Enabled: No
Justification: End
Format Mask: $99,990.00
Calculation Mode: Formula
Formula: :QuantitySold*:SalePrice
Database Item: No
Column Name: (blank/delete)
Query Allowed: No
Insert Allowed: No
Update Allowed: No
Prompt: Value
```

Repeat the copy/paste process to add the Subtotal column. However, the properties are quite a bit different. Figure 6.21 shows the properties you will need. The calculation properties are the most important. Choose Summary as the calculation mode, then choose the Sum function because you want the total. The item to total is the Value column you recently created, and it is in the SaleItem block. Again, make sure that this new field is not part of the database; otherwise, updates will fail. You also want to make this column invisible, and for layout purposes, it is easier if you assign it a minimal width and height. If you leave the column visible, it will show the same total value for each row, which is distracting. The next step is critical and falls into the category of a magical incantation. Oracle will not allow you to use summary calculations in the data block unless you set a specific property for the SaleItem data block. You must set Query All Records to Yes. If you forget, you will receive an error message when you run the form.

By now, you are probably asking: "If the total is invisible, how will the users see it?" The answer is that you have to create another text box on the main form that will retrieve and display the value from the subform. Why not just put the calculation into this new text box in the first place and skip the subform invisible column? Because Oracle will only compute the total

FIGURE 6.21

```
Name: SubTotal
Enabled: No
Justification: Right
Keyboard Navigable: No
Data Type: Number
Format Mask: $999,990.00
Calculation Mode: Summary
Summary Function: Sum
Summarized Block: SALEITEM
Summarized Item: VALUE
Database Item: No
Height: 1
Width: 5
Visible: No
Prompt: Subtotal
```

FIGURE 6.22

Name: Subtotal
Enabled: No
Justification: Right
Data Type: Number
Format Mask: $999,990.00
Calculation Mode: Formula
Formula: :SaleItem.Subtotal
Database Item: No
Prompt: Subtotal

within the original data block that holds the rows of data. To add a text box to the main form, click on the Sale data block in the object navigator, then use the toolbox to add a text box to the Sale form. Figure 6.22 shows the properties you need to assign to the new text box. The key step is the formula, which copies the value from the subform control and displays it in this text box. Be sure to remember the colon in front of the subform name. You will also want a total form that adds the sales tax value to the subtotal. Simply copy the new subtotal text box and change its properties to rename it as SaleTotal. Set the formula to: :Sale.Subtotal + :Sale.SalesTax. At this point, you should save the form and run it to check for errors. You can put these two text boxes anywhere on the form. They do not have to be in the Sale frame. But if you move them, you should also move the SalesTax and Payment-Method boxes.

Action

Copy and paste the SalePrice column in the subform to create a Value column. Assign properties so that it multiplies SalePrice by QuantitySold.
Copy and paste this new column to create a subtotal column.
Assign properties to make it a Summary calculation for Sum of the Value field.
Add subtotal and total fields to the Sale data block to display the subtotal and add the sales tax.

The next finishing step is to recognize that no one is going to memorize values for CustomerID. It would be helpful to include the customer name and phone number on the Sale form. Since these items reside in the Customer table, you must be careful when displaying them on the Sale form. In particular, if you simply build a query to pull data from the Sale and Customer tables, neither table will be updatable and the form will not allow anyone to change or insert data. Oracle allows you to use a query to display related data, but you must be careful to mark this data as nonupdatable. You must also make sure the primary key column (SaleID) is identified.

To add the query to the Sale data block, find the block's Query Data Source properties. First, make sure the Source Type property is set to Table. Then add a query to the Source Name property. To be safe, you should test this query first in SQL Plus to ensure that it retrieves exactly the data you want with no syntax errors. Figure 6.23 shows the query along with the other Sale data block property changes. Notice that the query must be enclosed in parentheses. Also, note that columns retrieved from other tables (Customer) must be given a single-name alias (such as cLastName).

Action

Edit the Sale data block properties and create a query as the data source to load the customer name and phone. Add text boxes to the Sale form to display the name and phone.
Set the SaleID property to Primary Key.
Set properties of the customer items so the database cannot change them.

You must also add the new columns to the field list by entering them into the Query Data Source Columns property. Figure 6.24 shows the edit form that pops up when you click the More button. Add the three aliased

FIGURE 6.23

Sale Data Block Properties:
DML Data Target Type: Table
DML Data Target Name: Sale
Query Data Source Type: Table
Query Data Source Name:
(SELECT SaleID, EmployeeID, SaleDate,
Sale.CustomerID, ShipAddress, ShipCity, ShipState,
ShipZIP, SalesTax, PaymentMethod,
Customer.LastName as cLastName,
Customer.FirstName as cFirstName, Customer.Phone
as cPhone FROM Sale INNER JOIN Customer ON
Sale.CustomerID=Customer.CustomerID)

column names (cLastName, cFirstName, and cPhone) that were defined in the query.

Back on the main Sale form, you must also set one property for the SaleID column. You have to set the Primary Key value to Yes so the forms processor knows how to update the table properly. The next step is to add the three new columns as text boxes to the main Sale form. You can add them with the text box icon in the tool box, or simply copy and paste an existing text box. Figure 6.25 shows the properties you need to set for the First Name text box. Adjust the Name, Column Name, and Prompt for the other columns.

FIGURE 6.24

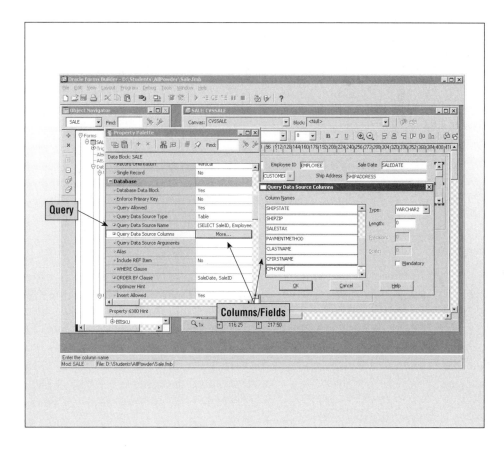

FIGURE 6.25

```
Name: cFirstName
Enabled: No
Database Item: Yes
Column Name: cFirstName
Query Only: Yes
Insert Allowed: No
Update Allowed: No
Prompt: First Name
```

The main properties are the Query Only (Yes), Insert Allowed (No), and Update Allowed (No). These settings prevent Oracle from trying to update both tables through the query at the same time.

The form is almost done. You should add one more item to improve its usability. What if there is a new customer or what if a clerk needs to change some data for an existing customer? You have a design choice to solve this problem. You could have created three levels on the form: Customer, Sale, SaleItem. The customer data would be displayed at the top, where selecting a customer would list all of the sales. Choosing a sale, or adding a new one, would show all of the items purchased at that time. While this approach works, it requires a relatively large screen to display all of the data. In some ways, it is the easiest type of form to create since each set of data resides in its own data block and the data blocks are automatically linked. However, for situations where you cannot fit dozens of subforms on a screen, it makes more sense to try the second approach.

Action
Add a button to the Sale form to edit customer data.
Add the two lines of code.
Add more code to the Customer startup trigger.
Save, compile, and test all forms.

First, make sure that the Sale form contains an Execute_Query; statement in the WHEN-NEW-FORM-INSTANCE trigger. Now add an Edit button to the Sale form. Clicking the button brings up the Customer form that was already created—with it displaying the data for the customer currently selected on the Sale form. Make sure you associate the button with the Sale data block by clicking the Sale data block name in the object navigator before adding the button to the form from the toolbox. Give the button a reasonable name (btnEditCustomer) and a label (Edit). Then create the two lines of code needed to open the Customer form. Figure 6.26 shows the code for the WHEN-BUTTON-PRESSED trigger, but notice that the folder name will probably be different on your system. A better approach is to set the environmental variable FORMS90_PATH to the folder that holds your form files. Then you can use just the name of the form so the application is easier to move to a different system. However, this change requires that you have some control over the server computer to set environmental variables.

The Customer form also requires some modifications. When the form opens, it has to look to see if the CustomerID is already given. If so, it should open the form with data for that specific customer. Figure 6.27 shows the code needed in the WHEN-NEW-INSTANCE event for the Customer form.

FIGURE 6.26

```
:global.CustomerID := :Sale.CustomerID;
Call_Form('D:\Students\AllPowder\Customer');
```

FIGURE 6.27

```
DECLARE
  sWhere VARCHAR2(200);
BEGIN
  -You should assign a null value to this in the startup form
  IF (:global.CustomerID IS NOT NULL) THEN
    sWhere := 'WHERE CustomerID=' || :global.CustomerID;
    set_block_property('Customer', DEFAULT_WHERE, sWhere);
  END IF;
  go_block('Customer');
  execute_query;
END;
```

Open the Customer form and add the trigger code. Essentially, when the form starts, if it finds a value waiting in the global variable (:global.CustomerID), then it uses that value to restrict the rows displayed in the form. If there is no value, it executes the main query without any constraints.

Figure 6.28 shows the final design screen for the Sale form. Your layout might be different, particularly if you choose to put the totals at the bottom of the form. Double-check the form to ensure that some text boxes are disabled, such as the customer data and the Value column. This is also a good time to check the tab order. It is easy to forget to set, but you will drive users crazy if the focus bounces all over the screen.

FIGURE 6.28

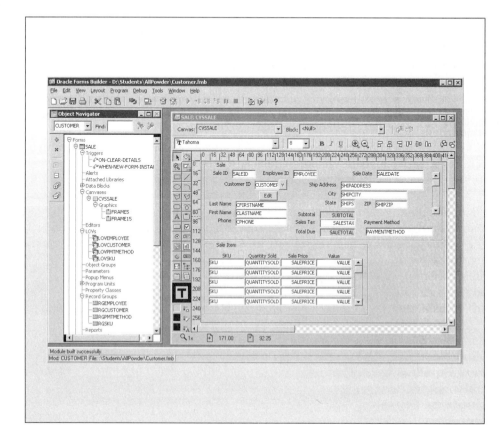

FIGURE 6.29

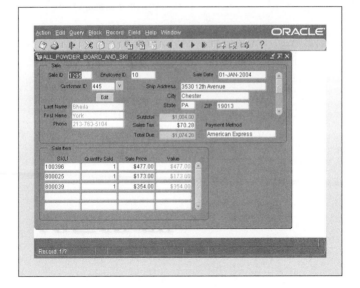

Figure 6.29 shows the form running in the browser. You should test the form and make sure you can change data, enter new rows in the subform, edit customers, delete rows, and create new sales. Testing forms is critical and time-consuming. Remember that it is always better to find problems now, while you still remember how to fix them. You should also consider having other users run your forms, because they might try combinations that never occurred to you. Since the forms run on a Web browser, it is relatively easy to set up a simple HTML page with links to your forms. When you start the form inside the designer, simply copy the URL from the browser when the form opens, then paste it into a plain HTML page and give users the address of that simple page.

All Powder Basic Reports

Activity: Create Reports with Subtotals

Most managers want reports so they can evaluate the progress of the business. Today, much of the business data could be displayed within forms—if the managers have sufficient access to the online system and if they are comfortable with reading the data on the screen instead of paper. However, reports are also useful when managers need to see lists of items with subtotals. Remember that queries can print detailed data rows or summary totals, but not both at the same time. And query results are difficult to format. Instead, you want to use the report writer to format the results, draw lines, and compute subtotals.

The first issue in building a report is to identify the level of detail that will be needed. The report writer can always compute subtotals across groups, but you need to ensure that your query retrieves the level of detail desired by the managers. As an example, consider a basic sales report by customer. Managers want to list each customer, followed by the sales placed by that customer. If they also want to include the individual

Action
Create a new report with the wizard.
Set the title and choose Group Above.
Build the SQL query using the Customer, Sale, and SaleItem tables.
Add the column Value AS QuantitySold * SalePrice to the SQL.
Set the group fields so Customer data is at Level 1 and Sale data is at Level 2.
Display all fields.
For totals, compute Sum(Value).
Choose a template.
Test the report and save it.

FIGURE 6.30

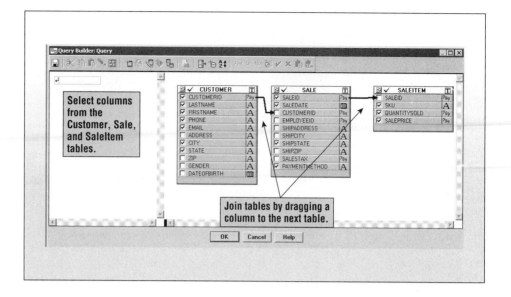

items purchased on each sale, that level of detail is different than if they simply want to see the total value of the sale. For now, assume that they want to see the detailed item list.

You can use the report wizard to build this report. Oracle has several options for building reports, but the underlying process is similar for all of them. After you start the report builder, select the option to let the wizard build the report, then enter a title. For this report, choose the Group Above style. You will now be asked to build the query to select the data for the report. You could build this query ahead of time and save it as a view, which makes it easier to test. However, this example is small enough that you can use the query builder. Figure 6.30 shows the main elements of the query builder—selecting tables, joining them, and choosing columns.

You could have written (copy pasted) the SQL directly and skipped the query builder. In this example, you need to add one element that the query builder does not provide. As shown in Figure 6.31, you need to create the Value field that multiplies QuantitySold by SalePrice. For example, if a customer bought two units of some item, the Value would reflect the total price for those two items. This calculation is entered in the SELECT

FIGURE 6.31

```
SELECT ALL CUSTOMER.CUSTOMERID,
CUSTOMER.LASTNAME,
CUSTOMER.FIRSTNAME, CUSTOMER.PHONE,
CUSTOMER.EMAIL, CUSTOMER.CITY,
CUSTOMER.STATE, SALE.SALEID, SALE.SALEDATE,
SALE.SHIPSTATE, SALE.PAYMENTMETHOD,
SALEITEM.SKU, SALEITEM.QUANTITYSOLD,
SALEITEM.SALEPRICE,
SALEITEM.QUANTITYSOLD*SALEITEM.SALEPRICE AS VALUE
FROM CUSTOMER, SALE, SALEITEM
WHERE ((CUSTOMER.CUSTOMERID = SALE.CUSTOMERID)
AND (SALE.SALEID = SALEITEM.SALEID))
```

FIGURE 6.32

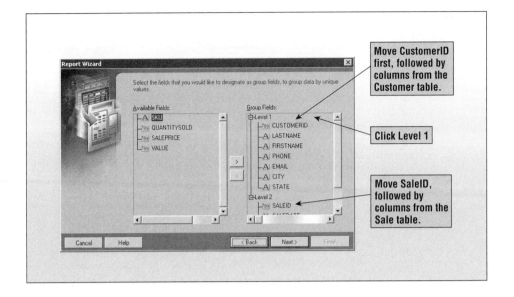

statement and identified with the alias Value. Be sure to include the comma before typing in this line. Notice that the query builder uses the older JOIN syntax. The wizard does support the newer INNER JOIN syntax, so you can use it instead if you type the entire query by hand.

Figure 6.32 shows one of the more important steps in the process—establishing groups. At this step, you create a listing that shows which columns will be grouped together on the report and which ones will trigger group breaks. For this example, you want two major groups: Customer and Sale. Indirectly, a third detail group is created from the SaleItem columns. Figure 6.32 shows what you want the groups to look like, but it is slightly tricky to create this grouping. At the beginning, all columns are in the left-side window. You need to carefully move them to the right-side window. First, move CustomerID, then move the other columns from the Customer table. Next, click the "Level 1" heading in the right-side window so that it is highlighted. Now, move the SaleID, followed by the other columns in the Sale table to the right-side window. This process will place the Sale columns into a Level 2 grouping. A Level 2 group means that it falls beneath the Level 1 (Customer) group. Customers with more than one sale will have their names listed only once at the Level 1 heading. The Level 2 Sale group data will be displayed within the overall Customer group.

Figure 6.33 shows the next step in building the report. You select the columns to be displayed. Generally, you will want to include all of the columns you selected with the query. However, sometimes you will simply choose all columns in the query, but then decide to display only a limited number of columns on the final report. You can also try to set the order of the items using this screen. Generally, the report builder will place items on the report in the order they are selected at this screen. However, you cannot control the number of columns displayed on a line, so you will still have to make adjustments later.

As shown in Figure 6.34, the next step is to choose the initial items that will be totaled or averaged on the report. In this report, you will need to total

FIGURE 6.33

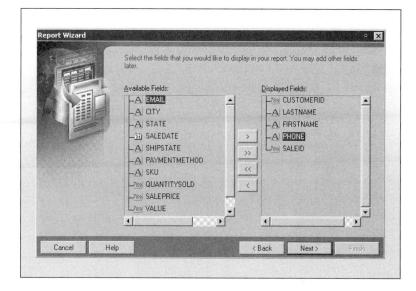

the Value column. Selecting it here will generate a total by Sale, by Customer, and for the overall report. Although you can create your own totals later, it is easier to create them at this point and then delete them later if they are not needed.

The next step is also not critical since you can modify the report later using properties. However, as shown in Figure 6.35, it is convenient to set the initial labels and display widths at this point because all of them are in one place. For the most part, you will want to correct the capitalization and add spaces to the labels. The widths are rough estimates in terms of the number of characters to be displayed in each column field. You need to make each column wide enough so that data is not truncated on the display. Yet, if you choose too large of a width, the initial layout will be squeezed with tiny fonts and will

FIGURE 6.34

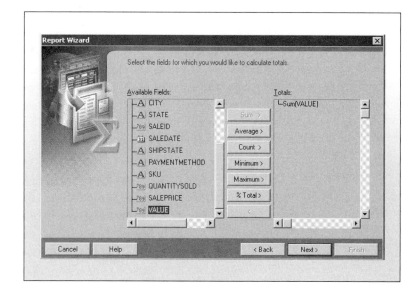

FIGURE 6.35

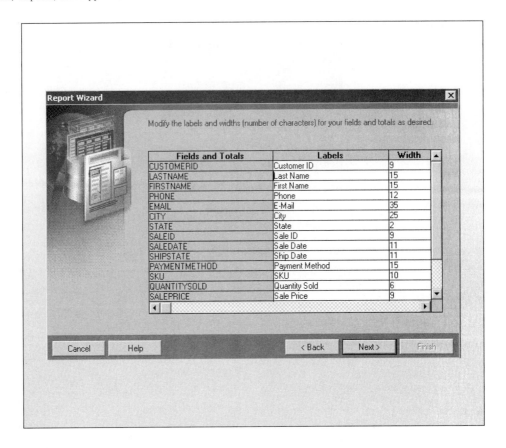

be difficult to alter later. It would be useful if Oracle examined the data to find the current maximum size necessary, but such a command is not available so you will have to estimate the width. You can always adjust it later; the goal at this stage is to be close so the wizard can create a decent first-pass version of the report and minimize your layout redesign efforts.

You will be given the option to select a template. A few default templates are shipped with Oracle, but you can always create your own version. Templates are useful to ensure consistency of style throughout an organization. The example here was created with the beige template, but you should experiment with the others to find a style that works well for your situation. Figure 6.36 shows the initial form created by the wizard. Notice the groupings that were created for Customer and Sale. The report breaks on Customer and Sale, which means that a new section is created whenever a different Sale is found for a customer. This page of the report has only single sales for each customer, but scroll through your report and you will see several examples. The detail section is repeated for each sale, but the customer data is listed only once. Also, notice the total Value calculations at the end of the detail section in the Sale footer. The Customer footer contains total sales for that customer—generally across multiple sales. At the end of the report, you will also see a total for the entire report.

The current report has the desired layout, but the formatting is missing and it is a little hard to read. For example, you need to format the price, value, and total fields so that they contain dollar signs and two decimal

FIGURE 6.36

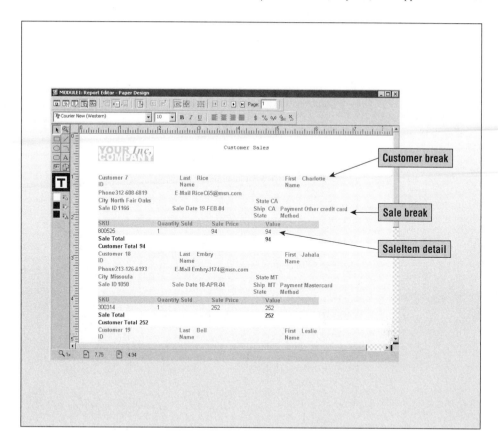

places. Figure 6.37 shows that you can change the layout and the individual formats from the Design view. The left-most buttons in the menu at the top switch from Design to Display mode. Notice that each field is placed in the appropriate section, based on the groupings that you established using the wizard. You can move fields into a different group, but you must be careful. To reduce errors, Oracle initially prevents you from moving fields to a different section. Turn off the confinement if you want to drag fields to a different section. More importantly, you can use the individual properties to set font sizes, change the display width, and format the display. In particular, you need to set the display format for the currency items. You should consult the online Help documentation for details on specifying formats.

To understand the report designer, it helps to look at the underlying data model. Figure 6.38 shows the data model that was created for this report. All of the data is retrieved with one query. There are three levels: Customer, Sale, and SaleItem detail. The boxes show the data columns that will be displayed at each level. This model was created by the wizard when you specified the grouping levels. It is the reason you had to be so careful about selecting items in each group. The basic report structure is built from this model. If you build a report manually, you have to create this model yourself. Generally, it is easier to let the wizard build the initial model, and then you can edit it by moving columns to different levels, or even creating new levels. Even if you do not need to edit the model, it is an easy-to-read

FIGURE 6.37

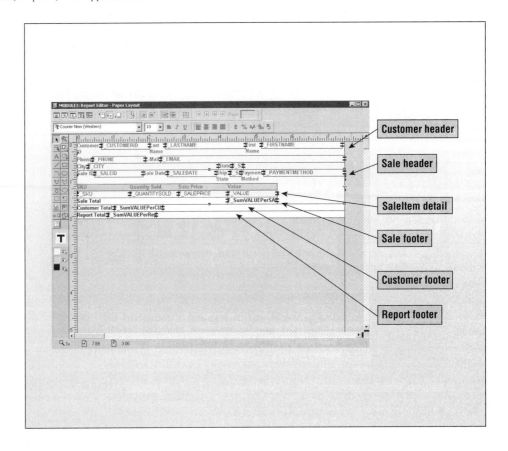

graphical depiction of the report that will help you understand the structure of complex reports.

Figure 6.39 shows the object navigator for the report. It is another powerful tool to help you understand and edit the report. Every item placed on the report is also displayed in the object navigator. Again, the object navigator shows the

FIGURE 6.38

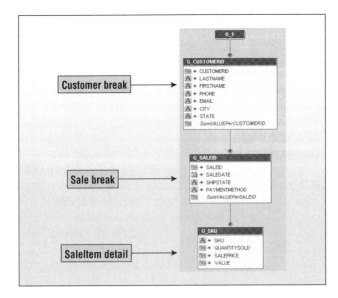

FIGURE 6.39

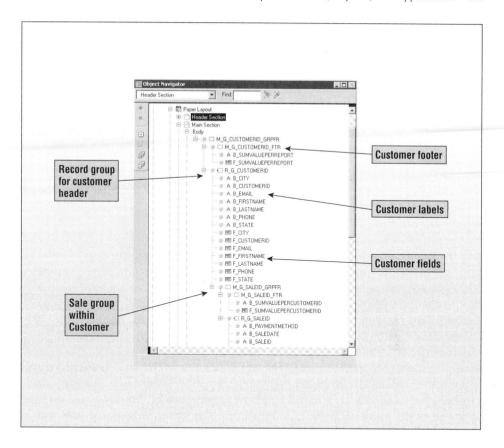

layout structure. For instance, in this portion, you can see the Sale group nested within the Customer group. More importantly, because the object navigator lists all of the items in a section, you can easily see which section holds an item and set the properties. Beyond formatting, one of the properties you should set with this report is to turn on Page Protect for the three main customer sections: M_G_CUSTOMERID_GRPFT, M_G_CUSTOMERID_FTR, and R_G_CUSTOMERID. This property setting will prevent data for a customer from being split by a page break. Since customer data generally fits on one page, it makes it easier to read by keeping all data for a customer on a single page.

Figure 6.40 shows the final design for the customer sale form. Notice the cleaner layout of the controls. The font has been reduced and the controls resized so the items fit better on the page with more white space. However, whenever you reduce font sizes below 10 points, you will have to check with the report users to ensure they can still read the report.

Figure 6.41 shows a page from the final report. Notice that it breaks cleanly at the end of a customer. Instead of trying to start the next customer on this page, it keeps the customer data together and moves it all to the next page. Observe that it has a generic logo file on the report (Your Company, Inc.). The template automatically included this image. It is stored in the main reports folder (for example, C:\OracleDAta\Ora92DS\reports\docroot\images). For this template, the file is named rwbeige_logo.gif. You can replace this file with your own

---

Action

Move items around to improve the look.
Set currency formats.
Set Page Protect in all customer levels.
Verify the data model is correct.
Run and test the report.

FIGURE 6.40

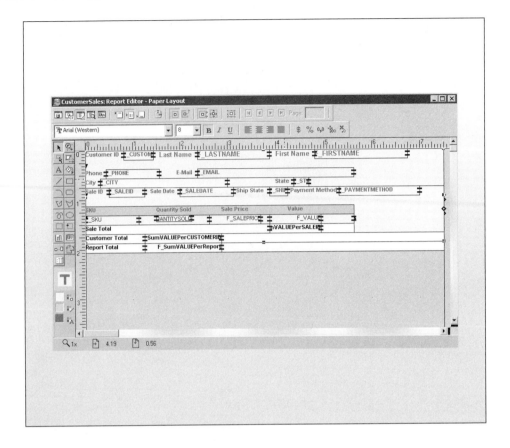

logo. To find where it is referenced in the designer, you need to look at the HTML design and search for the gif file. You could also remove or rename the file at that point.

It is possible that managers do not want the detailed list of items sold. Perhaps they need only the total value of the sale for each customer. The report would certainly be shorter. Because this level of report requires a different level of detail, you will first have to create a query that extracts the main data and computes the sales value and the total value for each sale. The report writer will then compute the totals per customer.

Figure 6.42 shows the query used to create the total value of the items for each sale. The design is straightforward: Add the desired columns from the Customer, Sale, and SaleItem table. Then add the computed column Value to compute SalePrice by QuantitySold. Save the query and build the report based on that query. Be sure that the wizard creates a group break based on the CustomerID. You can clean up the report in Design view. Move the columns for LastName, FirstName, Phone, and Email from the detail section to the Customer header section.

Figure 6.43 shows the Design view for the new report after it has been cleaned up. Set the formats for the Value column and the totals. A little rearranging provides additional white space, to make the report easier to read. Again, you can set Page Protect to prevent a page break from arising in the middle of one data for one customer.

Action
Create a new query to total sales by customer.
Create a new report based on the query.
Use the Group Above style.
Choose the No Template option.
Create a Level 1 group with the customer columns.
Build the report and clean it up.

FIGURE 6.41

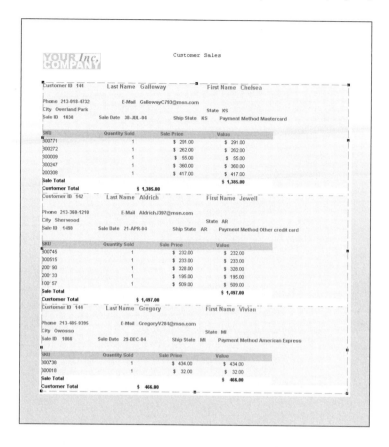

Building the All Powder Application

Activity: Create the Switchboard Form

Once you have created the forms and reports, you need to combine them into an application. A startup or switchboard form is a key element of an application. It is a form that contains links to the other forms and reports. Generally, it is easy to create—the challenge lies in determining how to organize all of the forms and reports. In most cases, users will only see the application through your forms. They will almost never want to open forms directly from the Access forms list. You have to create a structure, beginning with the switchboard form that guides them through their tasks. This process

FIGURE 6.42

```
SELECT Customer.CustomerID, Customer.LastName,
Customer.FirstName, Customer.Phone, Customer.EMail,
Sale.SaleID, Sale.SaleDate, Sale.ShipCity, Sale.ShipState,
Sum(SalePrice*QuantitySold) AS Value
FROM (Customer INNER JOIN Sale ON Customer.CustomerID =
Sale.CustomerID) INNER JOIN SaleItem ON Sale.SaleID =
SaleItem.SaleID
GROUP BY Customer.CustomerID, Customer.LastName,
Customer.FirstName, Customer.Phone, Customer.EMail,
Sale.SaleID, Sale.SaleDate, Sale.ShipCity, Sale.ShipState
ORDER BY Customer.LastName, Customer.FirstName;
```

FIGURE 6.43

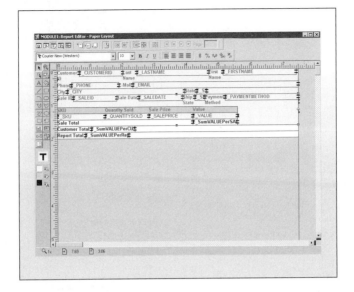

Action
Create a blank form without the wizard.
Add command buttons to open other forms: Open_Form('name');
Add links to the reports in the navigator.
Add buttons to open the reports.
Add code to open the reports.
Use colors and graphics to make the form appealing.
Run the form and test all buttons.

will often include links on other forms as well. You will have to test this sequence with the users to make sure that it matches their job workflow.

To create a switchboard form, begin with a new form and do not use the wizard. Do not create data blocks because you will not connect to the database. You can use Edit/Import to place images on the form. Use labels and properties to improve the appearance of the form and make it easy to use. Add command buttons to open other forms. The code for the trigger event WHEN-BUTTON-PRESSED is straightforward: Open_Form('form name'); Be sure to remember the semicolon at the end. You will probably have to use the full pathname of the form unless your server has already established the path using environmental variables. Figure 6.44 shows a simple example of a main form for the All Powder case. The purpose of the form is that it provides a starting point for users. All users should open this form, and it will direct and control their operations to use the application. In large applications, you might want to create additional forms that would function as submenus. For instance, you might have a special menu form just for administrators. This approach reduces clutter on the main form and hides details from other users to make their job easier.

Because Oracle Forms and Oracle Reports are two separate products, it is more complicated to add a button to print or display a report. Ultimately, you most likely will need to be running on Oracle 9i/AS to get this approach working. An Oracle whitepaper (http://otn.oracle.com/products/forms/pdf/277282.pdf) provides details on several approaches. Figure 6.45 shows the button code needed to generate a report from within a form. You can also pass additional parameters to the report if desired. For example, you might want to print the report for only one customer where the value is selected by the user on the form, so you create an additional property parameter. Note that you must declare the report inside the form object navigator. Add an entry to the Reports node and browse to find the .rep file. Be sure to

FIGURE 6.44

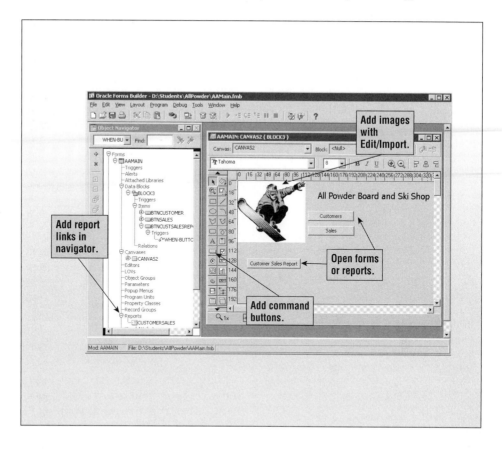

rename the new item node. You then place this name in the find_report_object function call. One other useful feature that you could use is that the buttons can open any standard Web document. The function call is a relatively simple: Web.Show_Document('URL', '_target');

Since all of the forms and reports are Web-based, you might also consider using a simple HTML page as a switchboard. You use basic HTML links to open the desired forms and reports. To get the name of the link and the

FIGURE 6.45

```
declare
  report_id       Report_Object;
  report_job_id   VARCHAR2(100);
begin
—Note: You must define the report file in the Reports node
  report_id := find_report_object('CustomerSales');
  SET_REPORT_OBJECT_PROPERTY(report_id,
    REPORT_EXECUTION_MODE, RUNTIME);
  SET_REPORT_OBJECT_PROPERTY(report_id,
    REPORT_COMM_MODE, ASYNCHRONOUS);
  SET_REPORT_OBJECT_PROPERTY(report_id,
    REPORT_DESTYPE, PREVIEW);
  SET_REPORT_OBJECT_PROPERTY(report_id,
    REPORT_SERVER, ' ');
  report_job_id := run_report_object(report_id);
end;
```

options, you can run the form and report in the designer, then cut and paste the resulting link into your HTML document. One serious drawback is that the system does not keep the login data between the various links, so users will have to log on each time a form or report is opened. Note that there is a way around this problem, but you have to be careful about security—the standard approach lists the password in plaintext in the URL link.

Activity: Build Menus and Toolbars

Switchboard forms and command button links help users navigate from one form to another, but in complex applications, users might need additional support. Menus are another method of displaying available actions to the users. Menus are usually displayed at the top of the application to provide quick links to common activities that are needed in any form. For instance, you can include a Print button for all reports, so users always know they can click one button to print whatever report they are viewing. You can also create secondary toolbars that are customized for each form. Oracle includes tools that make it relatively easy to create menus. You can also create pop-up menus that appear when the user selects a certain task. The challenge is to identify the tasks and options that users need to have available on the menu.

Menus can contain icons or submenus with additional items. Figure 6.46 shows the basic steps for creating a menu. Use the Create button or Edit/Create to add a menu module. Be sure to give it a better name, such as CustomerMenu. Within this module, you should create two menus: Customers and CustomerSub. The main customer menu is shown in the figure. You can double-click the icon to open the Menu Editor, or you can simply add items to the object navigator. Add the four items shown: AAMain, Customers, Close, and Help. Open the item property palette to assign actions to these items. Set the Menu Item Type to Plain and the Command Type to PL/SQL, then enter the command code. For AAMain, use the Open_Form('AAMain'); command, but be sure to use the pathname of the form—unless the forms environmental variable is set properly on the server. Compile the code. For the Close item, use the Exit_Form; code. Since the Help forms have not been created yet, simply add a Message('Help is not available yet.'); line. The Customers entry is a little trickier since it should open a submenu. Set its command type to Menu and select CustomerSub as the submenu name. Now modify the CustomerSub menu and add entries there to open the Customer and Sale forms. You can also add items to print the two customer sales reports. For the reports you need to copy the code from the switchboard section (Figure 6.45).

When you have created the two menus, save the module and use Program/Compile Module to convert it to a compiled menu (.mmx) file. You can now associate this menu module with any form. Since it will become the main menu, eventually you will want to associate it with all of the forms. For now, open the Customer form and open the

Action
In the object navigator create a new entry in the Menus section and rename it (CustomerMenu).
In the newly created Menus subsection, create a new entry and rename it Customers.
In the object navigator, in the same Menus sublist, add a new item and rename it CustomerSub.
Double-click the icon to open the Menu Editor.
Add entries for AAMain, Customers, Close, and Help.

Action
For each item, set the Command Type (PL/SQL or Menu).
Add the Command Text code, such as Open_Form('Name');
For the Customers item, set the submenu to CustomerSub.
Edit CustomerSub to open the Customer and Sale forms and print the two reports.
Save and compile the menus (Program/Compile Module).
Add the filename to the Customer form Menu Module property.
Compile and test the form and menus.

FIGURE 6.46

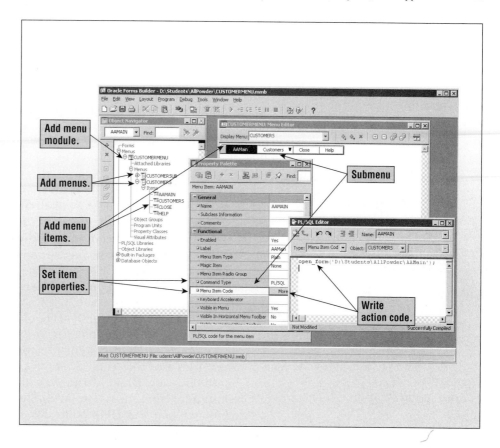

property palette for the form itself. Enter the full pathname of the .mmx file into the Menu Module property, replacing the DEFAULT&SMARTBAR entry. Recompile the form and run it. Figure 6.47 shows that you should see the new menu and be able to use its options.

FIGURE 6.47

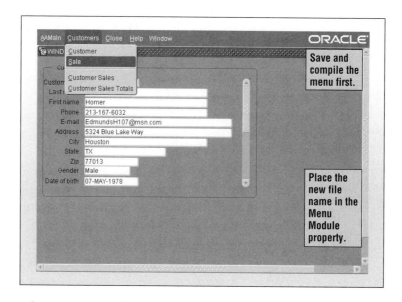

Activity: Write Help Files

A finished application also needs customized Help files. Users should be able to press the F1 key or select the Help menu option and receive additional information to help them perform a task or understand the data that needs to be entered. Detailed Help systems can become complex, with large applications requiring hundreds of pages of Help text and instructions. On large projects, companies often hire a special team just to create and edit the Help files. For these situations, you will want to purchase a dedicated Help system editor. However, you can build Oracle Help files with a text editor and a couple of free downloads. Search the Oracle OTN site for the Java Help or Oracle Help (OHW) files (http://otn. oracle.com/software/tech/java/help/htdocs/utilsoft.htm).

Action
Create at least three HTML Help files for the All Powder forms using an HTML editor or Wordpad.
If necessary, download and install the Oracle Web Help and Java Help systems.
Create the Map, Index, TOC, and Link files.
Build the search.idx file.
Create the new HelpSystem .hs file.
Edit the ohwconfig.xml file to add your helpsystem project.
Copy your files to the server and test the project.
Add the Web.Show_Document command to a custom menu to open a context-sensitive Help page.

Figure 6.48 shows the basic steps involved in creating a Help system. First you write individual Help pages as HTML text files. These pages can have links to each other and to external websites. One of the pages should be the startup page. You should also keep a list of keywords and topics for each page so you can create the index and table of contents (TOC) later. You should also create a mapping file that assigns a topic identifier to each page. The Help system file contains links to these other files so the Help system can find everything. Finally, in each Oracle form, you define a custom Help menu item that uses the Web.Show_Document command to open the Help topic for that form. The Help form also includes a Table of Contents page, as well as an index of keywords, and a full-text search engine so users can find additional information.

Figure 6.49 shows that you can create Help pages using a simple text editor, or you can use most HTML editors. You should consider using the existing Oracle style sheet for Help files. It is included with the Oracle

FIGURE 6.48

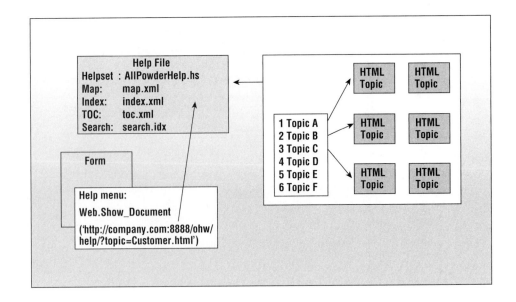

FIGURE 6.49

```
<HTML><HEAD>
<TITLE>All Powder Board and Ski Shop</TITLE>
<LINK rel="stylesheet" type="text/css" href="Styles.css">
</HEAD><BODY>
<H1>Introduction to the All Powder Board and Ski
Shop</H1>
<TABLE><TR>
<TD><IMG SRC="BoardLogo1.gif" border="0"></TD>
<TD>All Powder Board and Ski Shop sells and rents
snowboards and skis for all levels of riders and
skiers.</TD>
</TR></TABLE>
<H2>The Board and Ski Shop</H2>
<UL>
<LI><A HREF="Customers.html">Customers</A></LI>
<LI><A HREF="Sales.html">Sales </A></LI>
</UL>
</BODY></HTML>
```

download, but you will have to move it to your folder. One important consideration: You must use double quotes in the HTML file or the links will not work in the Help system.

Once you have created the individual HTML pages, you should create the mapping file that assigns a name to each topic. In HTML, you refer to each topic by the name of the file, but Oracle references topics by a name. The name should contain only letters, numbers, and underscores. As shown in the sample in Figure 6.50, you can assign almost any name, but it is common to simply replace the dot in the filename with an underscore. If you want to use it, Oracle has a tool to make this substitution for you.

Unless you have an automated Help editor, you will have to create the table of contents and index files manually. They are separate xml files with considerable flexibility. You can provide multiple levels of indented listings. Essentially, you enter a heading, followed by individual items. The individual items can link directly to a Help Topic page. Of course, you do not have to use headings, and you might not need them in the index. Figure 6.51 shows a sample TOC file. Notice the indentation used to show the levels of the final contents. The text entry is what the user will see, while the target entry is the name of the topic to be displayed. The topic must match an entry in the map file.

FIGURE 6.50

```
<?xml version='1.0' ?>

<map version="1.0">
 <mapID target="AllPowder_html" url="AllPowder.html" />
 <mapID target="Customers_html" url="Customers.html" />
 <mapID target="Sales_html" url="Sales.html" />
</map>
```

FIGURE 6.51

```
<?xml version='1.0' ?>
<toc version="1.0">

 <tocitem text="Introduction to All Powder Board and Ski Shop">
   <tocitem target="AllPowder_html" text="The Board and Ski Shop" />
   <tocitem text="Sales Options" target="Sales_html" />
 </tocitem>
 <tocitem text="Customer Options">
   <tocitem target="Customers_html" text="Adding New Customers" />
   <tocitem target="Sales_html" text="Sales Options" />
 </tocitem>
</toc>
```

Figure 6.52 shows a sample index file. In general, index files can be quite long. Automated generators are sometimes useful in creating an initial word list. However, it helps if someone goes through and adds synonyms or other search topics that might be more useful to users. Again, the text entry provides the list of words the user will see, and the target is the topic that is displayed when the user selects a keyword. The IndexEntry values provide a simple hierarchical list of items, enabling the indexer to group related topics together. For example, you might have a Customer topic, with Add, Delete, and so on as subtopics.

The search index is a little trickier, because it is a proprietary binary file. You need a tool to create the file for you. Commercial help editors can build it automatically. Oracle's Java Help system also has a Java-based tool to create the file. If you install the Java Help system (which is separate from the Oracle Web Help system), you can run a command-line Java program that reads the HTML files and builds the full-text index automatically. Figure 6.53 shows the two basic commands you need. However, you must customize the CLASSPATH variable and the folder name for your particular system. Hit the Enter key after you have entered the full CLASSPATH statement, and at the very end. Do not put line breaks in the middle of either command. The long

FIGURE 6.52

```
<?xml version='1.0' ?>
<index version="1.0">

<indexitem target="AllPowder" text="All Powder" />
<indexitem target="AllPowder" text="Management" />
<indexitem target="AllPowder" text="Start" />
<indexitem target="Customers" text="Client" />
<indexitem target="Customers" text="Customers" />
<indexitem target="Sales" text="Sales" />
<indexitem text="Introduction">
   <indexentry target="AllPowder" text="The Company" />
   <indexentry target="Customers" text="Customers" />
   <indexentry target="Sales" text="Sales" />
</indexitem>
```

FIGURE 6.53

```
set CLASSPATH=%CLASSPATH&;c:\program files\ohelp\help4-indexer.jar
java -mx64m oracle.help.tools.index.Indexer -l=en_US =e=8859_1
D:\Oracle\ohw\oc4j\j2ee\home\applications\ohw-
eapp\ohw\helpsets\AllPowder search.idx
```

folder name (D:\Oracle\...) is the full pathname of the folder holding your HTML files. The search.idx parameter is the name of the file to be created. You can change the name, but search.idx is a reasonable name for most applications.

As shown in Figure 6.54, the next step is to create the HelpSystem file. This is another XML file, although it is typically saved with an .hs suffix. It contains links to the other important files. For the most part, you can simply copy this example and change a couple of lines. For instance, you will want to change all of the <title> entries. But, as long as you stick with the standard names for the other files (map.xml, toc.xml, index.xml, search.idx, and link.xml), you can leave most of the file alone. The Links file is a little different. In many cases, you will not need it. It provides a way to consolidate several items into one associative link. You can simply copy the Oracle sample Link file; it will be ignored unless you need to create these special links.

The next step is to copy your Help system to the server and install it. This process might be slightly easier if you are using the full Oracle 9i/AS. In this

FIGURE 6.54

```xml
<?xml version='1.0' ?>
<helpset version="1.1">
 <title>All Powder Board and Ski Shop</title>
 <maps>
  <mapref location="map.xml" />
 </maps>
 <links>
  <linkref location="link.xml"/>
 </links>
 <view>
  <label>Contents</label>
  <type>oracle.help.navigator.tocNavigator.TOCNavigator</type>
  <data engine="oracle.help.engine.XMLTOCEngine">toc.xml</data>
 </view>
 <view>
  <label>Index</label>
  <type>oracle.help.navigator.keywordNavigator.KeywordNavigator</type>
  <title>All Powder Board and Ski Shop</title>
  <data engine="oracle.help.engine.XMLIndexEngine">index.xml</data>
 </view>
 <view>
  <label>Search</label>
  <title>All Powder Board and Ski Shop</title>
  <type>oracle.help.navigator.searchNavigator.SearchNavigator</type>
  <data engine="oracle.help.engine.SearchEngine">search.idx</data>
 </view>
</helpset>
```

FIGURE 6.55

```
<books combineBooks="true" useLabelInfo="true">
  <helpSet location="AllPowder/AllPowderHelp.hs" />
  ... other help set files
</books>
```

case, the Help Listener service should already be installed (or you can install the Help system's Deploy tool). A special folder and the ohwconfig.xml file should already exist. Create a new subfolder under the helpsystem folder, and edit the ohwconfig.xml file to add a line pointing to your new Help system (.hs) file. If you are running 9i/DS, you will have to install yet another 0C4J servlet, find the helpsystem subfolder, and locate the ohwconfig.xml file. Figure 6.55 shows the portion of the configuration file you need to edit. Simply add a row that lists the location of your new .hs file.

You can now open the Help file with a Web browser. On most systems, the Help file will open with the link: http://yoursystem.com:8888/ohw/help. Figure 6.56 shows the initial Help file for the All Powder case. Notice the tabs for Contents, Index, and Search. Clicking these tabs displays the appropriate forms that you created. You should test each one to ensure that they work properly. Also, be sure to test all links. The configuration file enables you to set a few additional options. For instance, you can change the branding text ("Oracle Help for the Web") and even add an image.

The final step is to link your Help topics into the database forms. Because Oracle has changed Help systems several times, the Oracle forms are configured to support an older version of the Help files that appears to be inconsistent with the new HelpSystem format. Oracle recommends that you switch to the new format, but the context-sensitive activation may not work yet. If you look at the form properties, you will see an entry for Help Book Title. Likewise, an individual text box will have a property for Help Book Topic. In theory, you should be able to enter the name of the Help System file in the form property, and individual topic names for each control on the form. In the 9.0.2 version of Oracle, this approach is not likely to work. Instead,

FIGURE 6.56

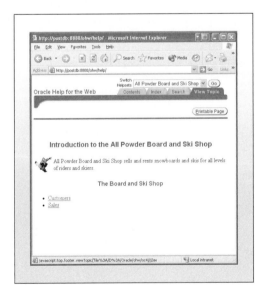

FIGURE 6.57

```
Web.Show_Document('http://yourserver.com:8888/ohw/help/?topic=Customers_html');
```

you can create a custom menu entry for Help. Then, set the PL/SQL trigger code to open the Help system for the specific topic you want to display. Figure 6.57 shows the command needed to open the Help file for a specific topic (Customer_html). Simply replace this topic with a name from your Map file. If you want, you can also capture an F1 key press and attach this same code to any control on the form.

Particularly if you are running Oracle 9i/DS and the OC4J servlets, you will find there is one more problem with this approach. The forms OC4J servlet and the help OC4J servlet cannot be run at the same time, and even if they could, would not share data. This problem should be minimized if you are running the full Oracle 9i/AS system. If not, you will have to read Oracle's documentation carefully to configure the forms OC4J servlet to process both the forms and the Help applications. Hint: Begin by finding and editing the server.xml file, and then move the Help folders into the Forms hierarchy. In real life, the Oracle DBA would have already configured the system to support the Help files. You would simply copy the files into the designated folder on the server, and then create the links within your forms.

Exercises

Crystal Tigers

The Crystal Tigers club is mostly interested in tracking members and events. The officers who will use the system do not know much about computers, but they can enter data into forms. They are also interested in a few key reports. For instance, they want to be able to get totals for the number of hours members devoted to charity events. They also want monthly summaries of the amount of money raised. The vice president also wants to be able to print a simple listing of the officers, their phone numbers and e-mail addresses. Sometimes, she also wants a similar list for members who have participated in the initial steps of an event. She wants to be able to carry the list with her when the event starts so she knows who to contact if problems arise.

1. Create the basic forms needed to enter data into the database.
2. Build a form similar to the one defined in Chapter 2.
3. Create the main reports needed by the organization.
4. Build the forms and reports into an application with a start-up form.
5. Create the Help files for the system, and remember that the users have limited computer experience.

Capitol Artists

Job tracking is the most important aspect of the application needed by Capitol Artists. In particular, the employees need to be able to quickly select a job and enter the time and expenses for the task performed. This data is then used to create a monthly billing report for the client. Consequently, you need to focus on creating the forms to capture this data. You need to make sure they are fast and easy to use. The managers also want weekly reports showing the hours and money generated by each employee so they can use the data in personnel evaluations.

1. Create the basic forms needed to enter data into the database.
2. Build a form similar to the one defined in Chapter 2.
3. Create the main reports needed by the managers.
4. Build the forms and reports into an application with a start-up form.
5. Create Help files for the system.

Offshore Speed

Special orders have always been a complex problem for the Offshore Speed managers. Customers come to the shop because it is one of the few that can obtain the custom parts they want. But the company has always had problems training employees to collect all of the order data and to keep track of getting the orders placed and delivered in a timely manner. Some of these orders include contracts with other local firms to perform customization and finish work on the boats. Although these firms do excellent work, most are terrible at keeping records. Consequently, the managers want to use the system to generate reports on individual boats for each contract shop that can be used to remind the other owners of the details. The company also needs reports on the inventory status of the specialized parts. They are having trouble keeping some items in stock, and other items seem to sit on the shelves forever; but they have no good way of keeping track at the moment.

1. Create the basic forms needed to enter data into the database.
2. Build a form similar to the one defined in Chapter 2.
3. Create the main reports needed by the managers.
4. Build the forms and reports into an application with a start-up form.
5. Create Help files for the system.

Final Project

The main textbook has an appendix with several longer case studies. You should be able to work on one of these cases throughout the term. If you or your instructor picks one, perform the following tasks.

1. Create the main forms needed for the database, including forms that will be used by administrators.
2. Build the forms similar to the ones used to define the project. That is, build database forms that match the existing user forms.
3. Create the main reports needed. Think about the analysis that managers will want to do and provide reports that help them. Consider adding charts to compare data.
4. Build the forms and reports into an application with a start-up form.
5. Build a toolbar that makes the application easier to use.
6. Create Help files for the system.

Chapter

Database Integrity and Transactions

Objectives

- Define customized functions.
- Improve forms by responding to form events.
- Execute customized SQL statements from code.
- Define transactions.
- Create new rows and use the generated key value.
- Write cursor-based programs that compare data across rows.
- Set up and handle optimistic and pessimistic locking conditions.

Program Code in Oracle

Oracle supports code in the form of triggers that are fired when specific events occur. These triggers can be attached to the database itself or can be user events within a form. Triggers in the database are powerful, and thus, potentially dangerous. For example, you can create a procedure that runs whenever a row is inserted into the Employee table. This one piece of code might be simple and easy to understand. The danger arises when your database has hundreds or thousands of these triggers. A simple change to one table could cascade to dozens or hundreds of additional updates propagated through the trigger code. This cascade of events can be difficult to trace and understand—particularly when the code sections have been written by dozens of different programmers. On the other hand, database triggers are an important tool to provide additional security and ensure that certain tasks are performed correctly. The code is created in one location and it cannot be circumvented. Once the events and code are defined, it does not matter what users and application developers create—the trigger updates are processed behind the scenes without additional intervention.

Oracle also uses form triggers to provide customized responses to user events. You can create simple or detailed code when a user presses a key, clicks a form button, or changes a piece of data. Dozens of events can accommodate your customized code, but generally you need to write only a couple of lines of code for one or two primary events. The other event triggers are available in case you need them for a special feature.

In all cases, Oracle stores code in procedures. A procedure contains a declaration section and a body. The declaration section lists the variables used within the procedure. With Oracle 9i, you can write the code using Oracle's language (PL/SQL), or you can write procedures in the standard Java language. This chapter will use PL/SQL, but the examples are not that complex and the syntax differences between the two languages are minor, so it is straightforward to convert them to Java. Oracle also supports packages, which are collections of procedures. If your application needs a group of related procedures, you should create a package and store all of the procedures together. The main advantage is that it makes the code easier to find and modify later.

To understand how the code and event models work, this chapter begins with some easy examples. Pay close attention to the code and where it is located. For example, code written in a module can be accessed throughout the application, but code written within a form is generally only called in response to events on that form.

Case: All Powder Board and Ski Shop

Figure 7.1 shows the Sale form developed in the last chapter. Notice that it has a box to enter the sales tax. If you look at the underlying Sale table, you will see that it contains a column to hold the sales tax amount for each sale. You could argue that the sales tax does not have to be stored, since it can always be computed from the other sales data. But what happens if the tax rate changes? Or, what if the round-off computation is modified? Then the company's sales tax records will no longer exactly match the data filed with

FIGURE 7.1

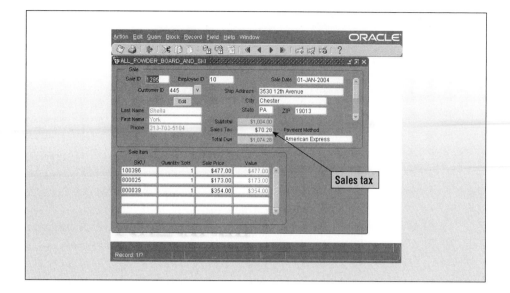

the state and local governments. It is safer to store the actual tax amount collected to ensure consistency. However, now you need a method to compute the sales tax on each sale; you certainly cannot expect clerks to compute the amount, or even look it up correctly in a table. Instead, you need to write a function that will compute the sales tax correctly and transfer it to the form and the database. Sales taxes can be highly complex. Some items might be taxable, while others are not. Since each state and local district is different (and there are several thousand tax districts in the United States alone), this presentation is simplified and assumes a single tax rate that is applied to all sales and to rental items.

The first question you must answer when creating custom code is to determine where it belongs. In this example, you might consider putting it on the Sale form, but since the code will also be useful for rentals, it makes more sense to generalize it and place it in a module so that it is available to any form, query, or report within the application. Placing the code in a package also makes it easier to find later.

Lab Exercise

All Powder Board and Ski Data

Like almost everything else in Oracle, functions and procedures are created in SQL. Although it is not necessary for this single function, you should get in the habit of storing functions and procedures in packages. Packages are simply containers for related functions and procedures. They make it easier for developers and users to find specific functions.

Activity: Create Sales Tax Function

In this case you will create a package named Taxes that will eventually hold other tax-related procedures. When the auditor asks to see all of the tax-related calculations, you can quickly find them in this one package. Figure 7.2 shows the PL/SQL code used to create the package header and the

FIGURE 7.2

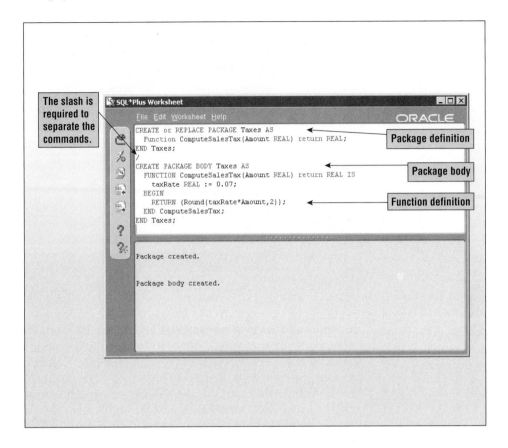

package body. If you run the two commands together, make certain they are separated by a slash (/) or it will not accept them. Right now, the package body contains only the simple function to compute sales taxes.

The tax calculation function is deliberately simple to highlight the process instead of the accounting rules. Be sure to use a variable for the tax rate, since it makes the code easier to understand, which reduces errors when someone tries to modify it later. Also, make sure you use the Round function to truncate the tax due at two decimal places. Run the commands to create the package and the function. You can now use this function in queries and forms just as you would use any other function. You can test the function in SQL using the special system table called dual. This tiny table contains one column and one row of data, making it useful for testing functions and calculations because it returns only a single value. Figure 7.3 shows the command and the correct result. Since the function is stored within a package, you include the name of the package when you call the function Taxes.ComputeSalesTax.

Action
Use SQL to create the Compute SalesTax function within a new Taxes package. Test the function with an SQL statement.

The next step is to use the formula to automatically compute the sales tax on the Sale form. The challenge at this step is to identify when you want to compute the tax. Why does that matter? The problem is that there are times you do not want to compute the tax. For example, if a sale has been completed and a manager is simply reviewing the form, you should not recompute the tax because the rate might have changed. So you only want

FIGURE 7.3

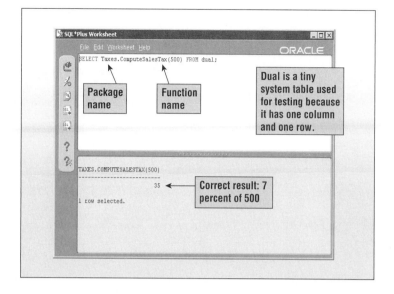

to compute it for a new sale. Realistically, it only needs to be computed when all of the sale items have been selected. However, the form has no good way to know when the sale is completed. Probably the easiest solution is to compute the sales tax due when the user clicks on the SalesTax box. For new orders, a simple click generates the correct value and the order total.

You need to attach a line of code to the PRE-TEXT-ITEM trigger of the SalesTax box. However, you must make sure that you are logged into the All Powder database or the compiler will not be able to find the function. Either run the form and then exit, or use File/Connect. On the form design or the object navigator, right-click on the text box and choose the PRE-TEXT-ITEM trigger from the Smart Trigger options. As shown in Figure 7.4, enter the command carefully: :Sale.SalesTax := Taxes.ComputeSalesTax(:Sale.Subtotal). Be sure to include the colons in front of the text box names and the assignment equals sign. Compile the trigger code to make sure you typed it correctly. Save and run the form. Test the code by clicking or tabbing to the SalesTax box. The current value displayed is probably based on the 7 percent tax rate already, so you might have to change the value, click away, and then return to the box to see the value change. Or just create a new sale.

To test the code, run the form and create a new order. Select an employee as the salesperson and choose the customer from the list. Check to ensure that the total box also updates correctly—it should be the sum of the subtotal and the newly generated sales tax value. Think about the steps you performed to create this trigger, and consider why it is so important to use the global ComputeSalesTax function. If you had buried this calculation on the form, the next developer that had to change it could search for days trying to find the calculation. With packages, developers can quickly scan the functions and procedures to find the appropriate function. Of course, good documentation is also important.

Action
Edit the Sale form.
Right-click the SalesTax box and select the PRE-TEXT-ITEM trigger.
Add the code:
:Sale.SalesTax :=
Taxes.ComputeSalesTax(:Sale.Subtotal);
Run the form.
Click on the SalesTax box to test the calculation.

FIGURE 7.4

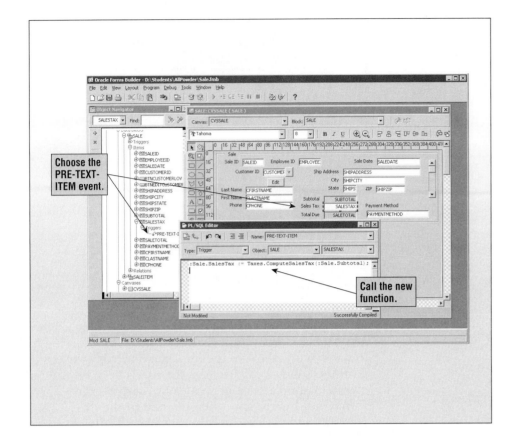

In real life, program code rarely runs correctly the first time. To find mistakes, you need to use the debugger. Open the Sale form in Design view and open the code window by double-clicking on the icon in the object navigator window. Double-click the gray column to the left of the one line of code. Select Debug/Debug Module from the main menu and click on the SalesTax box to trigger the code. The debugger will stop on the marked line. As shown in Figure 7.5, you can use the Debug/Debug Windows to see the values stored on the form and for any variables you might have created. You can single step through the code and evaluate the variables to see exactly how your code runs. Choose the Stop button on the toolbar to close the debugging session.

Activity: Update Inventory with Data Triggers

Maintaining quantity on hand statistics for inventory is one of the trickiest elements in programming business forms. Reexamine the Inventory table and notice that it contains the column QuantityOnHand. This value represents the current number in stock for a specific item. The value of the column is that clerks can quickly check the column to see if certain sizes are available. Also, managers can get a quick look at the list of items that might be under-or overstocked. Technically, this value would not have to be stored in the database—if you have a complete list of all purchases, sales, and adjustments, you could use a query to compute the total number currently in stock. However, with thousands of items and sales, this query might take

FIGURE 7.5

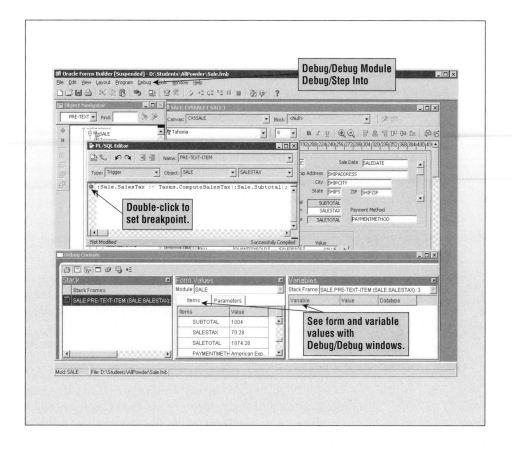

Action
Insert a new row into the Sale table with a SaleID of 3000, CustomerID of 582, and EmployeeID of 5.
Create the AFTER INSERT trigger for the SaleItem table.
Insert a new row into the SaleItem table (3000, 500000, 1, 100).
Check the value of QuantityOnHand in the Inventory table for SKU=500000 and ensure it was decreased from 10 to 9.

too long to run. Consequently, you need a mechanism to update this value on the fly. Whenever an item is sold, the corresponding quantity should be subtracted from the quantity on hand. In Oracle, this subtraction can be handled with triggers on the data tables. These data triggers are simply code that is executed whenever a specified event occurs. The three events are DELETE, INSERT, and UPDATE. You can attach a trigger before or after the change is written to the database. In the inventory situation, you want to attach your code to the AFTER event so that you do not change the quantity on hand (QOH) until after the change has truly been made.

The first step is to examine the tables and understand how they are related. You need to change the Inventory table whenever changes occur to the SaleItem table. The SaleItem table specifies the SKU value that matches exactly one row in the inventory table. Also, when testing, remember that you need a matching entry in the Sale table to provide the SaleID key. You should look at some sample data in the three tables so you can enter consistent values to test. In this case, a new SaleID of 3000 to CustomerID 582 by EmployeeID 5 should work. SKU values of 500000 and 500010 both have an initial QOH of 10 units.

The next step is to think about the events that can occur and determine what they mean and how they will affect the QOH. It is easier to understand

FIGURE 7.6

```
CREATE OR REPLACE TRIGGER NewSaleQOH
  AFTER INSERT ON SaleItem
  FOR EACH ROW
BEGIN
  UPDATE INVENTORY
  SET QuantityOnHand = QuantityOnHand - :NEW.QuantitySold
  WHERE SKU = :NEW.SKU;
END;
```

the process by considering one event at a time. Think about the first step in a sale. A row is entered into the Sale table: INSERT INTO Sale (SaleID, CustomerID, EmployeeID) VALUES (3000, 582, 5). You could enter the data for SaleDate and so on, but since this data is temporary, these three items are sufficient. Now, the next logical step that occurs in a sale is that the SKU for the item being purchased is entered into the SaleItem table: INSERT INTO SaleItem (SaleID, SKU, QuantitySold, SalePrice) VALUES (3000, 500000, 1, 100). At this point, the QuantitySold of one unit means that the system should subtract that value from the quantity on hand. To accomplish this task automatically, you need to establish an AFTER INSERT trigger on the SaleItem table. Figure 7.6 shows the SQL used to create this trigger. First the trigger is given a unique name. The second line specifies that the trigger should be fired after a row is inserted into the SaleItem table. The third line indicates that the code body should be executed once for each row being inserted. The begin/end block holds the main code, which consists of a single SQL UPDATE statement. The UPDATE statement should look familiar, with a small twist. The twist is that it refers to the values being inserted into the SaleItem table using the :NEW syntax to reference the data that was just added to that table. The statement simply tells the database to subtract the new quantity sold from the existing quantity on hand for the SKU value just entered into the SaleItem table. When you have successfully created the trigger, issue the INSERT statement to add the row to the SaleItem table. Now verify that the QOH was modified with the query: SELECT SKU, QuantityOnHand FROM SaleItem WHERE SKU=500000.

Action
Delete the SaleItem row (SaleID=3000 And SKU=500000).
Check the quantity on hand.
Add the AFTER DELETE trigger.
Insert the SaleItem row again.
Check the quantity on hand.
Delete the SaleItem row.
Check the quantity on hand.

You could continue to issue INSERT commands for different quantities, and the quantity on hand will decrease. Everything seems to be fine. However, what happens if there is a data entry error? Try deleting the row you inserted: DELETE FROM SaleItem WHERE SaleID=3000 And SKU=500000. Check the QOH in the Inventory table and you will see that it does not change. Why is that bad? Because the delete statement implies that the item was not actually sold, and since you have already subtracted the quantity, you need to add that value back to the QOH. In other words, you need another database trigger—one that fires when a row is deleted in the SaleItem table. Figure 7.7 shows the statement to create the trigger. This code is similar to the after insert version. The only differences are that the quantity sold is added back to the quantity on hand, and the syntax uses the :OLD reference. The :OLD reference simply means to use the values that existed before the row was deleted. In this case, there are no :NEW values because the Delete

FIGURE 7.7

```
CREATE OR REPLACE TRIGGER DelSaleQOH
  AFTER DELETE ON SaleItem
  FOR EACH ROW
BEGIN
  UPDATE INVENTORY
  SET QuantityOnHand = QuantityOnHand + :OLD.QuantitySold
  WHERE SKU = :OLD.SKU;
END;
```

command does not create anything. To test the new trigger, insert the SaleItem row again and check the quantity on hand. If you are using the SQL Plus Worksheet, you can use the Back and Forward query buttons to bring up the SELECT statement that you used before. Now, delete the SaleItem row and check the quantity on hand again. It should be restored to its value before the latest INSERT command.

The two triggers you created are powerful tools. Once they have been defined, you never need to think about them. Anytime a process inserts or deletes a row, they are activated and inventory is changed immediately. You could test these actions using the Sale form, and you should see the same results. However, there is still something missing. One of the trickiest aspects to event programming is that you need to think hard about possible actions by users—and the consequences. In the inventory situation, what happens if a clerk goes back and changes a value? Originally, an SKU and quantity were entered, then the clerk sees an error or a customer changes his mind. Try it first with a change in quantity. Check the current value for QOH, then insert the row to sell 1 unit. Check the QOH again to see that it was reduced by one, say from 9 to 8 units. Now consider what if the customer actually purchased two units. Issue the statement to change the QuantitySold to two units: UPDATE SaleItem SET QuantitySold=2 WHERE SaleID=3000 And SKU=500000. Check the QOH and you will see that it still shows only one item was removed from inventory (8 units remaining instead of 7).

You need to add an UPDATE trigger to the SaleItem table to handle this problem. Figure 7.8 shows the code to create the trigger. Again, it uses a familiar UPDATE statement. However, check the use of the :OLD and :NEW references carefully. They contain the heart of the logic. The :OLD values are the data that was stored in the SaleItem table before the update was initiated. The :NEW values are the data in the row after it has been changed. In this case, the QuantitySold changed from one (old) to two (new). For the specified product SKU, this query adds the old value back and subtracts out the

FIGURE 7.8

```
CREATE or REPLACE TRIGGER ChangeSaleQOH
  AFTER UPDATE ON SaleItem
  FOR EACH ROW
BEGIN
  UPDATE Inventory
  SET QuantityOnHand = QuantityOnHand + :OLD.QuantitySold -
  :NEW.QuantitySold
  WHERE SKU = :OLD.SKU;
END;
```

Action
Add the **ON UPDATE** trigger.
Check the quantity on hand.
Issue an update to change the
QuantitySold in the SaleItem table.
Check the quantity on hand.

new value instead. Remember that a change in quantity means that the original subtraction was incorrect, so it is restored while the new value is subtracted. Again, you should test this trigger by checking the current QOH value, issuing an Update statement to the SaleItem table to change the quantity sold value, and then examine the new QOH to see that it holds the proper total.

If you look closely at the Update trigger code and think about the problem for a minute, you will see that one additional situation has to be handled. What happens if a clerk changes the SKU? In this case, you need to add the QuantitySold back to the original SKU item, then subtract the QuantitySold from the new SKU item. Of course, the QuantitySold might have been changed at the same time, so you need to be careful about which one you add and subtract.

Figure 7.9 shows a revised version of the AFTER UPDATE trigger. At this point, it is useful to point out the value of the CREATE or REPLACE clause in Oracle. Since the trigger already exists, you cannot simply issue another CREATE statement with the same trigger name. Normally, you would have to DROP the original trigger and then create the new one. The CREATE or REPLACE statement essentially combines these two operations to save you a step. The IF statement divides the trigger so that it handles the two cases separately. Actually, you could have created two completely separate triggers using a WHEN condition, but it is easier to see the code with all of the cases in one trigger. The IF statement is true when the SKU was not changed. This Update statement is the same as the simple update trigger. The ELSE condition handles the case where the SKU was changed (and the QuantitySold might or might not have been altered). The first UPDATE statement restores the old quantity subtracted from the original SKU value (old quantity, old SKU). The second UPDATE statement subtracts the new QuantitySold from the new SKU inventory level.

These three triggers should now handle all of the sales situations that affect the inventory quantity on hand. You should reset the QOH value and

FIGURE 7.9

```
CREATE  or  REPLACE  TRIGGER  ChangeSaleQOH
  AFTER  UPDATE  ON  SaleItem
  FOR  EACH  ROW
BEGIN
  IF  (:OLD.SKU  =  :NEW.SKU)  THEN
    UPDATE  Inventory
    SET QuantityOnHand = QuantityOnHand + :OLD.QuantitySold — :NEW.QuantitySold
    WHERE  SKU  =  :OLD.SKU;
  ELSE
    UPDATE  Inventory
    SET  QuantityOnHand  =  QuantityOnHand  +  :OLD.QuantitySold
    WHERE  SKU  =  :OLD.SKU;
    UPDATE  Inventory
    SET  QuantityOnHand  =  QuantityOnHand  —  :NEW.QuantitySold
    WHERE  SKU  =  :NEW.SKU;
  END  IF;
END;
```

Action
Create the full **ON UPDATE** trigger.
Check the quantity on hand.
Change the QuantitySold and SKU (to 500010) in the SaleItem row.
Check the quantity on hand for SKU 500000 and 500010.

test all of the changes. In particular, in the SaleItem row change both the QuantitySold and the SKU.

Of course, if you have created purchase order and purchase item tables, you would have to add similar triggers to the purchase item table. The only difference is that a purchase adds quantity to the QOH instead of subtracting it, so you have to reverse the signs in the code.

Activity: Define Transactions

Transactions consist of multiple changes that must succeed or fail together. One of Oracle's strengths is its support to ensure that transactions are completed correctly. In particular, all changes are written to journal logs. If the system crashes in the middle of a transaction, the system can still recover the transactions that were interrupted or roll them back to the point where the changes began. The other important aspect of transactions is the ability to prevent or handle collisions of two processes altering the same data at the same time.

Katy, the manager at All Powder, has noticed that many customers do not like being charged for damages caused to the rental equipment. Some of them believe that the equipment is simply wearing out and failing. She also notices that there can be several complaints about a specific rental—particularly when it involves multiple items. David, the rental manager, agrees, but still wants to be able to track the cumulative charges. He has suggested that any reduction in the damage charge be recorded as a discount to that customer. That way, he can track the total damages, as well as which customers might receive the most discounts. Katy also likes the discount idea, because she wants to implement a discount program for employees who rent equipment. Since multiple discounts can be applied to a single rental, a new table is needed. Figure 7.10 shows the table keyed by both RentID and DiscountDate.

You can build a form to handle data entry for the employee discounts, but do not do that now. It is a little more complicated to correctly handle the

FIGURE 7.10

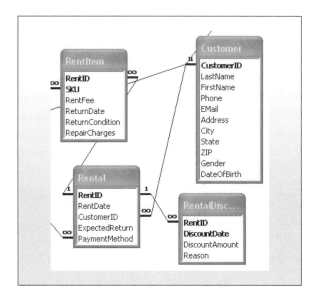

FIGURE 7.11

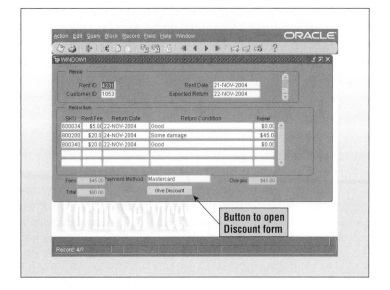

Action

Create the Rental form.
Create the Rental Discount form with no data.
Add the text boxes and button.
Save the form.
Add a button to the Rental form that opens the Discount form.

---

customer discounts for disagreements over the damage charges. You need a transaction that decreases the repair charges and adds a row to the RentalDiscount table for the same amount. To begin, you need to create a Rental form similar to the Sale form. Figure 7.11 shows a standard Rental form. Notice that it needs subtotals for the rental amount and for the charges. Any repair charges would be entered when the items are returned. Eventually, you also need to add a standard command button to open the form to give the discounts, but it is easier to create the form first and then return to add the button on the Rental form.

Figure 7.12 shows the Discount form (GiveRentDiscount). It is built from Design view and not tied to the database. Add the text boxes by hand. Set

FIGURE 7.12

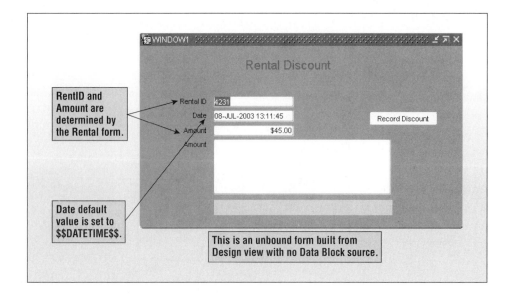

FIGURE 7.13

```
:global.RentID  :=  :Rental.RentID;
:global.Amount  :=  :Rental.SubCharges;
Call_Form('D:\Students\AllPowder\GiveRentDiscount');
```

the default value on the date field to $$DATETIME$$, so the current date and time are entered by default.

The next step is to place a button on the Rental form that will open this Discount form and transfer two values automatically: RentID and Amount. Figure 7.13 shows the code used on the Rental form button WHEN-BUTTON-PRESSED trigger. The values are transferred to global variables, which will be loaded when the Discount form opens.

Figure 7.14 shows the code for the two trigger events in the discount form. The form trigger is fired when the form first opens, so it retrieves the values stored in the two global variables and places them onto the form as the default values. The second code is triggered when the button is clicked to save the changes. First, it zeros any charges for that rent, and second, it adds a row to the new discount table to record the rental, the date of this action, the amount of the discount, and the reason for the discount. In terms of business policy, the first step might be overkill. It is possible that the rental manager would want to give only a partial discount to the customer. If so, he can first run this routine, then return to the Rental form and enter the remaining value of any charges. If this activity is common, you should change this form and code so that only the partial amount is subtracted from the charges.

Figure 7.15 shows one more important addition to the button code that handles the discount. What happens if something goes wrong between the two DML commands? The EXCEPTION line traps all errors and rolls back any changes made. Without this code, it is possible for the UPDATE command to change the value to zero and then the INSERT command could fail and it would never record the reason for the change. With the exception handling and the transaction code, both changes will commit or fail together. Notice that you do not have to declare the start of a transaction. In Oracle, a transaction begins and a rollback segment log is created when the first SQL statement is executed.

Action
Edit the Rental Discount form.
Add the specified code to the WHEN-BUTTON-PRESSED trigger.
Test the forms.

FIGURE 7.14

```
Form:  WHEN-NEW-FORM-INSTANCE
:RentalID  :=  :global.RentID;
:Amount  :=  :global.Amount;

Button:  WHEN-BUTTON-PRESSED
UPDATE RentItem SET RepairCharges=0
WHERE RentID = :RentalID;

INSERT INTO RentalDiscount(RentID, DiscountDate,
DiscountAmount, Reason)
VALUES (:RentalID, :TransDate, :Amount, :Reason);
Commit;
:txtMessage :=  'Changes recorded.';
```

FIGURE 7.15

```
BEGIN
  UPDATE RentItem SET RepairCharges=0
  WHERE RentID = :RentalID;

  INSERT INTO RentalDiscount(RentID, DiscountDate, DiscountAmount, Reason)
  VALUES (:RentalID, :TransDate, :Amount, :Reason);
  Commit;
  :txtMessage := 'Changes recorded.';
EXCEPTION
  WHEN OTHERS THEN
  Rollback;
END;
```

Database Cursors, Keys, and Locks

Activity: Read Rows of Data

Direct SQL commands are useful for DML issues where you need to change or delete rows of data. When you need program code that needs to examine several rows of data, you need to use database cursors. Consider the business question of sales by week. Katy wants to know if weekly sales increase more in the first part of the year or in the last part. In particular, she wants to know the average percent increase in weekly sales for the first weeks (1 to 15) compared to the last 15 weeks (38 to 52). Remember that SQL can perform calculations on data within the same row. SQL can also compute subtotals for groups of data. However, it is difficult to get SQL to compare data by subtracting values across two rows. Instead, it is easier to write a query that does the main computations, and then use cursor code to do the comparisons.

Action
Create a new query.
Tables: Sale and SaleItem.
Create column TO_CHAR(SaleDate, 'ww') AS SaleWeek.
Create column QuantitySold*SalePrice AS Value.
Sum the Value column by week.

Begin by creating a query that computes total sales by week. Figure 7.16 shows the query. Note that you need to format the SaleDate using the TO_CHAR function with a format of 'ww' to get the number of the week. Make sure you compute the Sum of the price times quantity and that the total is computed for each week with the GROUP BY clause. A couple of entries have missing dates, so they can be removed from this query. Use the CREATE VIEW line at the top to save the query, but make sure you test the query before you add this line.

The next step is to compute the percentage change between the rows. The code for this step will be created within a function in a new SalesAnalysis

FIGURE 7.16

```
CREATE VIEW WeeklySales AS
SELECT TO_CHAR(SaleDate, 'ww') AS SalesWeek,
  Sum(SalePrice*QuantitySold) AS Value
FROM Sale INNER JOIN SaleItem ON
Sale.SaleID=SaleItem.SaleID
WHERE SaleDate Is Not Null
GROUP BY TO_CHAR(SaleDate, 'ww');
```

package. Eventually, you can add a button and result box to a form to display the computation, but for now, it is faster to build the command and test it in PL/SQL.

The next step is to write the code that computes the average percent increase. For each pair of rows, the code needs to subtract the two values and divide by the value in the prior row to yield a percentage change. This percentage needs to be summed and eventually divided by the number of calculations to obtain the average percent increase. Figure 7.17 shows the main code. The SQL statement is opened as a cursor, which retrieves one row of data at a time using the loop. The Avg1 variable keeps the running total of the percentage increase, while *N* counts the number of operations. The role of the PriorValue variable is the most important. At the end of the loop, it is assigned the value obtained from the current row. When the next row is retrieved, the program can now compare the current (new) value to the old (PriorValue) value. This trick is useful for many cursor-based programs, so you should study the code until you understand it. Use a basic SELECT statement to test the function in the package. Note that you need to use the FROM dual clause so you can see the result. Depending on the actual values in your database, the result should be about 13 percent. Note that this routine does not quite provide the detail Katy wants, but it is straightforward to restrict the query using starting and ending week parameters and call the function twice.

Action

Create the SalesAnalysis package with the AvgPercentWeeklyChange function. Use SQL to call the function: SELECT SalesAnalysis.AvgPercentWeeklyChange FROM dual.

FIGURE 7.17

```
CREATE OR REPLACE PACKAGE SalesAnalysis AS
    FUNCTION AvgPercentWeeklyChange return REAL;
END SalesAnalysis;
/
CREATE or REPLACE PACKAGE BODY SalesAnalysis AS
    FUNCTION AvgPercentWeeklyChange return REAL IS
        CURSOR c1 IS
            SELECT SalesWeek, Value FROM WeeklySales;
        Avg1 REAL;
        N Integer;
        PriorValue WeeklySales.Value%TYPE;
    BEGIN
        Avg1 := 0;
        N := 0;
        PriorValue := -1;
        FOR recSales in c1 LOOP
            IF PriorValue > 0 THEN
                Avg1 := Avg1 + (recSales.Value-PriorValue)/PriorValue;
                N := N + 1;
            END IF;
            PriorValue := recSales.Value;
        END LOOP;
        RETURN (Avg1/N);
    END AvgPercentWeeklyChange;
END SalesAnalysis;
/
```

Define the SELECT statement for the cursor to trace through.

Create variable to hold the value from the previous row with the same data type as the column in the table.

Skip the first week because there is no prior value.

Compute the percent change and keep a running total.

Save the current row value and move to the next row.

FIGURE 7.18

```
CREATE SEQUENCE seq_Sale
INCREMENT BY 1
START WITH 10000
NOMAXVALUE
NOCYCLE
CACHE 10;
```

Activity: Generate and Use Keys

Oracle uses sequences to generate unique key values. Sequences have some nice properties that make them highly efficient for multiple users and heavy loads. However, the act of generating a new number does not automatically store it in the table. On the other hand, triggers provide a means of automating the number generation when you need it the most—inserting a new row.

Action
Create a sequence to generate key values for the Sale table beginning with a value of 10000.
Create a trigger for the Sale table that generates a new sequence value and uses it for the SaleID.
Test the process by inserting a row into the Sale table without using a SaleID.

Figure 7.18 shows the PL/SQL code to generate a sequence of numbers that will be used for the Sale table. Notice that the command contains no overt indication that it is for the Sale table. Only the name that you provide gives a clue. The point is that sequences are technically independent from a table. Your code, either through a trigger or through other INSERT code, is what ties a sequence to a table. Notice that several options are available for generating sequences of numbers. This example starts at 10000 to avoid collisions with the existing data.

One of the easiest ways to use a sequence is to automatically generate a new value whenever a row is inserted into the table. Figure 7.19 shows the trigger that will generate sequenced key values for the Sale table. Each time a row is added to the Sale table, this trigger is fired and it generates a unique key value by selecting it off the sequence list. The trigger must be fired before the row is inserted, because you cannot insert a row without a primary key. There are some potential drawbacks to this approach. In particular, what happens if someone wants to insert a new row without using the generated key? This situation arises when you need to import existing data that already has key values that should not be changed. If this situation is common, you should consider not using this automated system. If it is relatively rare, or at least controllable, you can always disable the trigger (ALTER TRIGGER GenKeyForSale DISABLE), load the data, and then reenable the trigger.

You should test all sequences and triggers using SQL. Figure 7.20 shows the statements needed to test this particular trigger. The first line inserts a row into the Sale table. Notice that it does not specify a value for the SaleID.

FIGURE 7.19

```
CREATE OR REPLACE TRIGGER GenKeyForSale
  BEFORE INSERT ON Sale
  FOR EACH ROW
BEGIN
  SELECT seq_Sale.NEXTVAL INTO :NEW.SaleID
FROM dual;
END;
/
```

FIGURE 7.20

```
INSERT  INTO  Sale  (CustomerID,  EmployeeID)  VALUES  (582,  5);
SELECT  seq_Sale.CURRVAL  FROM  dual;
SELECT  *  FROM  Sale  WHERE  SaleID=10000;
```

If you did specify a value, the command would be accepted, but the SaleID value would be discarded. The second line retrieves the value that was generated by the sequence. You will use this value (probably 10000) in the third statement to retrieve the Sale values to ensure the row was created correctly.

For many common operations, this key-generation process works well and is mostly invisible to the user and developer. However, some cases cause more problems—particularly when you need to perform operations outside the common forms. Consider a case where you need custom code to generate each sale and enter the sale items. For example, perhaps you have a bar-code scanner and want to automate as much of the checkout process as possible.

Figure 7.21 outlines the basic events that will occur. Notice that when the new Sale is created, the Oracle trigger will generate a new key value. The catch is that you need to get this value so that you can save it in the SaleItem table for each scanned item. The immediate question is, How do you get this value? Notice that you call seq_Sale.NEXTVAL to generate a new value in the sequence. Sequences also support seq_Sale.CURRVAL to retrieve the most recently generated value. This value is unique to each database process, so the value you obtain is based on any keys you just created and is not affected by the fact that another user might also have just generated a key.

Now consider the issue of the bar-code scanner. Even if you have a scanner handy, you probably do not want to write the interface code for it. To simulate the data from the scanner, begin by creating a form in Design view that has text boxes for the three main keys: CustomerID, EmployeeID, and SKU. Figure 7.22 shows a sample form with default values that will work. Add a command button and delete the main wizard code. Also, add a text box to display the SaleID that will be generated within the code.

Figure 7.23 shows the code that runs the process. First, the row is inserted into the Sale table using the current date. This insertion automatically generates a new key value. Second, this generated value is retrieved and held in a temporary variable. Third, the list price of the item being scanned is retrieved and also placed into a temporary variable.

FIGURE 7.21

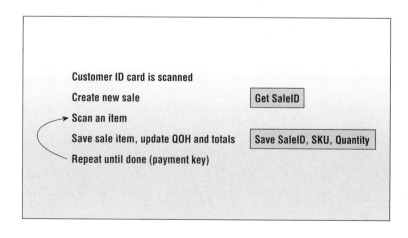

FIGURE 7.22

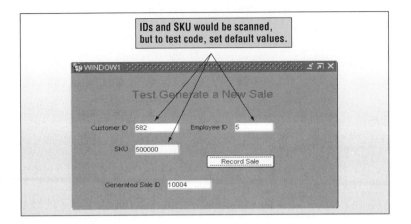

<table>
<tr><td>

Action

Create a new form with no data.
Add boxes for CustomerID,
EmployeeID, SKU, and txtSaleID as the
generated key.
Create a command button and add the
indicated code.
Test the form.
Place a breakpoint at the top of the
code and step through the code.

</td></tr>
</table>

Finally, a row is added to the SaleItem table using the generated SaleID value to link it to the Sale table and the retrieved list price so clerks do not have to memorize prices. To be safe, exception handling code is added to catch any problems and roll back the transaction in case of a failure.

The last step is to display the newly generated SaleID on the form so you can see it. You should be able to use a SELECT command to retrieve the inserted Sale and SaleItem values. You could also use the Sale form and search for the new sale. Of course, you could modify the code to handle multiple items being scanned, along with a screen to add the payment data, but they are not needed at this point.

FIGURE 7.23

```
DECLARE
    tmpListPrice ItemModel.ListPrice%TYPE;
    tmpSaleID Sale.SaleID%TYPE;
BEGIN
    INSERT INTO Sale (CustomerID, EmployeeID, SaleDate)
    VALUES (:CustomerID, :EmployeeID, SYSDATE);

    SELECT seq_Sale.CURRVAL INTO tmpSaleID FROM dual;

    SELECT ListPrice INTO tmpListPrice
    FROM Inventory, ItemModel
    WHERE Inventory.ModelID=ItemModel.ModelID
    AND SKU=:SKU;

    INSERT INTO SaleItem (SaleID, SKU, SalePrice, QuantitySold)
    VALUES (tmpSaleID, :SKU, tmpListPrice, 1);
    :txtSaleID := tmpSaleID;

EXCEPTION
    WHEN OTHERS THEN
        Rollback;
END;
```

FIGURE 7.24

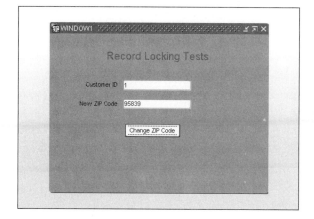

Activity: Compare Pessimistic and Optimistic Locks

The issue of locking records to prevent concurrency errors could be applied to the Rental Discount form. Think about the possible errors if one clerk enters new values for damages while a second one is offering a discount. However, the differences between pessimistic and optimistic locking are difficult to understand, and it is better to start with a simple problem that is independent of the other forms. Consider a program that changes ZIP codes for customer data.

Create a new form that is not bound to the database. As shown in Figure 7.24, add a box to select a customer. You should consider adding an LOV for practice, but you will need a second form that will also provide the Customer ID in a list. Add a text box to enter a new ZIP code. Create a command button that will execute the code to change the ZIP code for the selected customer.

Action
Create a new form with no data.
Add a text box and LOV for Customer ID.
Add a text box to enter a new ZIP code.
Create a button and add the indicated code for it.
Test the form.
Use the wizards to create a second form that displays CustomerID and ZIP code in a tabular list.

Figure 7.25 shows the code used to update the ZIP code for the selected customer. The SQL statement selects the desired customer through the WHERE clause, and the new ZIP code is assigned using the UPDATE command. For the moment, the goal is to keep the code simple.

You need two processes changing the same data to test the data locks and concurrency. To be able to see the effects of locks, create a quick and simple form to view a few of the columns of the Customer table. Use the Form wizard to create a form based on the Customer table showing CustomerID, LastName, FirstName, and ZIP. Choose the tabular layout so you can see several rows at one time. Figure 7.26 shows the basic form. Keep the form small so you can display it on the screen along with the TestLock form. Open both

FIGURE 7.25

```
BEGIN
  UPDATE Customer
  SET ZIP = :ZIPCode
  WHERE CustomerID = :CustomerID;
  Commit;
END;
```

FIGURE 7.26

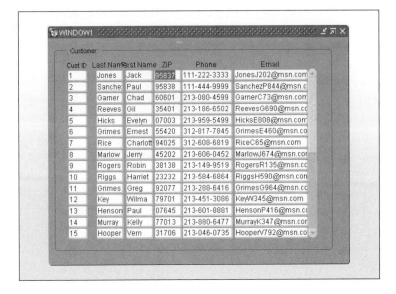

forms and arrange them on the screen so you can see both at the same time. You might want to start two separate browser windows and open each form separately.

Oracle does not support optimistic locking. It contains a sophisticated mechanism to handle concurrency issues as automatically as possible. These forms will illustrate how the system works. Begin with the List form, click on the ZIP code for the first customer and change the last digit. But, keep the cursor inside the ZIP box. That is, do not press the Tab or Enter keys, and do not save the changes. Switch to the CustomerLocks form, enter the Customer ID for the same customer you selected in the list form (the ID is probably 1 if you sorted the form). Enter a new ZIP in the text box, then click the button to submit the changes. You should not receive any error messages. However, the changes will not be saved, and the form will go into a waiting mode as shown by the hourglass cursor. Oracle recognizes that the change from the List form is pending, and it will not write the new change until the first one is finished. Switch to the List form and save the changes. When you return to the test form, the change will be committed and the hourglass cursor will be gone. If you issue a simple SELECT command using SQL Plus, or return to the List form and execute the query, you will see that the ZIP code you entered on the testing form is the current value stored in the database. This result is not an error; it simply indicates that two different people changed the data—one after the other. The delay in updating the second change simply arose because it had to wait for the first change to be completed.

Now try the collision from the other side. Refresh the List form by clicking the Execute Query button. Switch to the Lock Testing form and enter a new ZIP code. Click

Action
Open both forms so they are both visible on the screen.
In the list form, change the last digit but do not save the changes.
In the test form, enter the same Customer ID and a different ZIP code, then click the Save button.
You should see the test form go into wait mode (hourglass cursor).
Return to the list form and save the changes.
Determine the final value of the ZIP code.

Action
Execute the query in the List form to obtain current database values.
Alter the ZIP code in the testing form and save the new value.
In the List form, try to change the matching ZIP code.
You should receive an error message.

FIGURE 7.27

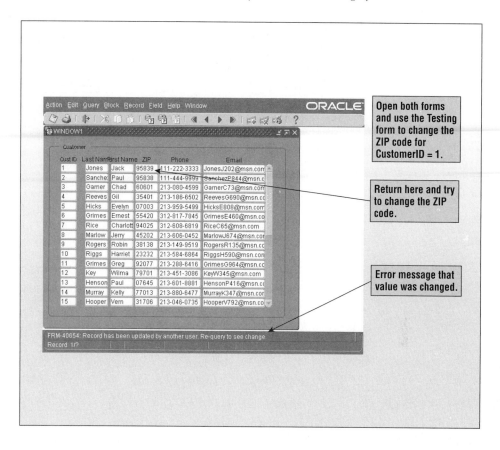

the Save button to write the new value to the database table. The List form read the data before it was changed by the Testing form. As shown in Figure 7.27, this form is still showing the older value from the database. Consequently, the form warns you that the data has changed and suggests that you requery the database to obtain the current values.

For some applications, it will be useful to have the same effect in the Testing form. Exit the forms and return to Design view with the Lock Testing form. The waiting and hourglass cursors are useful, but you might want an even stronger lock setting, or at least the ability to provide a message to the users and give them the chance to not make the changes. Figure 7.28 shows a modified version of the code for the Save button on the testing form. The main difference is that the transaction level is set to serializable, which means all transactions will operate as if they were performed in sequence. In this case, it means the transaction will generate an error when it encounters the incomplete changes made from the List form. Consequently, exception handling code has been added to catch the error and display a message. Users are then free to retry the update or to go on to a different task. Notice that the concurrency error is not predefined within Oracle, so the pragma EXCEPTION_INIT is used to attach a name to the error based on its number. Using an explanatory name makes the exception handling code easier to understand.

Compile the new code, save the form, and reopen both the List and Testing forms. Again, make a change to a ZIP code in the list form but do not save the change—to force a collision of updates. Switch to the Testing form,

FIGURE 7.28

```
DECLARE
  concurrency_hit EXCEPTION;
  PRAGMA EXCEPTION_INIT(concurrency_hit, -8177);
BEGIN
  SET TRANSACTION ISOLATION LEVEL SERIALIZABLE;

  UPDATE Customer
  SET ZIP = :ZIPCode
  WHERE CustomerID = :CustomerID;
  Commit;

EXCEPTION
  WHEN concurrency_hit THEN
    message ('Data has been changed by another process.');
  WHEN OTHERS THEN
    message ('Unknown error.');
END;
```

Action
Change the code in the testing form. Save and recompile the form. Reopen the list and testing forms. Repeat the first experiment by changing one digit of the ZIP code on the List form. Enter a new ZIP code on the Test form and click the button to save it. You should receive an error message. Return to the List form and save the changes. Determine the current value of the ZIP code in the data table.

enter the same Customer ID and a new ZIP code, then press the Save button.

Figure 7.29 shows the result of the stronger isolation level. Recall that the first time you ran this experiment, this form went into wait mode until the update from the List form was completed. Then this form wrote out its value, replacing the change made by the List form. Now, with the serializable isolation level, this PL/SQL update recognizes that the data row is in the process of being changed. Consequently, it cancels the update, raises the error, and displays the message at the bottom of the screen. You should return to the List form and save the changes. Now use SQL Plus or refresh the List form data to see that the current value stored in the

FIGURE 7.29

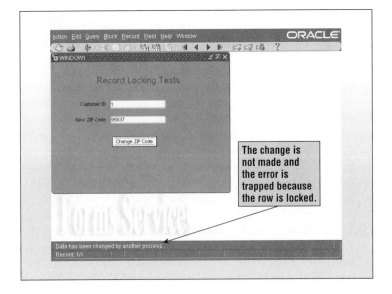

database came from the changes just made on the List form. Remember that earlier, the Test form overwrote this value. The stronger isolation level prevents that second change. Of course, the user can still decide to click the Change button again and the value from the list form will be overwritten. The important difference is that a human made the decision—not the machine.

Exercises

Many Charms

Inventory control is a critical success factor for determining profitability at Many Charms. Madison and Samantha need to watch the quantity on hand—particularly for the high-cost items. The suppliers are a complicating factor. Some of them are known for being inconsistent in delivering items ordered. As a result, Samantha and Madison have to carefully check every shipment they receive and cross-match it to the orders. Many times the shipment is missing items, and once in a while, the companies send items that were not ordered. These items have to be returned, but the supplier billing is just as bad. Madison has to continually watch the supplier bills to ensure that they are only billed for items they actually ordered and received. As a result of problems, she also wants to track the unordered items that were sent back, so if they show up on a bill, she can provide the details of when the item was returned.

1. Create a form to handle purchase orders to suppliers. Create a second form to handle received shipments. Be sure that it can handle receipt of partial orders and track the day that each partial order arrives. It must also handle receipt of unordered items (which should be stored in a separate table).

2. Add a button to the Received Orders form so that if they receive an interesting unordered item, it can be added to the orders and inventory and paid for. Create it as an entirely new order and be sure to handle optimistic locks and transactions.

3. Create a form that enables Madison to select a product category and metal, and then enter a percentage price increase. Write the SQL update code so that this increase is applied to the list price of the selected categories.

4. The company often ships orders to three states, each of which charge different sales tax rates. Write a function that takes the state code and the amount and returns the tax due.

5. Create a form and write a program that for a given type of charm and type of metal, computes the average of (1) the number of days between sales of that item, and (2) the average number of days between purchase orders for that item.

Standup Foods

While food items and celebrities are important aspects of the business, the day-to-day operations depend on managing the employees. In particular, Laura wants to reward the workers who continue to do well. The evaluation and rating system she has implemented is a major component of this plan.

Now she has to set up the system to make it easy to use so everyone can enter the necessary data. She also needs a way to analyze the data to help managers select the best employees for the next job, and to reward people who do well.

1. Create a form to enter data about an event, with an emphasis on the jobs performed by the employees and their evaluations. Make sure the form includes the revenue received from the event, the costs, and the dates involved. Create a separate form to enter and display data about employee specializations.

2. Create a form for Laura that lets her select a job category and then displays the top-rated employees in that category. (*Hint:* Create a subform and modify its Record Source query using code.) Create a text box so Laura can enter an average rating as a cut-off value. Create a second text box so Laura can enter a percentage raise increase. Add a button and write the code to give that raise increase to all of the selected employees.

3. Sometimes managers need to hire part-time workers on the spot. Create a simple form that lets managers add basic employee data without allowing them to see or change data for other employees.

4. Workers often want to estimate how much money they will make after all withholdings are deducted. Calculating withholdings is a complex process, but create a simple version to use as an estimate. The function should have number of exemptions, wage rate, and hours worked as inputs. It returns an estimate of the take-home pay. Use sample paychecks or research the Internet to estimate the tax withholding based on the number of exemptions. Create a simple form so employees can plug in these three values and receive the estimate.

5. Laura needs to provide some documentation to the bankers regarding the firm's growth. Create a new table with columns for month, revenue, costs, and percent change for revenue and cost. Write a query to compute the total revenue and costs per month and insert those values into the new table. Write a cursor-based program to compute the percent changes and insert the values into the appropriate columns.

EnviroSpeed

Tracking the knowledge of the workers and experts along with recording the experiences obtained in the many clean-up situations is a primary element of the company. You need to create forms that make it easy for workers to enter the data and knowledge gained. However, for the company to stay in business, you also need to track costs and revenue. Revenue is generally straightforward—the company bills based on the underlying costs, but payments are generally received over time. You will need a form to record the receipt of payments by the customers.

1. The company is trying to standardize its fee structure. Write a function that has inputs for the cost of the crews, the cost of expert time, the cost of chemicals, transportation costs, equipment, and miscellaneous costs. Compute a billing fee based on a percentage profit from each of these costs (crews: 20 percent, experts: 30 percent, chemicals: 15 percent, transportation: 10 percent, equipment: 50 percent, miscellaneous: 15 percent). Also include a $50,000 fixed cost for overhead.

2. Create a form that enables managers to quickly put together a crew in an emergency. The form will have selection boxes for specialty and years of experience (subtract date hired from today). Clicking a button will retrieve a list of crew members meeting the desired conditions. Double-clicking on a name should add that person to the crew required for this disaster.

3. In the middle of an incident, crew members still need to record all of the details so they can be retrieved later. Create a form that enables them to enter the needed information. Be sure to include a way to quickly add a list of chemicals encountered in the incident. Mostly they should be able to select from a known list, but they sometimes encounter new chemicals. Be sure to control for concurrency, since several people may be entering data at the same time.

4. Write a program that evaluates payments by each customer. Assuming payments are due at the end of each month, assess an interest charge of one-half percent of the outstanding balance. Also, assess a late fee of $200 for each month that a payment is late. Automatically add these values to the customer's balance. *Note:* You will have to enter several payments and late or missing payments to test the function.

5. Enter enough sample incident data to cover at least a year. Write a cursor-based program to calculate and display the percent increase in revenue per month.

Final Project

The main textbook has an appendix with several longer case studies. You should be able to work on one of these cases throughout the term. If you or your instructor picks one, perform the following tasks.

1. Make the forms easier to use by automating as many tasks as possible.

2. Examine the case for situations where you can use SQL to update records selected by the users. For example, consider price increases, employee raises, and automated inventory orders.

3. Look for potential reports that require comparing data over time. Write the cursor-based code to generate the necessary change data.

Chapter

Data Warehouses and Data Mining

Chapter Outline

Objectives

- Extract data from spreadsheets and import it to a data warehouse.
- Create and browse an OLAP cube.
- Analyze time-series data.
- Analyze geographic data.
- Analyze data with statistical tools.

Data Warehouse

Data warehouses have evolved because of the need for online analytical processing (OLAP) and its conflicts with online transaction processing (OLTP). The goal of a data warehouse is to hold consistent data, possibly obtained from several sources, which can be quickly searched and analyzed. Only recently has Oracle added data warehouse and OLAP capabilities. Many of the data warehouse and data mining tools are designed to be used by programmers. They are not easy-to-use tools designed to quickly build systems. On the other hand, most large-scale data warehouse and OLAP projects require detailed specialized coding to automate data extraction and cleaning. Most business intelligence problems also require highly customized data models. The tools Oracle sells make sense in this context. The drawback is that they are probably too hard to use for these short exercises. Oracle has also added the Discoverer tool that provides a more interactive browsing environment with some analytical capabilities. It is specifically designed for managers to use to examine data from their perspective without having to write SQL queries.

Oracle has taken a slightly different approach than the rest of the industry to creating data warehouses and converting transaction data into a format that can be quickly analyzed by OLAP systems. Instead of building a new storage mechanism, Oracle keeps the original data in relational tables. Figure 8.1 shows the basic concepts involved in this method. First, you have to import all of the necessary data into Oracle tables. Second, you define the OLAP business perspective queries in terms of a star (or snowflake) design by creating dimensions that are related to the fact measures. You often have to create hierarchical groupings on the dimensional data. Although this process appears similar to the traditional OLAP approach, the big difference is that the new star design does not hold any of the data. It is simply a metadata definition that describes how to retrieve data from the relational tables. But since data stored across multiple tables requires joins that can be slow

FIGURE 8.1

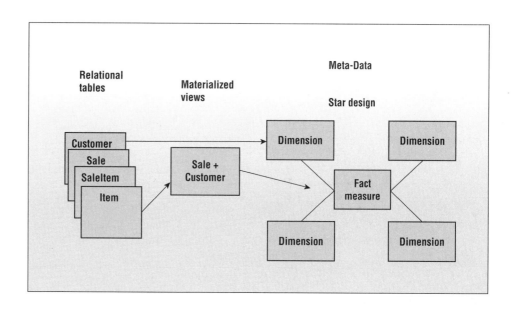

to compute, Oracle introduced materialized views. A materialized view is essentially a temporary, nonnormalized table. When extensive joins or complex calculations are needed, you can create a materialized view that holds the results of the computations and joins. The OLAP system then pulls the data from this temporary view instead of returning to the original tables. To improve performance, Oracle relies on snapshots of the data called materialized views. For the most part, Discoverer can automatically create these snapshots and refill them as needed.

Case: All Powder Board and Ski Shop

Like most businesses, the managers of All Powder need to analyze data to spot trends and solve problems. One of the most challenging aspects of a board and ski shop is the huge variety of inventory needed. As vendors produce even more styles and variations, it becomes difficult to stock all of the items in a collection of sizes. Yet, if the store does not have items in stock, it will lose sales. This balancing act between inventory costs and sales revenue has destroyed many other firms. The owners of All Powder are committed to running a large enough shop so that they can afford to carry a large selection of snowboards and skis. However, managers need to constantly evaluate styles and products so items can be cleared out if needed. For that analysis, one of the main tools they need is an OLAP cube browser or perhaps the Microsoft PivotTable that shows sales split by several features and categories. Figure 8.2 lists some of the main dimensions that managers want to examine in terms of sales. They are not certain about the validity of the last three, so they are displayed with question marks.

Managers also occasionally raise some more challenging statistical questions, such as whether customers who rent equipment are likely to buy that equipment, and whether skiers buy certain types of poles or boots with their skis. They also need to forecast sales by categories. In particular, they often argue about whether certain styles are increasing or decreasing in popularity. Some of these analyses might require the help of a statistician to build a formal model, but the managers would at last like to see some rough analyses.

FIGURE 8.2

Sales Dimensions
State (ship)
Month
Category
Style
SkillLevel
Size
Color
Manufacturer
BindingStyle
WeightMax?
ItemMaterial?
WaistWidth?

Lab Exercise

All Powder Board and Ski Shop

As organizations grow over time, the internal processes undergo changes, data changes, systems improve, and number systems rarely stay the same. Consequently, most information systems consist of a mix of technologies and databases. Rarely is the data consistent across all of these systems. For the All Powder shop, before the database was created, the managers kept limited records in Microsoft Excel. These records are not perfect: They are organized by Sales and by Rentals and the data is not normalized. Also, they are focused primarily on the equipment and did not keep data on customers. From our more modern database perspective, the records are a pain, but at least they are electronic and not paper so you do not have to enter all of the data by hand.

Nonnormalized data is common in business, and you will often be asked to convert this data into a relational database. Fortunately, you can use the power of SQL as a magical super tool to impress mere mortals with your skills. Figure 8.3 shows the layout of the data in the two worksheets. Again, notice that lack of normalization. Each row represents an item that is sold or rented. Fortunately, the worksheets repeat the SalesID and RentalID so you can still recover which items are grouped onto a single sale or rental. Likewise, they repeat the descriptive item data for each time the model was sold. To ensure your information is really accurate, you should eventually check to see that the managers were consistent in recording this data. For

FIGURE 8.3

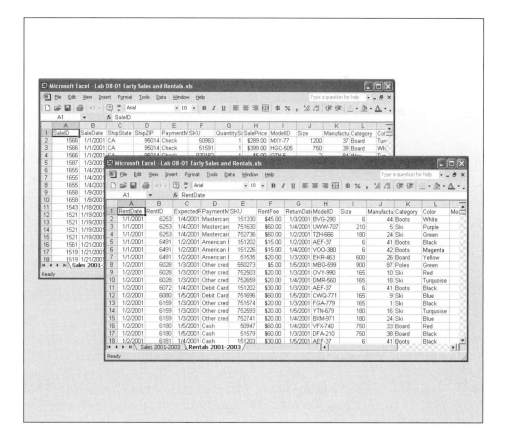

example, ModelID BVG-290 might have been given a different description at different times. If there are many inconsistencies of this type, it will be difficult and time-consuming to clean up this data. Most of the corrections would have to be handled manually, unless you have a third source of data that you know is correct. These are the types of problems you often face when extracting data from diverse systems.

Activity: Extract and Transform Data

The first step in extracting and transforming this data is to get it into the database where you can use SQL to work on it. Oracle now provides two related tools to import data from text files: the SQL * Loader and external tables. SQL * Loader is a command-line utility (sqlldr) that reads data from a variety of text files and transfers it into SQL tables. It uses a sophisticated control file to specify the location of the data and the format of the data in the files. The files have to be plain text files but can have delimited or fixed-width columns. It often takes considerable time to set up the control file correctly. However, once the control file is correct, you can use it to extract data from the same source time after time. It is a useful tool for transferring data on a regular basis.

Action
Delete all sales with SaleID>2000. Disable the trigger that creates SaleID keys: ALTER TRIGGER GenKeyForSale Disable; Modify and run the code to create the external tables for the old Sale and Rental data. Insert CustomerID 0 and EmployeeID 0.

External tables have similar capabilities—since the data reader is based on the SQL * Loader engine. However, data is not really transferred out of the flat files. Once you define the data format and declare it as an external table, you can use SQL and treat the data as if it were stored in a regular Oracle table. Because an external table is declared using PL/SQL, it is a little easier to set up and to work with interactively until you get the definition correct. At that point, it takes a simple SQL SELECT INTO command to transfer all of the data from the external file and copy it into a standard Oracle table. Oracle also provides the Warehouse Builder tool that has similar features to import data from flat files. This tool is actually better at handling other tasks, such as cleansing addresses and rebuilding OLAP cube dimensions. Since the older sale and rental data only needs to be loaded one time, and it requires some effort to split it into normalized form, it is easier to do the transformation one time.

Because they are a little easier to set up, you should use an external table to extract the data for this activity. Unfortunately, the loader cannot read an Excel worksheet directly; consequently, the two worksheets have been saved as comma-separated value (CSV) files. CSV files are a common format used to transfer data. The files are simple text files that hold one row of data on a line. The values for each column are separated by commas (hence the name). Although the system is relatively easy, you must be careful that the text data does not contain additional commas that would throw off the parser.

In the All Powder case, some of the earlier exercises have added new data to the Sale table. You need to ensure that the sales being imported do not have SaleID values that conflict with the existing data. To be safe, delete any sales with a SaleID greater than 2000 in the existing Oracle database. A related problem arises from the trigger that automatically generates a new key value for SaleID whenever a row is inserted. This trigger should be disabled while you import the new data: ALTER TRIGGER GenKeyForSale Disable.

You are now ready to create external table links in Oracle that point to the two CSV data files. The data files and the PL/SQL code to create the links are

FIGURE 8.4

```
rem change the folder to point to the location of the CSV
files create or replace directory csv_dir as
'D:\students\BuildAllPowder\AllPowderSampleDataCSV';

create table OldSale_Ext
(SaleID               INTEGER,
 SaleDate             DATE,
 ShipState            VARCHAR2(50),
 ShipZIP              VARCHAR2(50),
 PaymentMethod        VARCHAR2(50),
 SKU                  VARCHAR2(50),
 QuantitySold         INTEGER,
 SalePrice            NUMBER(10,2)
 ModelID              VARCHAR2(250),
 ItemSize             NUMBER,
 ManufacturerID       INTEGER,
 Category             VARCHAR2(50),
 Color                VARCHAR2(50),
 ModelYear            INTEGER,
 Graphics             VARCHAR2(50),
 ItemMaterial         VARCHAR2(50),
 ListPrice            NUMBER(10,2),
 Style                VARCHAR2(50),
 SkillLevel           INTEGER,
 WeightMax            NUMBER,
 WaistWidth           NUMBER,
 BindingStyle         VARCHAR2(50)
)
organization external (
   type oracle_loader
   default directory csv_dir
 access parameters (
   records delimited by newline
   fields terminated by ','
   optionally enclosed by '"' lrtrim
   missing field values are null
   (
      SaleID,
      SaleDate char date_format date mask "mm/dd/yyyy",
      ShipState, ShipZIP, PaymentMethod, SKU, QuantitySold,
      SalePrice, ModelID, ItemSize, ManufacturerID, Category,
      Color, ModelYear, Graphics, ItemMaterial, ListPrice,
      Style, SkillLevel, WeightMax, WaistWidth,
      BindingStyle
   )
 )
 location ('Lab 08-01 Early Sales.csv')
)
   reject limit unlimited;
```

on the student CD. Copy these three files to a folder on the server. Figure 8.4 shows the code for the first half of the ReadOldSalesAndRentals.sql code file. At the top of the file, you will have to edit the name of the folder that contains the two CSV files. Then you can save and run the program to create the links. Before running the code, it is worth examining it so that you can modify it to handle similar problems in the future. The first section is just a standard CREATE TABLE command that identifies the columns and data types used in the table. These elements are necessary because they describe the table as it will be accessed by SQL. The phrase "organization external" and the associated parameters are the features that establish the link to the actual data file. Notice the specification of oracle_loader and the directory. If you look near the bottom of the code, you will see the actual name of the file specified in the location parameter. The main section describing the parameters indicates that each record is stored on a single line and the fields are separated by commas. Some CSV systems place quotation marks (" ") around text items, so that option is specified to be safe. The null values note is probably not needed, but it makes it clear how missing data should be handled. The listing of the fields must match the order and type of data as it is listed in the table. Note that you will almost always have to specify a mask for dates, since Oracle reads only dd-MMM-yyyy formats by default, and most other software uses the mm/dd/yy format. Numeric and character fields generally do not need formatting hints, but you can provide them if necessary. One final note of warning: Currency data must not contain a $ character. Many export systems, including Excel, use them by default, and you must remove them from the file before trying to load it. Generally, you can quickly remove all dollar sign symbols using global search and replace in a text editor. You should now be able to save and run the code to attach to the two files.

Once the external files have been defined, you can access them with SQL as if they were Oracle tables. Without indexes, they will be a little slower, but you need SQL to extract the data correctly and move it into the main relational tables. Once the data has been extracted, you can delete the links to the external tables.

Looking through the temporary Sale table, you will see that the data needs to be split into four tables: SaleItem, Sale, Inventory, and ItemModel. Go back and examine the relationships for those tables, and you will see that because of the dependencies, you will have to enter data first into the tables for ItemModel, Inventory, Sale, and finally SaleItem. The relationships and foreign keys require that data be entered in that order. You must also be careful with the Customer and Employee data. If you try to create a row in the Sale table, the system will try to set a value of zero for the CustomerID and EmployeeID. But there is no matching data for a zero ID in either of these tables. So, either you try to force a blank CustomerID and EmployeeID, or you create a new Customer and new Employee called "walk-in" and "staff." This latter approach is slightly better than relying on blank data. So your first task is to create these new entries in the respective tables. Figure 8.5 shows the basic SQL commands needed to create these two entries.

SQL makes it relatively easy to extract the new model data and copy it to the ItemModel table. The first step is to create a SELECT query that retrieves the model data from the temporary tables and removes the duplicates. This

FIGURE 8.5

```
INSERT  INTO Customer  (CustomerID,  LastName)
Values  (0,'Walk-in')

INSERT  INTO  Employee  (EmployeeID,  LastName)
Values  (0,'Staff')
```

FIGURE 8.6

```
SELECT DISTINCT OldSale_ext.ModelID,
OldSale_ext.ManufacturerID, OldSale_ext.Category,
OldSale_ext.Color, OldSale_ext.ModelYear,
OldSale_ext.Graphics, OldSale_ext.ItemMaterial,
OldSale_ext.ListPrice, OldSale_ext.Style,
OldSale_ext.SkillLevel, OldSale_ext.WeightMax,
OldSale_ext.WaistWidth, OldSale_ext.BindingStyle
FROM OldSale_ext;
```

process is slightly complicated because of the two tables. It is possible that a model has been sold but not rented and vice versa. The easiest way to handle this problem is to write two queries and use UNION to combine the results. Figure 8.6 shows the basic query to retrieve the model attributes from the OldSale table. Move this query to the side and build a similar one from the OldRentals table. Be extremely careful to list the columns in exactly the same sequence.

Add the data rows from the two queries with the UNION statement. Figure 8.7 shows the basic structure of the query, but yours will contain several more columns. Save this query as qryOldModels so you can use it as one set of data.

Action

Create a new query that retrieves DISTINCT values from the saved UNION query.
Verify that it works.
Add an INSERT INTO statement above the SELECT statement to copy the data to the ItemModel table.
Run the query.
Use a similar process to add SKU, ModelID, and Size to the Inventory table.
Follow a similar process to copy the Sale, Rental, SalesItem, and RentalItems tables.

Now that you can retrieve the new model data, it is relatively easy to write a query to insert these rows into the base ItemModel table. Build a new SELECT query using the qryOldModels query with all of its columns. Add the DISTINCT keyword to be absolutely certain that all duplicates are removed. Run the query to make sure it retrieves the data. As shown in Figure 8.8, at the top of the query add the phrase INSERT INTO Item Model (ModelID, . . .). Because you do not have data for all of the columns, you must list them in the parentheses and they must be in the order of the columns being selected. Run the query and all of the new models will be added to the ItemModel table.

Follow a similar process to add the SKU, ModelID, and Size data to the Inventory table. Note that you should set the QuantityOnHand to zero for each of these items since the store probably does not have any of the old models in stock. If they do happen to have a few items around, the quantity can be entered by hand later. Figure 8.9 shows the final step that inserts the data into the Inventory table. Remember that you have to create the UNION query first. Notice the use of the column alias to force a zero value into the QuantityOnHand column for each row.

The Sale and Rental data is considerably easier because they are separate and you will not need the UNION command to merge the two sets of data.

FIGURE 8.7

```
SELECT DISTINCT ModelID, ManufacturerID, Category, ...
FROM OldSales
UNION
SELECT DISTINCT ModelID, ManufacturerID, Category, ...
FROM OldRentals
```

FIGURE 8.8

```
INSERT INTO ItemModel (ModelID, ManufacturerID, Category,
Color, ModelYear, Graphics, ItemMaterial, ListPrice, Style,
SkillLevel, WeightMax, WaistWidth, BindingStyle)
SELECT DISTINCT qryOldModels.ModelID,
qryOldModels.ManufacturerID, qryOldModels.Category,
qryOldModels.Color, qryOldModels.ModelYear,
qryOldModels.Graphics, qryOldModels.ItemMaterial,
qryOldModels.ListPrice, qryOldModels.Style,
qryOldModels.SkillLevel, qryOldModels.WeightMax,
qryOldModels.WaistWidth, qryOldModels.BindingStyle
FROM qryOldModels;
```

In fact, you can copy the Sale (or Rental) data with one SQL command. First, build a query to retrieve the distinct sales data from the OldSale_ext table. Be sure to include the DISTINCT keyword in the SELECT statement. After you test the SELECT statement, add the INSERT INTO line above it. Figure 8.10 shows an additional trick that is often helpful. If you added new rows of data to your Sale table, the system might have generated values that would conflict with the values from this older dataset. To avoid this problem, you can add an offset number to the old SaleID (+5000 in this example). If you choose a large enough offset, this step will ensure that all of the new ID values will be safe. However, you must also remember to add the same calculation in the final step of transferring the SaleItem rows.

Figure 8.11 shows that the query for the SaleItem table is almost identical to the query that copied the sale data, but with slightly different columns. Remember that if you transform the SaleID in the Sale table, you must make the identical transformation for the SaleItem table. Otherwise, the data will never match and cannot be joined. If you forget, you will usually receive several error messages. But some of the data might be joined to your existing Sales data, making it difficult to reverse the query. Finally, you need to do the same two steps for the Rental and RentalItem tables. The Rental table uses columns RentID, RentDate, ExpectedReturn, and PaymentMethod. The columns for the old rental table do not include repair charges and are limited to RentID, SKU, RentFee, and ReturnDate. At this point, you have successfully imported the old data and cleaned it up so it can be used within your database. Finally, now that the data loading is finished, you might want to reenable the data trigger that generates keys for the sale table (GenKeyForSale). At this point, you should also drop the two external tables because they are no longer needed. You can use a simple DROP TABLE OldSale_ext command.

Activity: Use Discoverer Administrator to Create a Business Area

Investigating sales by a variety of dimensions is an important task for the managers and owners of All Powder. It would be difficult to train all of them to build queries to examine all of the items that might be of interest. A faster

FIGURE 8.9

```
INSERT INTO Inventory (ModelID, SKU, Size, QuantityOnHand)
SELECT DISTINCT qryOldInventory.ModelID, qryOldInventory.SKU,
qryOldInventory.ItemSize, 0 As QuantityOnHand
FROM qryOldInventory;
```

FIGURE 8.10

```
INSERT INTO Sale (SaleID, SaleDate, ShipState, ShipZIP,
PaymentMethod)
SELECT DISTINCT OldSale_ext.SaleID+5000,
OldSale_ext.SaleDate, OldSale_ext.ShipState,
OldSale_ext.ShipZIP, OldSale_ext.PaymentMethod
FROM OldSale_ext;
```

Action

Use Discoverer Administrator to create a new Business Area.
Select your schema.
Add base tables: Sale, SaleItem, Inventory, ItemModel, and Manufacturer.
Add lookup tables: BindingStyle, Customer, PaymentMethod, ProductCategory, SkiBoardStyle, and SkillLevel.
Check the box to build the LOVs.

and more flexible solution is to create an OLAP cube that contains the sales value (price times quantity) as the factor, along with the dimensions. Using Oracle Discoverer, the cube can be manipulated to see subtotals and sort or filter the dimensions. Managers can also create charts that let managers select the data to be displayed, or perform some statistical analyses on the data. Discoverer essentially contains two pieces: the administrative tool (Administrator) and the client tools (Desktop or Plus). As the developer, you will use the Administrator tool to create business areas and select the data tables that belong in each area. Essentially, a business area translates the database terms into names and calculations that can be understood by managers. Managers will use the client tools to browse the data, create charts, and perform statistical analyses. The critical first step is to interview managers to determine what types of data they need to see and how it will be analyzed. For this example, you will create a simple business area that enables managers to analyze sales by various dimensions.

Begin the process by running the Discoverer Administrator. The first time you run it, you might be asked to install the End User Layer. This step creates several new tables in the database that hold the metadata to translate the database tables into your designs. You will never edit the tables directly, but they have to be created so Discoverer can use them. The main step is to create a new business area. Give the area a name, such as Sales Analysis, that is meaningful to the managers. Eventually, you will have many business areas, and each will contain various items. They should be able to glance at the screen and identify exactly which section they need. A wizard helps you build the business area. The first step is to select the database schemas that hold the tables you need. In this example, you only need to select your schema (for example, Powder). In a large company, you might need to retrieve data stored in several different schemas, so you simply place check marks to select the ones you need.

The next step is to choose the tables that you will need within this new business area. To analyze sales by product, you will need the basic tables: Sale, SaleItem, Inventory, ItemModel, and Manufacturer. You will also need lookup tables so Discoverer can provide lists for users to make detailed selections, so include the tables: BindingStyle, Customer, PaymentMethod,

FIGURE 8.11

```
INSERT INTO SaleItem (SaleID, SKU, QuantitySold, SalePrice)
SELECT DISTINCT OldSales.SaleID+5000, OldSales.SKU,
OldSales.QuantitySold, OldSales.SalePrice
FROM OldSales;
```

FIGURE 8.12

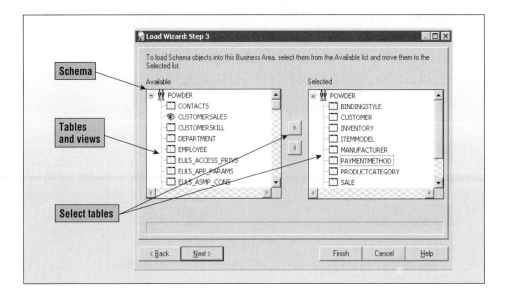

ProductCategory, SkiBoardStyle, and SkillLevel. Figure 8.12 shows the main wizard page to select tables. Simply choose a table on the left side and use the button to move it to the right side.

As shown in Figure 8.13, you can have the wizard automatically create some useful features for the business area. In particular, you do want the

FIGURE 8.13

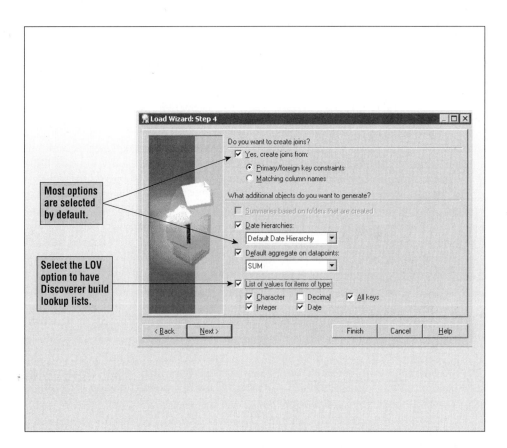

FIGURE 8.14

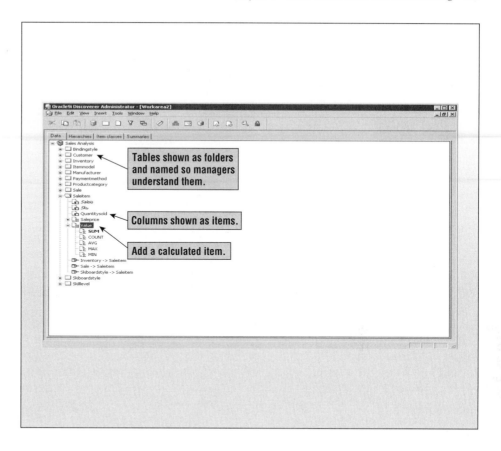

system to create the joins, to build date hierarchies (year-quarter-month-day). Most of these choices are selected by default, but you should check the box to request that the list of values be created automatically. The system understands how foreign keys relate to lookup tables, so it will build a list of values box that will pop up when users need to select something like Category.

Figure 8.14 shows the resulting business area that contains the tables you selected under the Data tab. This is the list of items that the managers will see, so you should check the names and consider renaming anything that might be confusing to them. Also, remember that the SaleItem table contains QuantitySold and SalePrice. For the most part, managers will want to see the total sales value of items, which is obtained by multiplying those two values together. The business area makes it relatively easy to perform this calculation. Open the SaleItem folder and insert a new item. Change its name to Value and use the calculation builder to create the formula. Click on SalePrice and click the Paste button to move it into the calculation window. Click on the Multiply button, then paste the QuantitySold item into the window and click the OK button to accept the new item. Managers can use this new item like any other item.

Hierarchies within the data are important to managers. The classic time hierarchy (year-quarter-month-day) is commonly used to compare sales over time periods. These time hierarchies are automatically generated by the Load wizard. Other hierarchies may also be useful to managers. For instance, sales are sometimes grouped into states, regions, or countries. In the All Powder case, enough detail exists to create a hierarchy for State-City, and a second

FIGURE 8.15

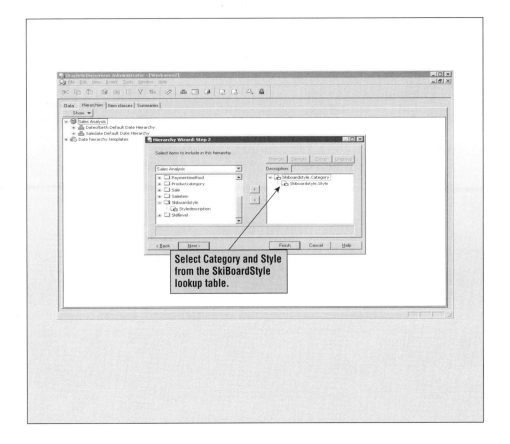

Select Category and Style
from the SkiBoardStyle
lookup table.

hierarchy that divides categories into styles. You should define these two hierarchies so managers can use them to drill down or consolidate totals when analyzing the data. Figure 8.15 shows the basic process for the Category-Style hierarchy. Under the Hierarchies tab, open the Sales Analysis folder and insert a new hierarchy. Using the wizard, open the SkiBoardStyle lookup table and select the Category and Style items. When you have finished creating this hierarchy, add one for customer location (Customer.State and Customer.City) and one for shipping location (Sale.Shipstate and Sale.Shipcity).

If you open the tab for Item classes, you will see several entries created automatically by the load wizard. For the most part, these items are used to generate the list of values (LOV) data. You can create your own lists, but the wizard probably generated more than enough to handle most applications. The Summaries tab will probably not contain any items yet. This section is used to hold materialized views, which are snapshots of query data, including calculations and totals. With the appropriate permissions established on the EUL tables, Discoverer Administrator can analyze the tables and create summaries to improve performance. However, you should read the details in the Administrator documentation to determine how to set up schedules that will refresh the data on a regular basis.

Action

In the Data tab, expand SaleItem.

Add a new calculated item: Value = SalePrice*QuantitySold.

Double-click the SUM option to set the default.

In the Hierarchies tab, create a new hierarchy for Category Style: Category, Style from SkiBoardStyle.

Create new location hierarchies from Sale and Customer based on the state and city.

Activity: Browse the Sales Data with Discoverer Desktop

Once the administrator has created business areas that identify tables and items, managers can use the client tools to browse the data. Oracle has several client systems, depending on which system is used for production. All of the tools have essentially the same capabilities. The developer version includes the Discoverer Desktop client tool, so start it from the main menu. To the manager, all data is analyzed and examined inside worksheets. A workbook can hold several worksheets, and the Desktop client can save the workbook in the database itself or on a local or network disk. If you want other users to access the workbook using Oracle 9i/AS across the Web, you need to save the workbook in the database.

To begin, create a new workbook and select the Page-Detail-Crosstab option. As shown in Figure 8.16, the next step is to select the columns to analyze. In this particular case, the goal is to evaluate changes to the SaleItem. Value, which is the main fact item. You can add as many dimensions as the users want to evaluate at one time. If you put too many dimensions on each row and column, it will be difficult to read the data. In this case, the main table will consist of the Sale State and Category as rows and the time data (year, quarter, month) as columns. You can place additional dimensions on the page, and managers will be able to select subsets of the data from those lists. For example, you could include Color, Graphics, ItemMaterial, Style, and BindingStyle from the ItemModel folder. You might also include the manufacturer's name and the payment method. Ultimately, you will select

FIGURE 8.16

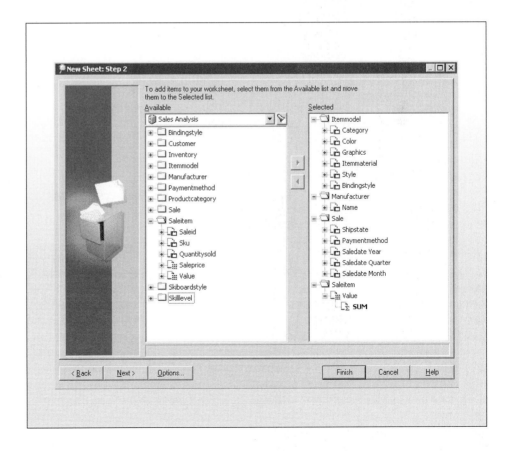

the columns based on the use needs. If a worksheet starts to get too large and difficult to deal with, simply create a second worksheet with a different set of dimensions. There is one trick you need to know when selecting folders (tables). Sometimes you have to select an intermediate table to be able to get to the final dimension you want. For example, the ItemModel dimensions are identified by the ModelID, but the ModelID is not in the SaleItem table. Initially, the ItemModel table will be grayed out in the list. To activate this table, you need to temporarily add the ModelID from the Inventory table, which forms a link between the SaleItem and ItemModel tables. Once you have selected items from the desired tables, you can remove the ModelID item and Discoverer will remember how to link the tables.

The next step is to define the initial layout of the Crosstab table by placing the attributes as rows, columns, and page items. The page items are not initially displayed on the table. Instead, the user can use the items to filter the data. For instance, if you place ItemMaterial on the page list, users can choose to select all item materials or any subset of the list. The entire table will change in response to the selection, but users will not see separate rows or columns of these items. Of course, users can always change the layout later by dragging items from the page onto rows or columns. The purpose of the page items is to provide a holding place for secondary items. By default, the initial layout will place the Value SUM as the main data item, because it is the only numeric data item in the list. You should drag the Category and Shipstate items onto the row section. Finally, you want the Year, Quarter, and Month items as columns. Drag everything else (except Value SUM) onto the page items section. Figure 8.17 shows the resulting layout. You can finish the wizard steps by ignoring the conditions for now. Conditions would be used if you wanted to limit the data, such as making data available only for 2004. Save your work.

FIGURE 8.17

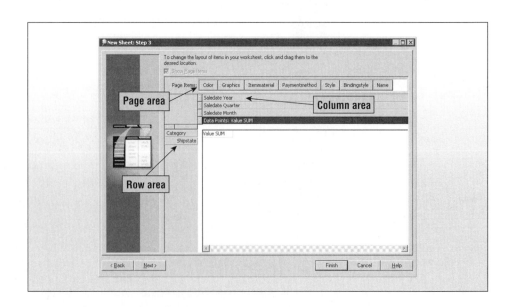

FIGURE 8.18

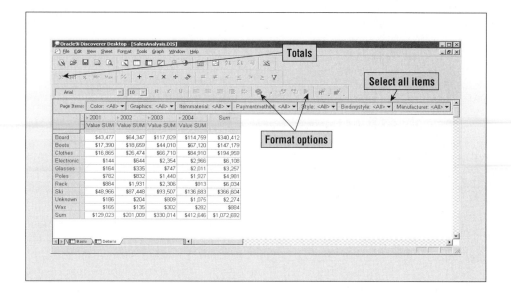

Action
Play with the worksheet by collapsing, formatting cells, and adding row and column totals.
Use the drop-down arrow to select all of the values for each page item box.
To collapse categories, mark the column and right-click to select collapse.
Collapse the time frame down to years.
Format the data using the buttons.
View the Analysis Bar.
Select the Category column and click the Sum Totals button.
Select the Year row and click the Sum Totals button.

To understand the power of this tool, you should play with the data as if you were a manager. First, you probably want to see all of the data from the page items instead of just one entry. For each of the items, click the small arrow and select the All option. Then collapse the chart so it displays aggregated data with less detail. Managers can always drill down later to see the detail. For example, select all categories by clicking the Category marker on the left-most column. Right-click it and select the Collapse option to hide the state data. Similarly, click on the small box to the left of the time listing, and collapse the time frame down to years. Mark the main data cells and format them as currency. Add totals for the rows and columns. Select the View/Analysis Bar menu option, then click the Category column on the left side. Click the sigma (Sum Total) button to get the totals of the row data. To get totals across the rows, select the years and click the Sum Total button. Figure 8.18 shows the resulting worksheet. Again, save your work on a regular basis.

Introductory Data Analysis

Activity: Analyze Time-Series Data

Oracle provides some relatively powerful data mining tools. However, they only work by building customized models with Java programming. Consequently, they would take too long to build for this lab. On the other hand, Oracle Discoverer provides some analytical tools that are easier to use and provide additional flexibility by enabling managers to experiment with the results in the worksheet. Companies can also purchase powerful data mining tools from independent firms.

Oracle includes some analytical functions that are useful for analyzing time-series data. For example, you might want to smooth monthly fluctuations using a moving average or compute growth rates as a percentage change from one quarter to the next. The AVG function solves the first problem, while the LAG function works for the second. This lab will use the AVG function because the

---

Action

Add a new worksheet using the table layout instead of crosstab.
Use items: SalesItem.Value SUM, Sale.Saledate Year, and Sale.Saledate Month.
On the worksheet, choose Tools/Calculations.
Click the Functions option button.
Expand Analytic and paste the AVG function.
Edit it to match: `AVG(Value SUM) OVER(PARTITION BY "Saledate Year" ORDER BY "Saledate Month" RANGE INTERVAL '2' MONTH PRECEDING).`

---

chart is more interesting. In situations involving calculations over time, you cannot use either of the two crosstab worksheets. Instead, you have to use the basic table display. The reason is that while crosstab does display monthly (or quarterly) detail values, it also displays subtotals for each grouping. The time-series analyses require a simple single listing.

Begin by creating a new worksheet and selecting one of the two table modes. The difference between them is that the page version enables you to place dimensions on the top of the page that can sometimes be used by managers to limit the data being displayed. For this example, the system is more reliable if you use the simple table display in the first choice. Use the SalesItem.Value SUM item as the main data element. Use Sale.Saledate Year and Sale.Saledate Month as the time intervals.

The goal of a moving average is to smooth a series of data by averaging it across an interval. This interval moves or slides along the time frame. For example, the first average would use months 1, 2, and 3. The next average would use months 2, 3, and 4. You need to create a new item using a calculation. Select Tools/Calculations from the main menu and create a new calculation. Name it MA3 to remind you that it will be a three-period moving average. You can click the Functions option button, and expand the items under Analytic to find the AVG function. Clicking the Paste>> button will place a prototype into the main calculation window. To reduce typing, you can click the Items option to select a list of items and paste them into the parameters of the prototype. The prototype is slightly different from what you need for a moving average. Ultimately, you want the function to look like AVG(Value SUM) OVER(PARTITION BY "Saledate Year" ORDER BY "Saledate Month" RANGE INTERVAL '2' MONTH PRECEDING). The '2' MONTH PRECEDING tells it to use a 3-month moving average because the system always includes the current row. You have to tell the function that the data is partitioned by year because the months repeat. Another option would be to create a new date column that includes both the year and the month, such as 2001-01. When you close the Calculation window shown in Figure 8.19, the worksheet will query the database and compute the values. If the values are blank, you need to edit the calculation and make sure the formula is correct.

The next step is to chart the two values. Figure 8.20 shows the chart. Notice how the moving average line smooths the data and reduces the variability. Statistically, this line would provide a better indication of the true sales over time.

Action

Select Graph/New Graph from the main menu.
Choose Line chart, with the 2D option.
Enter the chart title (Sales Moving Average).
Set font sizes to 8.
When the chart is drawn, resize and edit it to display enough data to make it useful.

To create the chart in Discoverer, select Graph/New Graph from the main menu. Choose a Line chart, and select the 2D option to keep it readable. Be sure to add a chart title. You can reduce the axes and legend fonts to the chart can show more data on the screen. Make sure the legend is displayed, and you should set the Y-axes scale to a fixed 2000-unit increment. All of these options can be set or edited after the Chart wizard finishes. You will have to drag the sides of the chart to resize it so you can see more of the data on-screen at a time. Rename the worksheet and save the workbook.

FIGURE 8.19

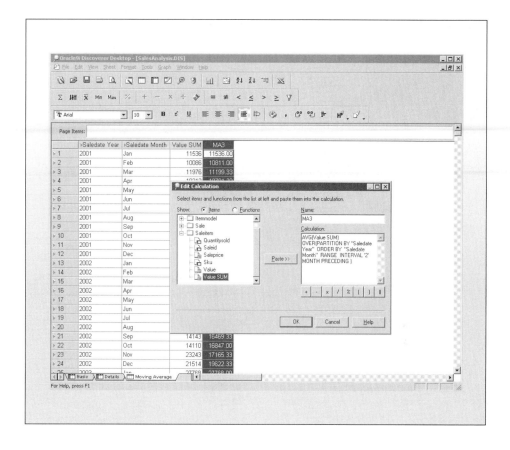

Activity: Analyze Data with Regression

Linear regression is a tool that is relatively easy to use and is supported by a variety of platforms, including Excel. With Excel, you need to install and select the Data Analysis tools. Linear regression can be used for many things, and many options and features exist in high-end tools. Its primary purpose is to compare sets of data in terms of closeness. In the classic multidimensional case, regression is used to determine how various dimensions (independent variables) statistically affect the fact (dependent) variable. In the All Powder case, the managers would like to analyze the state data and see if the total sales within a state are heavily determined by the income level or population of the state. In this case, the income and population are exogenous variables (predictors) and the sales total is the endogenous variable to be predicted. As a data mining tool, regression has some strengths and weaknesses. Its main strength is that it has been heavily analyzed and applied for many years, and the results are relatively easy to understand and interpret. Its main drawback is that the results are largely determined by averages, so the conclusions apply to the average or general group, but not necessarily to the outliers. Sometimes the most valuable insights come from understanding the outliers—such as the people who do not buy certain items, or the few leading-edge customers who pursue new sports before the crowd arrives.

Action

Read the demographic data into Oracle.
Create a query to combine the sales data by state with the demographic data.
Start Excel and retrieve the query data.
In Excel, choose Tools/Data Analysis/Regression.
Select the Value column as the Y-range and the population and income columns as the X-range.
Check the top row as label option.
Run the regression.

FIGURE 8.20

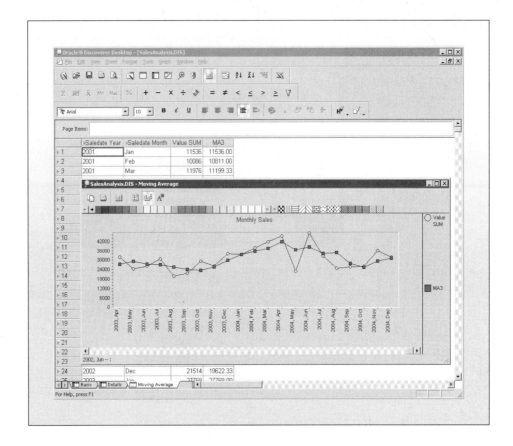

Demographics and economic data on states and counties can be found in the federal government publications. The http://www.fedstats.gov site contains links and search engines for an enormous amount of data. For this exercise, the 2002 population and 2001 total personal income by state have been saved in an Excel spreadsheet. As shown in Figure 8.21, a basic query can be used to compute the total sales by state for the year 2004. But, if you look closely at the results of the query, you will spot a problem. Only 47 states are represented in the sales data (and one null value). The spreadsheet file contains data on 51 states (including the District of Columbia). You will need to match the rows from the query with the data in the spreadsheet and discard the states for which your sales query has no data. Fortunately, SQL makes this process easy. Simply import the spreadsheet data into a table and use a query to join it to the sales query rows. The join condition will automatically match only the states that exist in the Sale table.

As with many data warehouse exercises, the first step is to load the state demographics data into Oracle. Since this is a one-time data transfer and the data is already in a flat CSV file, it is relativley easy to load the data by creating an external file. The student CD contains the data file and the PL/SQL code to create an Oracle StateDemographics table and load the data from the external table. When you have created and loaded the new table, use an SQL query to ensure that the table is loaded.

At this time, Oracle Discoverer supports only a simple two-variable version of regression. It can compute the correlation between one dependent variable

FIGURE 8.21

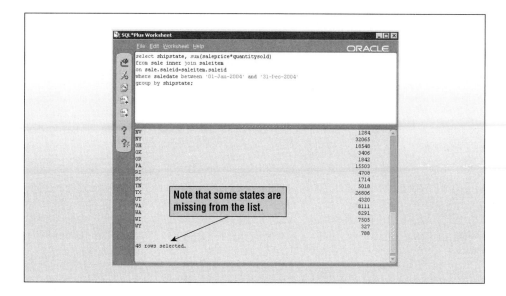

and one independent variable. Although the newer data mining tools provide more capabilities, the easiest way to solve this problem is to use Microsoft Excel to analyze the data. This approach is actually a common solution, because it enables managers to use a powerful tool that they use regularly.

Excel can easily retrieve data from an Oracle view, so the goal is to create a view that contains only the data needed for the problem. Figure 8.22 shows the query needed. Since you have income and population data for only one year, you should restrict the sales data to one year (2004). Also, remove the data with missing states because you will not have matching demographic data. Test the SELECT statement first, then create the view.

Open Excel and select the Data/Import External Data/Import Data menu option. Create a new source and choose the Oracle option. Save the connection file and open it. Excel retrieves the data dynamically from Oracle. If the data changes later, whoever opens the spreadsheet can automatically requery the database and get the current values.

The next step is to start the Excel regression wizard with Tools/Data Analysis/Regression. Note that if you do not see the Data Analysis option, you will first have to select Tools/Add-Ins and check the Analysis ToolPak option. If this option is not visible, you will have to install it from the original Office disks. Once the tool is installed, as shown in Figure 8.23, you will

FIGURE 8.22

```
CREATE VIEW StateSales2004 AS
SELECT StateName, Income2001, Pop2002,
Sum(SalePrice*QuantitySold) AS Sales2004
FROM Sale INNER JOIN StateDemographics
ON Sale.ShipState = StateDemographics.StateCode
INNER JOIN SaleItem ON Sale.SaleID = SaleItem.SaleID
WHERE ShipState IS NOT NULL AND SaleDate Between
'01-Jan-2004' And '31-Dec-2004'
GROUP BY StateName, Income2001, Pop2002
ORDER BY StateName;
```

FIGURE 8.23

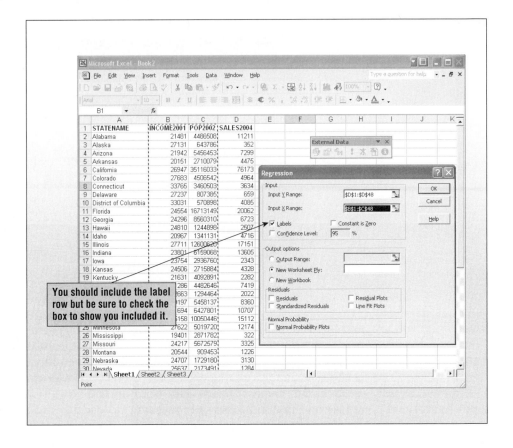

have to select the Y (dependent) variable as the Value column, as well as the X (independent) variables as the Population and Income columns. To make the results easier to read, when you select the data you should also include the top row that contains the label for the column. Then make sure that you check the Labels box in the wizard so it knows the first row is not part of the numeric data. Most of the time you will want to accept the default option to place the results in a new worksheet.

Figure 8.24 shows the results of the regression for this example. Notice that the R-square value is relatively high, indicating that this simple model describes a little under 90 percent of the variance in the sales. Second, notice that only the population coefficient is significantly different from zero at a 5 percent level of significance (P-value less than 0.05). The coefficient value is positive, indicating that states with higher populations tend to purchase more items from All Powder. In fact, the company receives about $1.76 in sales for every thousand people. In general, this population result is not too surprising. Larger states with more people mean that there will be more showboarders and skiers. The lack of significance on the income term is a little more interesting. There is a question of whether or not it really is insignificant or if there is simply too little data or too few variables in the model. These questions should always be examined for insignificant variables. But, if it is true, it means that the sport has changed. Historically, because of the costs, snow sports have generally appealed to wealthier people. In terms of the business and marketing, it would mean the company

FIGURE 8.24

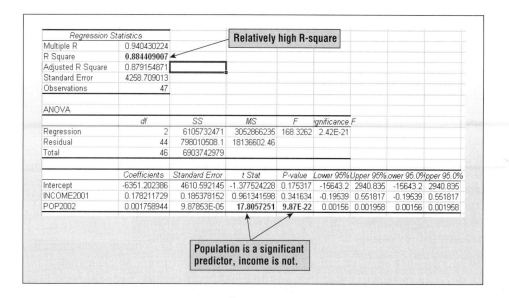

should consider a major shift in advertising and promotion if the sports now appeal to all income levels. Of course, considerably more data would be needed before making this commitment, but it is worth investigating. In truth, for this case, the customers were generated based on city populations, so the statistical results match the underlying data model. Actual sales data would provide more interesting results, but the process is the same.

Activity: Analyze Association Rules for Market Baskets

Although it requires some effort to use, the Oracle data mining package can provide some useful results. In particular, the association rule or market basket analysis is a classic data mining tool. The goal is to search for items that are likely to be purchased together. For instance, a person who purchases cross-country skis might commonly purchase gloves. Knowledge of these patterns could provide insight into your customers and give you tips on how to train your sales staff to increase sales. On the other hand, the correlations could be purely arbitrary. Managers must critically evaluate all results to see if they make sense and determine if they can be applied to the individual store.

Oracle's data mining system uses data from specially constructed tables but relies on custom code written in Java to do the analysis. Fortunately, you can leverage the sample files provided by Oracle. With a few modifications, these tools can be used to analyze your data. To run these tools, you need to find the location of several Oracle folders. Figure 8.25 lists the folders along with

Action
Find the folders with the data mining samples and the Java directory.
Copy the sample files to a new folder.
Edit the Sample_Global.property file.
If necessary, log in as DBA and create a new password for the odm and odm_mtr users and unlock the accounts.

FIGURE 8.25

Item to Find	Possible Location
Data mining samples	D:\Oracle\ora92\dm\demo\sample
ORACLE_HOME	D:\Oracle\ora92
JAVA_HOME	C:\OracleData\Ora92DS\jdk

FIGURE 8.26

Sample Files to Copy
| ```
compileSampleCode.bat
executeSampleCode.bat
Sample_AssociationRules.java
Sample_AssociationRules_Transactional.property
Sample_Global.property
``` |

their likely locations. Your drive letter will be different, but look for the ora92 folder. The Java folder is tricky because your machine might have several jdk folders. Go to the command line (DOS) mode and check the path. Several of the entries will include the jdk folder that you need to use.

When you find the sample files, copy some of them into a new folder so you can modify them without destroying the originals. Figure 8.26 lists the files that you will need for this exercise. The main code is in the Java file—you do not want to change this file. The two batch files are simple routines to compile the Java file and run it. The Transactional property file contains some basic titles that you could change, but by being careful, you can leave it as it stands. The only file you need to edit is the last one because it sets the log-in name and location of the data file.

You might as well edit the Sample_Global.property file now so you do not forget to do it later. Figure 8.27 shows the changes you need to make. For the URL, enter the name of the database server, the port (usually 1521), and the logical name of the database. These are the names you usually use to log in so they should be familiar to you. Second, there is a special user account called odm. The data mining must be performed with this user. Enter a password for this account. Your instructor or DBA should give you the password. If you are running your own system, you will have to assign a new password, so just make one up now. The last step is to specify the input and output schema names. This example does not use the output schema, so enter the same user for both. This schema is probably your username, since it will hold the data table to be analyzed. If you are running your own system, you must log in as system DBA and assign a new password for the odm and odm_mtr accounts. You must also unlock the two accounts. The easiest way to accomplish both tasks is to use the enterprise manager, expand the security tab, and click on each user to see and edit the main property page.

The next major step is to create a special table that will hold the market basket transaction data. Recall that the SaleItem table contains the SaleID

FIGURE 8.27

Sample_Global.property File
| ```
miningServer.url=jdbc:oracle:thin:@YourServerName:1521:DBName
miningServer.userName=odm
miningServer.password=password

inputDataSchemaName=powder
outputSchemaName=powder
timeout=120
``` |

FIGURE 8.28

```
CREATE TABLE MARKET_BASKET_TX_BINNED
(SEQUENCE_ID      INTEGER,
 ATTRIBUTE_NAME   VARCHAR2(35),
 VALUE            NUMBER
);
GRANT SELECT ON MARKET_BASKET_TX_BINNED TO odm;
commit;
```

Action
Create the MARKET_BASKET_TX_BINNED table.
Insert the data from the SaleItem table.
Insert the data from the Sale table.
Run the code to change dashes to underscores at least twice.
Run the code to reduce the size of the attribute column data.

and the SKU to identify each sale and each item purchased. This data forms the foundation for the table needed, but some additional data must be added. Ultimately, the association rules system needs a table that contains a Sequence_ID, an Attribute_Name, and a Value column. The SaleID can function as the Sequence_ID to identify each unique basket. The Value is generally set to 1 to indicate the presence of the specific item. The Attribute_Name is the name of the product being purchased. However, it does not make sense to analyze every single SKU. For example, it is unlikely that it would matter if a person buys a 180 cm ski versus a 190 cm ski. Plus, it is considerably more time-consuming (perhaps impossible) to analyze market baskets at the SKU level. Instead, the attribute will consist of the item style and category, such as a cross-country ski.

Figure 8.28 shows the code to create the MARKET_BASKET_TX_BINNED table with the three required columns. Be sure to use this table name with these exact column names. If you change any of the names, you will have to edit the Transactional.property table. Also, make sure that you include the GRANT statement. Remember that the data mining system will log in as the odm user, so this user needs to be able to read (SELECT) the data in the new table.

The next step is to insert the main SaleItem data into the new table. The Sequence_ID is simply the SaleID and the Value is easy since it is set to 1. The Attribute_Name is more difficult since it is a combination of the model category and style. Figure 8.29 shows that Oracle's concatenation operation (||) is used to create the new attribute by appending the style to the category—separated by an underscore. You have to use the GROUP BY statement because the query is consolidating data by the category and style, which reduces the table compared to the original SKU listing.

FIGURE 8.29

```
INSERT INTO MARKET_BASKET_TX_BINNED (SEQUENCE_ID, ATTRIBUTE_NAME, VALUE)
SELECT SaleID, ItemModel.Category || '_' || ItemModel.Style AS AName, 1
As Value
FROM SaleItem Inner Join Inventory
ON SaleItem.SKU = Inventory.SKU
Inner Join ItemModel
ON Inventory.ModelID = ItemModel.ModelID
GROUP BY SaleID, ItemModel.Category || '_' || ItemModel.Style;
```

FIGURE 8.30

```
INSERT INTO MARKET_BASKET_TX_BINNED
      (SEQUENCE_ID, ATTRIBUTE_NAME, VALUE)
SELECT SaleID, 'ID', SaleID
FROM Sale;
commit;
```

A careful investigation of the original Oracle sample data shows that you need one more element in the new table. A special row is added to identify each market basket. For each sale, you have to enter a row like 5, 'ID', 5 for the respective values. The first number is the SaleID, the name must be set to the ID characters, and the last (Value) number should match the SaleID. Since the data comes only from the Sale table, Figure 8.30 shows that the query is relatively easy.

In an ideal world, the data would now be ready to analyze. However, a few hidden issues in the analysis routines place some restrictions on the data for the Attribute_Name column. In particular, you cannot include dashes (minus signs) in the data itself. More importantly, the length of each element cannot exceed approximately 20 characters. Figure 8.31 shows the query that will remove any dashes that exist in the category and style names. You will have to run this query at least twice, because some names have more than one dash and it only removes one dash at a time. The query basically searches a line for the location of a dash and then rebuilds a new version by taking the first part of the name, adding an underscore instead of the dash, and then appending the remainder of the line.

Figure 8.32 shows the query to reduce the overall length of each Attribute_Name. Experimentation revealed that 20 characters work, but there is a chance you might need a smaller number. Note that the original Oracle sample contains a maximum of 12 characters. The code that crashes when the attributes are too long is buried deep within several Oracle assemblies. Perhaps at some point, Oracle will rewrite the assemblies to allow longer names.

You are almost ready to run the analysis. First, use **SQL PLUS** to log in as the odm user. Then, start the data mining engine by issuing the command exec odm_start_monitor; The next step is to compile the Java program. Figure 8.33 shows the main steps. First, you have to set the two environmental variables to tell the system where to find the Oracle libraries and the Java compiler. If you need to compile or run the files on a regular basis, you can place those two lines in the system startup so they are set automatically. The Compile command is straightforward, but remember to include the .java suffix. This command only needs to be run

FIGURE 8.31

```
UPDATE MARKET_BASKET_TX_BINNED
SET ATTRIBUTE_NAME =
substr(ATTRIBUTE_NAME,1,instr(ATTRIBUTE_NAME,'-')-1)
      || '_' || substr(ATTRIBUTE_NAME,instr(ATTRIBUTE_NAME,
      '-')+1)
WHERE instr(ATTRIBUTE_NAME,'-') > 0;
commit;
```

FIGURE 8.32

```
UPDATE MARKET_BASKET_TX_BINNED
SET ATTRIBUTE_NAME = substr(ATTRIBUTE_NAME,1,20);
commit;
```

Action
Open a command line (DOS) window.
Set the ORACLE_HOME and
JAVA_HOME environmental variables.
Compile the Java class.
Run the program.
Study the results and look for ideas.

one time—once the file is compiled you should see a Sample_AssociationRules.class program in the folder and not have to compile again. The last command is also straightforward but takes a while to type because the filenames are so long. Type the entire command as one line. The system might wrap it to a second line, but do not hit the <Enter> key until you have typed the entire line. The first parameter tells the system which class file to run. The second specifies the name of the start-up properties. For this program, the results will simply be displayed on the command line screen. If you want to capture these comments and place them in a file, you can add a redirection command to the line. Type >myfile.txt at the end of the command, using whatever filename you want. The results will be redirected into the file, and you can edit it or print it when the analysis is finished.

Figure 8.34 shows the results from analyzing the All Powder sales. Several statistics books explain the values in more detail. Remember that the system identifies items that people purchase at the same time. For example, the first rule (124) states that about 17 percent of the baskets include both boots and clothes (support). The confidence measure states that if a customer purchased boots, then about 45 percent of the time that customer also purchased clothes. From these results, it appears that two possible rules might exist: (1) People who buy boots also buy clothes, and (2) Half-pipe boarders and freestyle skiers are more likely to buy clothes. This latter rule could be the most useful. If those two types of customers prefer a certain type of clothing, it means the managers should focus the inventory toward that style. Of course, it is possible that the store already focuses toward that style, which could explain why those two types already buy clothes. In that situation, perhaps the store should consider expanding and carrying more styles that fit the other customers. Although this analysis might seem confusing, the point is that the conclusions require that you understand and analyze the existing state of the store. Association rules can show you patterns, but it does not explain why those patterns exist or if there is any way to gain from the knowledge. The minimum support and confidence levels can be set in the Transactional.property file. You can also set the name of the table that holds the data.

FIGURE 8.33

```
SET ORACLE_HOME = D:\Oracle\ora92
SET JAVA_HOME = C:\OracleData\ora92DS\jdk
compileSampleCode.bat Sample_AssociationRules.java

executeSampleCode.bat Sample_AssociationRules
Sample_AssociationRules_Transactional.property
```

FIGURE 8.34

```
Getting top 5 rules for model: Sample_AR_Model_tx sorted by support.
  Rule 124: If Boots_=1 then Clothes_=1 [support: 0.17285714, confidence:
  0.44814816]
  Rule 38: If Clothes_=1 then Boots_=1 [support: 0.17285714, confidence:
  0.35276967]
  Rule 101: If Board_Half_Pipe=1 then Clothes_=1 [support: 0.11357143,
  confidence: 0.4622093]
  Rule 9: If Clothes_=1 then Board_Half_Pipe=1 [support: 0.11357143,
  confidence: 0.23177843]
  Rule 100: If Ski_Freestyle=1 then Clothes_=1 [support: 0.09785714,
  confidence: 0.48070174]
  Get rules by support: Sample_AR_Model_tx, with minimum support of 0.16.
  Rule 124: If Boots_=1 then Clothes_=1 [support: 0.17285714, confidence:
  0.44814816]
  Rule 38: If Clothes_=1 then Boots_=1 [support: 0.17285714, confidence:
  0.35276967]
Get rules by confidence: Sample_AR_Model_tx, with confidence of 0.56 or more.
```

Exercises

Crystal Tigers

The Crystal Tigers club does not have a huge amount of data to analyze within the organization. However, club members are interested in comparing their service data and the organizations they work with to see if they are serving the needs of the community. Periodically, they survey people in the surrounding areas to determine if they have heard of the club, if they know what charities the club supports, and their overall opinion of the club. In the process, they also ask citizens about the events and problems that most affect their lives. A substantial part of the survey is a listing of support organizations with which the club is considering partnering. Crystal Tigers has collected this survey data every six months for the last three years, and they get several hundred responses each time. All of the data is stored in Excel spreadsheets.

1. Create two sample spreadsheets with the survey data. Create tables in Oracle to hold the normalized data. Write the SQL statements to transfer the data. Build this code into a form and button that will automate the transfer.

2. Create a query and a Discoverer worksheet that will enable managers to analyze the survey data.

3. Create a worksheet that will enable managers to analyze the existing club service data. Use two possible fact fields: hours worked and money raised. Include all of the dimensions you think managers might need.

4. Do a time-series analysis of the money raised. Managers are particularly interested in trends and in identifying the months that raise the most money.

5. Assume you have data on money raised for several years (make up monthly totals if necessary). Obtain personal income data for your state or metropolitan area over those years and see if the income level is correlated with the money raised.

Capitol Artists

The managers of Capitol Artists are primarily interested in identifying the best employees and the most profitable customers. The job-tracking system ultimately generates a considerable amount of data—at the hourly and daily levels. Note that all employee tasks are supposed to be recorded in the system based on the client, job, and task involved. The firm has considerable information on clients, including a size classification (tiny, small, medium, and large) and type of company (such as printing, marketing, retail, and medical). This additional client information is currently stored in a spreadsheet, with one page devoted to each client.

1. Create three sample client worksheets with sample data. Modify the tables as needed to handle this new data. Create a form that will enable a clerk to find the worksheet and transfer the data to Oracle.

2. Create a Discoverer worksheet that will enable managers to analyze the hours worked and revenue generated by employees, day of week, client, client size, and so on.

3. Create a Discoverer worksheet that compares employees based on billable hours by day during the past month.

4. Assume that you have approximate sales numbers representing the size of each of the clients (make up the data). Create a categorical variable for the client industry (for example, 1 = printing, 2 = marketing, and so on). Perform a regression to see if the client size or industry influence the amount of sales revenue Capitol Artists generates.

5. Analyze the data with the association rules to see if there are relationships between the items purchased.

Offshore Speed

Inventory control is critical for Offshore Speed because it has to stock thousands of small parts for different engines and drives. All of these parts are grouped into categories in terms of the manufacturer and the location within the engine or boat. Lately, the owners think there has been an increased demand for oil pump impellers, but they are not certain because there are several different brands. They also suspect that sales of electronic navigation devices have tapered off. Although they have the sales data available, they are not sure how to analyze and compare it. Of course, the sales data for the past three years is stored in Excel spreadsheets. One sheet for each month of sales, and each line contains a sale number, date, part number, quantity, and price. Unfortunately, the part numbers do not match the new ones entered into the database. However, there is a separate spreadsheet that maps the two numbers. The first column lists the old number and the second column contains the new number.

1. Create at least two sample spreadsheets for the older sales, and the spreadsheet that maps the old numbers to the new ones. Create a form that can be used by a clerk to pick a spreadsheet and import the data into the new database.

2. Create a Discoverer worksheet that will enable managers to analyze sales by category, manufacturer, and time. Note that category should be a hierarchy. For example, managers might want to see detailed parts, or just the parts that are used in engines (or drives, or steering, and so on).

3. Create a worksheet chart that analyzes sales of the major categories over time based on monthly sales.

4. For some reason, an employee of the company has kept records of the weather for the last three years. She has a spreadsheet that contains the date, the amount of rain on that day, and the high temperature for the day. Create a regression to see if there is a relationship between the weather and your sales. (Make up some sample weather data, or find it on the Internet for your area.)

5. If you have access to software that performs association or market basket analysis, this case would be a good application to see what types of parts might be purchased together.

Final Project

The main textbook has an appendix with several longer case studies. You should be able to work on one of these cases throughout the term. If you or your instructor picks one, perform the following tasks.

1. Identify at least one primary fact attribute that managers would want to track, along with several dimensions. Create the query and Discoverer worksheet to analyze the data.

2. Identify any data that could be analyzed over time, and create a Discoverer chart and an Excel spreadsheet to forecast the data.

3. Identify any data that could benefit from market basket or association analysis. If you have access to the software, create the queries and analyze sample data.

4. Identify any data that could benefit from geographic analysis. If you have access to the software, create the queries and analyze sample data.

5. Identify any correlations or regression analysis that might help managers better understand the operations and effects of various attributes. If possible, collect sample data and analyze it.

Chapter

9

Database Administration

Chapter Outline

Objectives

- Evaluate and improve the application performance.
- Establish backup and recovery methods and plans.
- Install simple security controls to provide basic protection of the data.
- Protect the forms, reports, and code form unauthorized changes.
- Protect the data with user-level security controls.

Database Administration Tasks

One of the powerful features heavily pushed by Oracle is its performance under a heavy load of users. However, obtaining this performance often requires detailed work by the database administrator. Oracle provides a variety of options to tune the storage, query execution, and control other features of the database. Additionally, these options change over time as Oracle finds new ways to improve performance. The job of an Oracle DBA is not easy and requires constant learning. However, a good DBA can make a tremendous difference in the database performance. Fortunately, Oracle is beginning to include more automated tools to help analyze the database and queries and recommend improvements.

Every DBMS maintains an internal list of all of the database objects, such as table, query, and report names. Only recently has the SQL standard proposed a common method to obtain these names. Consequently, most systems have proprietary tables and columns for the metadata tables. In Oracle, you can use the enterprise manager to identify table and column names, but it can be a little cumbersome. In many cases, you will want to be able to retrieve a list of tables or queries directly from the database. Oracle stores a considerable amount of metadata within system tables.

To make them easier to use, Oracle defines several synonyms that retrieve data from these static data dictionary views. Figure 9.1 shows some of the commonly used synonyms. Any of the three prefixes can be used with the command synonym to specify which level of objects you want to see. The All prefix lists all tables in any schema that you have rights to read. The DBA prefix specifies objects with permissions for the DBA. The USER prefix lists objects within the current schema. Each schema returns different columns. You can read the Oracle documentation to identify the columns, or simply run a short query: SELECT * FROM USER_TAB_COLUMNS WHERE rownum<5; The rownum constraint reduces the amount of data displayed to a small number of rows so you do not have to wait for thousands of rows of data. The sample query in Figure 9.1 provides a list of the tables in the schema along with the percentage of space remaining that is allocated to each table.

FIGURE 9.1

Prefixes	Synonym	Description
ALL_ DBA_ USER_	CONSTRAINTS	Table constraints and keys
	IND_COLS	Indexed columns
	MVIEWS	Materialized views
	SEQUENCES	Sequences
	SYNONYMS	Synonyms
	TAB_COLUMNS	Table columns
	TABLES	Tables
	TRIGGER_COLS	Trigger columns
	TRIGGERS	Triggers
	TYPES	User-defined data types
	USERS	Users
	VIEWS	Views (saved queries)
SELECT Table_Name, Pct_Free FROM USER_TABLES		

FIGURE 9.2

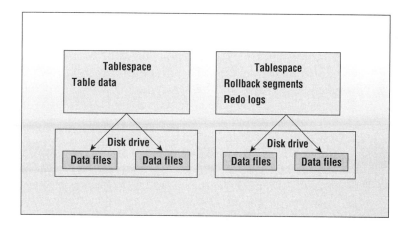

Performance is always a tricky issue in a DBMS. Small tables with a limited number of joins and a handful of simultaneous users rarely encounter performance problems. Also, with hardware improvements, performance improvements simply come down to "buy more processors and disk drives." However, since one of Oracle's strengths is its ability to handle huge amounts of data, you will encounter some databases that will need changes to improve performance. To understand some of the performance controls in Oracle, you need to be aware of how Oracle stores data on the file system. At the base level, the DBA allocates data files on disk drives. If you are not using a RAID system to automatically store data on multiple drives, you can accomplish a similar effect by creating separate storage files on different disk drives. Tablespaces are logical folders that can utilize multiple data files. Tables are assigned a specific tablespace to store the data. Oracle also uses rollback segments and redo logs to handle transactions and other situations where device failure might cause serious problems. As indicated in Figure 9.2, you get a substantial gain in performance if you store the table data and rollback segments in separate tablespaces on different drives. Two drives spinning independently means (1) the computer can write the data simultaneously, and (2) there is less chance of a loss in the event of a hardware failure. Oracle provides a tablespace map tool to help DBAs monitor the current storage allocation.

Backup and recovery are critical aspects to a database designed to handle thousands of users and processes running at once. In many cases, the database must run 24-7, so you cannot stop it to make a backup copy. Consequently, even while you are backing up data, new rows are being added and data is changing. Oracle has systems to protect all of this data, but if there is a hardware crash, you need to be careful about putting everything back together.

In some ways, security in Oracle is straightforward. Security and user identification are an integral component of the DBMS. By default, users have minimal access to any data in the database. Consequently, the major security efforts consist of identifying the access that people need and then enabling it with an SQL command. Of course, the security team will want to monitor system and database activity for potential breaches. Database triggers can be used to provide additional security controls by logging changes to sensitive tables.

Case: All Powder Board and Ski Shop

Ultimately, the owners of All Powder want to assign individual user permissions. Although the shop trusts its employees, it does often hire students to work as clerks, and the owners would like to limit what the clerks can do with the application. The issue is only partly a matter of trust. It is also useful to protect the database so clerks and other users cannot start changing form layouts or accidentally delete items.

The managers are also somewhat concerned about performance, particularly at the checkout machines. Sometimes the checkout lines get hectic, and the application has to be fast. Some of the issues can be handled by installing more computers; that way the salesperson can enter the basic customer data immediately, and the checkout clerk simply selects the customer and enters the product numbers. Of course, more computers mean that the company will need a network, and it means that more people will be simultaneously accessing the data, so the risk of collisions and locks increases.

Lab Exercise

All Powder Board and Ski Shop

DBMS developers learned early that indexes can significantly improve the performance of a relational DBMS. Primary key columns are almost always indexed because they often represent single-item lookups. Without an index, the computer has to search each row sequentially to find a match. Oracle automatically builds indexes on primary keys. However, you also need to think about building indexes on foreign keys to provide performance gains for joining tables.

Activity: Monitor the Application Performance

An index can exponentially reduce the number of lookups in a search. On the other hand, indexes have to be updated whenever data is changed, deleted, or added. As a result, placing too many indexes on a table can result in even worse performance. Your job is to find the balance with enough indexes to improve performance for key tasks, but not so many that other portions become too slow. This balance is unique to each application and can be difficult to find. Ultimately, you will have to fine-tune the application over time. A few simple rules help you begin: (1) All primary keys should be indexed; (2) Join columns should be indexed—particularly in large tables; (3) Heavily searched or sorted columns should be indexed; and (4) Transaction tables that are constantly changed (such as SaleItem) should have few indexes.

An important step for the query processor is to select the best approach for joining tables and restricting rows to retrieve data as quickly as possible. Part of this decision depends on the availability of indexes. Ultimately, the best performance depends on the amount and distribution of the data in the table. For these reasons, Oracle has implemented a cost-based optimizer that examines some statistics about the data to determine how to execute a query. This same optimizer can be used to help tune a query and identify which columns should be indexed.

Action

Log in as a DBA and run the script: Exec DBMS_STATS.Gather_Database_Stats.
Start the enterprise manager and log into your schema.
In the Diagnostics Pack, start the Performance Overview monitor.
Open an SQL session and issue several queries while you monitor the database performance.
Run some reports or get several people to alter data at the same time.

FIGURE 9.3

```
Exec  DBMS_STATS.Gather_Database_Stats
Exec  DBMS_STATS.Gather_Schema_Stats('powder')
Exec  DBMS_STATS.Gather_Table_Stats('powder', 'Customer')

You might have to run the catproc.sql script first.
```

To drive the optimization process, you must tell Oracle to analyze the database and collect statistics about each table. You can use the older Analyze Table command, but Oracle now recommends using a special procedure to analyze the entire database with one command. Figure 9.3 shows the three main commands in the DBMS_STATS package that gather statistics. Generally, you want to use the first version because it applies to the entire database. However, if your database has many schemas with relatively static data, you might want to update one schema at a time. Note that you might have to run the special catproc.sql script that installs the DBMS_STATS package. This script takes a while to run but only has to be done once. The DBMS_STATS commands should be run by a user with DBA privileges. Other procedures within the DBMS_STATS package will return the statistics to special tables that you can analyze to understand the structure of the database and manually tune the system.

Although you can run most of Oracle's administration tools through SQL, many of the more useful tools have been consolidated in the graphical enterprise manager. Figure 9.4 shows the schema for the All Powder case and

FIGURE 9.4

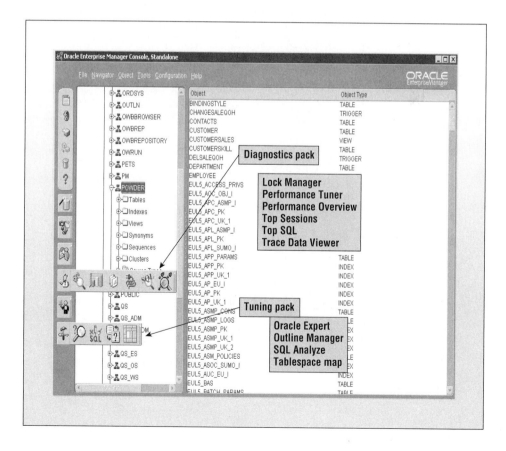

the two sets of diagnostic and performance tuning tools. Before examining some of these tools, notice that you can use the console to examine and alter properties for the schema objects (tables, views, and so on). With DBA permissions, you can also use the console's storage options to add new data files and tablespaces when you begin to run low on space in an existing tablespace.

The Diagnostics Pack tools are generally used to monitor the current performance of the database. A DBA would often monitor these tools on a daily basis to watch for problems. For example, the Lock Manager shows if deadlock problems are arising, or if one process is responsible for holding long locks on tables. These types of contention problems could be due to high traffic loads, poorly designed applications, or even network connection errors. If they persist, the DBA will have to find the specific cause by tracking the individual applications and users.

The Performance Overview chart shown in Figure 9.5 presents a relatively comprehensive overview of the current status of the database. The charts are

FIGURE 9.5

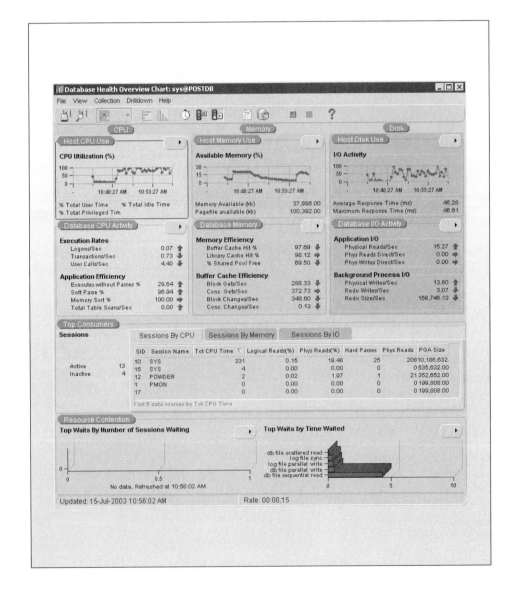

FIGURE 9.6

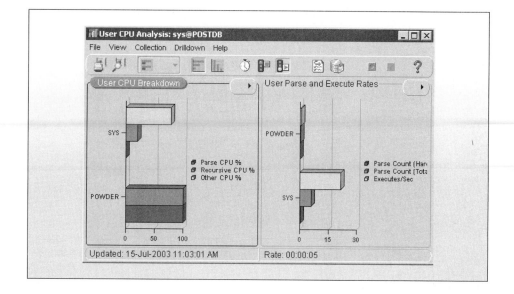

continually updated so they provide an immediate snapshot of the activity in the database. The CPU and memory indicators can help the DBA identify hardware bottlenecks. If the system is constantly low on memory or the processors maxed, you need to either improve the database performance or purchase additional hardware. The graphs on wait times indicate if some process is blocking others. The main point of the chart is that you should watch it over time to monitor trends and catch problems before they become huge. In a production environment, you will also want to write some procedures that periodically check some critical factors, such as percent free, and send automated warning notices when certain limits are exceeded.

If you identify a problem (say CPU usage has jumped), you can drill down or open related charts to identify the source of the problem. For example, Figure 9.6 shows the User CPU Analysis at one point in time to see which database users are bogging down the processor. As a simple experiment, open these charts and start an SLQ Plus session. Issue a query that retrieves a large number of rows. Also try a more complex query with several joins or perhaps a NOT IN statement. As the queries run, keep an eye on the performance monitors. If possible, get several students in the class to run queries or reports at the same time. You should see when using this small database that, most of the queries you throw at Oracle will execute very quickly. If you write some more complex copy commands or move to gigabyte- or terabyte-size tables, performance monitoring and tuning becomes more critical.

Action
Start the Oracle Expert and create a new repository if necessary.
Create a new tuning session and select all the options, including the comprehensive choices.
Under the Collect tab, use the Schema button to select the All Powder schema, then click the Collect button.
Under the Recommendations tab, click the Generate button.
Review the recommendations and create the indexes identified.

Activity: Expert Index Recommendations

Because of the complexity of managing large databases, Oracle provides several tools for tuning the database performance. Although it takes years of experience (and reading) to become an expert in tuning Oracle databases, you can practice with a couple of tools to learn some of the main concepts. From the

FIGURE 9.7

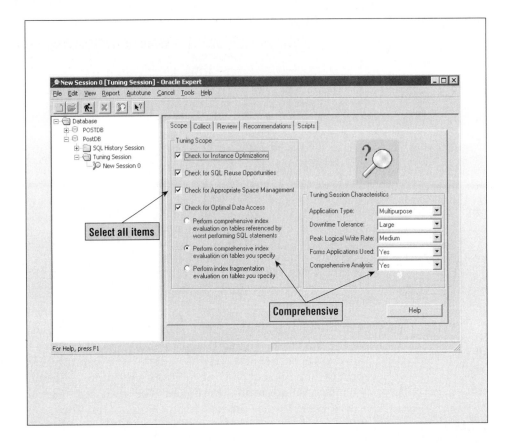

enterprise manager console, you can open the Oracle Expert. This tool provides a big-picture analysis of the database. Consequently, you will probably need **SYSDBA** privileges to run it. You will likely want to connect it to a stand-alone repository system. Large companies with multiple instances of Oracle running on several computers will ultimately install a single management server to control all of the copies. However, in a typical educational setting, you will most likely have access to only one copy of Oracle. If this copy of Oracle has not been used by the analysis expert yet, it will ask permission to create the repository. You have to allow this step to use the system. Once the repository tables are installed, you will be given the option to create a new tuning session or use an existing one. The first time through, you will have to create a new session. You should be able to accept the default options.

As shown in Figure 9.7, when you create a tuning session, generally you will want to add all of the options specified in the Scope screen. By choosing the detailed option, you can select your specific schema under the Collect tab. Many of the analyses will be more effective if users have been working with the system for a while to generate queries and create more realistic statistics and usage patterns. As long as you have executed most of the queries from the labs in Chapters 4 and 5, there should be sufficient statistical data for the expert to produce valid recommendations.

Figure 9.8 shows that all of the options are selected under the Collect tab. You might want to skip the Instance test for now (or interrupt it when it runs), because you most likely do not have many users on the system. More

FIGURE 9.8

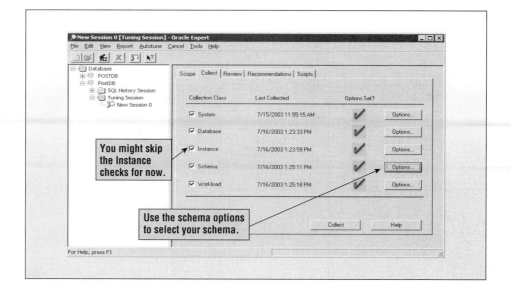

importantly, you need to set the options for the Schema to select your schema that holds the data tables for the All Powder case.

Figure 9.9 shows the selection tool where you find your schema and select it for analysis. Click the Get Schema button to obtain a list of all current schemas, then move yours to the window on the right. The system

FIGURE 9.9

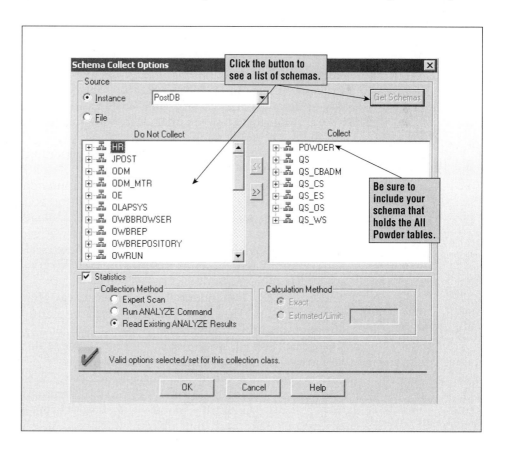

FIGURE 9.10

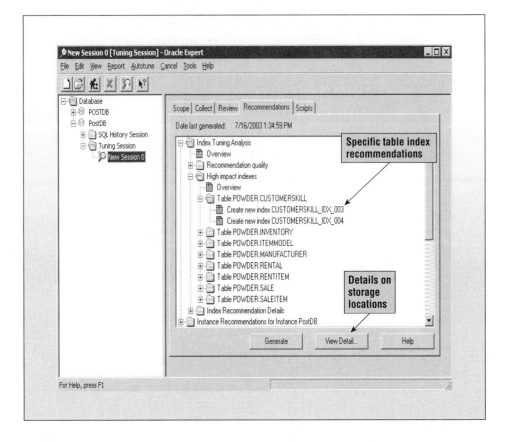

usually includes the quality of service tables by default. If you have recently executed the DBMS_STATS package, you can use the existing statistics option. Otherwise, you should select either the expert scan or the ANALYZE option to ensure that recommendations are based on current data.

Figure 9.10 shows the recommendations generated by the Expert analyzer. You need to click the Generate button: Be patient, it could require several minutes to run. Expand each recommendation to learn more details. Double-click the specific recommendation to read the accompanying notes. In this case, several indexes have been suggested—largely for foreign key columns. If you scroll down the list, you will also see storage recommendations on where to place the indexes. In this example, the system generally recommends that the indexes be created in the same tablespace as the tables.

The expert recommendations are an easy way to quickly identify good index candidates. However, you must still be cautious. Remember that adding indexes to a table speeds up queries but slows down deletes, inserts, and updates. Every time a row of data is changed, all of the indexes on the table have to be rebuilt. The expert analyzer tries to evaluate how the tables are used—based on recent queries, particularly the slow-running queries. However, you should still carefully evaluate its recommendations. Once the database is in production mode, you should keep good records of any changes you make and then observe the processing times carefully for a

FIGURE 9.11

```
SELECT Lastname, Firstname, Customer.CustomerID
FROM Customer, Sale
WHERE Customer.CustomerID = Sale.CustomerID
AND Customer.CustomerID NOT IN
(SELECT CustomerID FROM Rental)
ORDER BY Lastname, Firstname;
```

couple of weeks to see how your changes affected the overall database performance.

Activity: Analyze Query Performance

Many times as a DBA and as a developer, you will find that a few queries present the greatest performance issues. If a query is run once or twice a year, performance might not matter. If the query is an integral part of an application, or inside of a loop and executed thousands of times, it is worth the time to optimize the query. Oracle provides several tools to analyze queries. The Explain Plan command describes the tools that Oracle will use to generate the results. It indicates whether indexes will be used, the number of rows at each step, and the estimated "cost" of each step. The costs are an internal assignment by the query processor based on the statistics collected on each table and the estimated time to run the step. The query optimizer evaluates several approaches and chooses the one with the least estimated cost.

Although the optimizer is good, sometimes you can gain even more speed by rewriting the query—perhaps even breaking it into several pieces. You can manually review a query and the plan to look for potential gains. However, a better first step is to use the SQL Analyze tool. Figure 9.11 shows a query from Chapter 5 that returns a list of customers who have purchased items but never rented anything. As a challenge to the optimizer, it uses a subquery instead of a left join. Note that the actual join is written using the older syntax because the analyzer does not support the newer Inner Join version.

Start the SQL Analyze tool and log into the standalone repository. If you have not already created the repository, you will have to wait a few minutes while the system builds the necessary tables in your schema. Use the SQL/Create New SQL menu option and enter the SQL statement into the top window. You can now perform several analyses on the query using the buttons on the toolbar. Begin by selecting the Get Index Recommendations button. Figure 9.12 shows the results, and the suggestion is that you should add an index to the CustomerID key in the Sale table. It is not unusual to see this suggestion for foreign keys. The Virtual Index Wizard provides a slightly different approach to choosing indexes for this query. You can temporarily create indexes and test the performance to see if there is enough of an improvement to justify the overhead of the index. You do not need to run this tool now, but remember that it can help you analyze difficult questions about indexes.

Adding the index will help, but there are more critical issues with this query. Click the button to run the SQL Tuning Wizard. Figure 9.13 shows that the wizard found a substantial performance gain by rewriting the query.

FIGURE 9.12

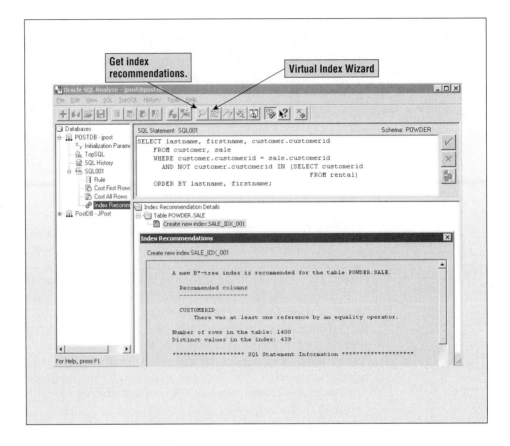

Figure 9.14 shows the recommendation made by the Tuning Wizard. Sometimes the wizard will make several suggestions, but this time, one change will improve the query. Click the Rule Details button to see a longer explanation. When the wizard is finished, it will add the modified version of the query to your tree list.

FIGURE 9.13

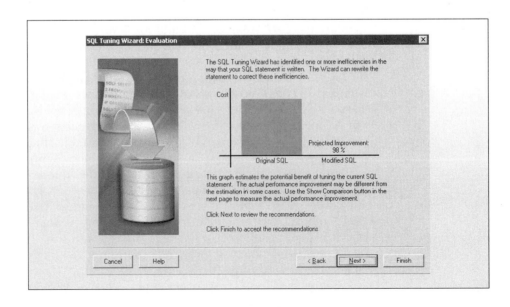

FIGURE 9.14

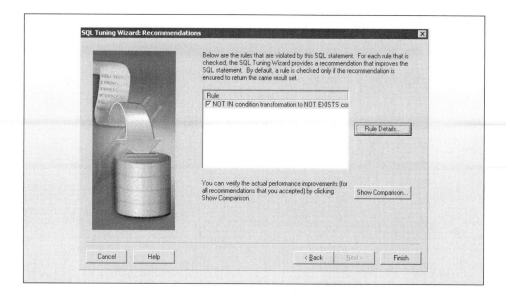

To see the effect of the changes, select the original query and click the button to Explain All Costs. Figure 9.15 shows the detailed results. Begin by looking at the Order column, which indicates where the query processor will start (step 1). Remember that the tables are relatively small, so the row counts are also small at each step. The biggest problem is that the final step (step 7) has a relatively high cost associated with analyzing so many rows.

Now select the new query that was created by the Tuning Wizard and run the same Explain All Costs command. The results shown in Figure 9.16 have some interesting features. First, observe that the revised (faster) version uses a correlated subquery. Looking at the plan, you can see why the query is faster in this situation: It sets up a second hash join instead of requiring a search of the entire table. Looking at the row counts and costs of the last three steps, you can see that this second hash join has quickly reduced the query result

FIGURE 9.15

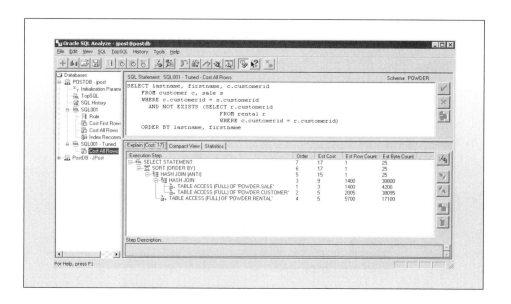

FIGURE 9.16

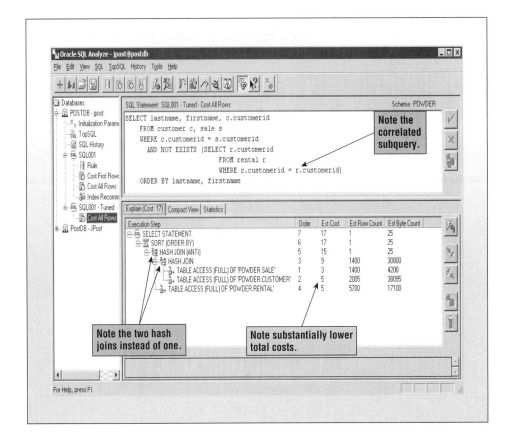

to one row that can be retrieved at considerably less cost than the original query. Unless your hardware is slow, you probably cannot observe the performance difference between the queries, but you should test them to ensure that they return the same results. The query analyzer also enables you to step through the queries and monitor performance at each step.

Improving performance of very large databases and complex queries can be a difficult process. Analyzing the tables is critically important for the query optimizer to function correctly. Even on small tables, the statistics can make an enormous difference in the performance. More detailed tuning is accomplished by using the index and tuning wizards. Just remember that adding too many indexes can cause problems with tables that have a high rate of change due to data entry or updates. Also, remember that it is important to monitor the daily performance aspects of the database. Keeping benchmarks on at least a weekly basis will enable you to spot long-term trends.

Action
Start SQL Analyze.
Create repository if asked.
Choose SQL/Create New SQL.
Enter the query into the top of the form.
Select Get Index Recommendations.
Run the SQL Tuning Wizard.
Explain all costs for the original query.
Explain all costs for the modified query.

Security and Privacy

Activity: Backup and Recovery

Backup and recovery of an Oracle database can be straightforward, or it can be complex. If you are able to shut down the entire database, you could simply use the operating system utilities to copy the underlying data files and the system control file. More realistically, the business will want to run the database without interruption. Oracle uses its redo logs to handle this situation. The underlying data is backed up at a certain point in time. Data that is being changed as the backup is taking place is written to the redo logs. These logs are also backed up, so the database can recover everything up to the point of the backup and then roll forward the additional changes from the redo logs.

In the Oracle Management Server, Oracle provides the RMAN (recovery manager) tool to automatically back up a database, as well as initiate the recovery steps if something happens to the database. To use this tool, you have to use the enterprise manager and connect it to the management server. It is not available if you use stand-alone mode. If you attempt this exercise on your own machine, you might have to return to the installation and set up the management server. Also, check the operating system administrative tools to ensure that the Management Server service is started. Finally, note that the first time you log into the management server, you will have to use the "sysman" username with a password of "oem_temp."

In order to back up the database while it is running, Oracle requires that the database be running in Archive Log Mode. By default, the initial database is usually running in No Archive Log mode. The easiest way to change this setting is to use the enterprise manager, select the database, the instance, and the configuration options in the tree view. Under the Recovery property tab, you can check the box to select Archive Log Mode. This action does mean that your database will continually use more disk space. As changes are made to the database, they will be permanently saved to a set of archive files. You will generally have to stop and restart the database for this change to take effect.

Action
If necessary, set up and start the Oracle Management Server. Start the Enterprise Manager and log in to the Management Server (use sysman/oem_temp for the initial login). Check the database recovery property to see if it is set to Log Archive mode. Use Tools/Database Tools/Backup Management/Backup to configure a backup process. If you have time, you can run the backup.

To perform an actual backup, start the enterprise manager and connect to the management server. Select the database in the tree and choose Tools/Database Tools/Backup Management/Backup from the main menu. Choose the customized backup strategy and you will see several options. Figure 9.17 is the primary customization form that you receive when you click the button to Edit Backup Configuration. If you have an automated tape system, you will want to define it under the Channels tab so backups are automatically written to the tapes. By default, they are written to new files stored on the same drive as the initial database. From there, you will want to copy the files to a portable system so they can be removed to a safe location.

Figure 9.18 shows one of the final steps in the backup process. Notice that you can manually schedule the backup to occur immediately. More importantly, you can specify automatic backup intervals. With these options, you can program the system to back up the database on a nightly basis when the database and the system are less busy. If your database receives thousands of changes a day, you can schedule backups more frequently. However, in these cases, you will want to use incremental backups to reduce the time and system load. You will also want to schedule full backups less frequently. Remember that full backups can take quite a while to run when the database is large.

FIGURE 9.17

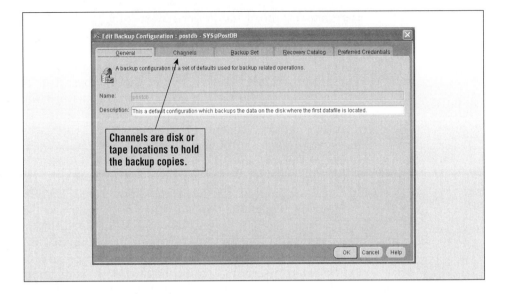

If a disk drive fails, the DBA can use the backup copies to restore the database to the point of the last backup. The enterprise manager contains a recovery tool that automatically loads the backup and rolls forward through the archive logs. If you need even greater protection, Oracle strongly recommends that you configure the database to store multiple copies of the log files on separate disk drives. Oracle uses the term *multiplexing* for this setup option. With enough disk drives stored in different locations, it is possible to have the bulk of the database running constantly under an automatic backup. If one device fails, Oracle can fairly quickly recover the changes from the duplicate log files. With multiple servers in a cluster, the entire system can continue running even if an entire machine fails. With these techniques,

FIGURE 9.18

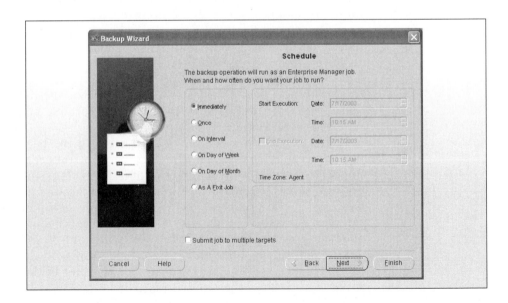

it is possible to maintain very high reliability systems that can run without interruption for extended periods of time.

Activity: Setting User-Level Security Controls

The Oracle database system is built and distributed with a complete security system. Users must log in to the system to see any of the data. The DBA can create new users and assign rights to the users or to groups of users. Initially, users have no permissions. Users and security rights can be created through SQL commands or by using the enterprise manager. The enterprise manager provides a relatively easy-to-use graphical interface, and is useful when you need to make simple changes or check on a particular item. However, if you need to set several security permissions at one time, it is often easier to write the SQL commands into a text file and execute the file in SQL Plus. If you do not happen to remember the exact SQL syntax, it is sometimes helpful to set up a test example using the enterprise manager interface, and copy the SQL command that it writes.

Action
Identify the SalesClerk and SalesManagers roles and determine what permissions are needed on the basic Sale, SaleItem, Customer, and Inventory tables.
Create three new users and assign them simple passwords.

The first issue to face is that Oracle needs to be able to identify the individual users. Figure 9.19 outlines the basic process. The main database application contains forms, reports, and tables. As the DBA, you want to assign individual permissions to separate users for each object. For instance, sales clerks would be able to read some supplier data, but not change it, and probably would not need access to the main supplier form. But before you can assign any permissions, the database application needs to be able to identify the user.

Identifying a user is an important step in securing a database or a computer system. Oracle has two primary means of identifying users: (1) Individual accounts can be created within the database, where users are assigned a unique username and a password, or (2) User accounts can be created on the computer that is responsible for handling the login and

FIGURE 9.19

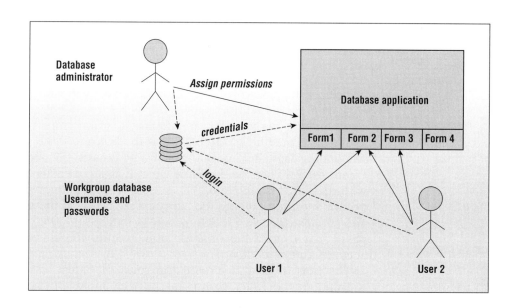

FIGURE 9.20

	Sales table	Customer table	Item table
Sales clerks	S,U,I	S,U,I	S
Sales managers	S,U,I,D	S,U,I	S
Rental managers		S,U,I	S

Sales managers   Sales clerks

Individual users

passing the username to Oracle. Each organization must balance the costs and benefits of the two methods. It is relatively easy to set up a new user account within Oracle. The main drawback to this approach is that users need to remember yet another username and password. Firms are increasingly looking for single sign-on systems where users log into a central directory and all computers and applications pull the user identity from this central server.

Before attempting to create users and assign security, you should write down a list of usernames and initial passwords that will be asked to enter into the workgroup database. While you are identifying users, you should also classify them in terms of tasks or groups. You almost never want to assign permissions to individual users. Instead, you place users into groups and assign database permissions to the roles of these groups. Figure 9.20 illustrates the main concept. By assigning permissions to the role, you should only have to set permissions once. As individual roles are added to or removed from users, their permissions automatically change.

Action
Create the SalesClerk and SalesManager roles. Assign appropriate table permissions to the new roles. Assign one of the roles to each of the new users. Use the Sales form to test the accounts and roles.

Creating a new user account is relatively easy with the enterprise manager tool. With DBA permissions, open the database and expand the Security node on the tree. Right-click the user list or icon and select the Create option. Figure 9.21 shows the screen used to create a new user account. If you select the password option, the database will validate the user based on the given username and password. If you choose External in the list, you must enter a username that matches a value from the operating system login. Click the Show SQL button at the bottom of the screen to see the corresponding SQL statement that actually creates the account. If you need to create several users at the same time, it is often easier to create a script file with these SQL statements. You simply edit the name and password for each person and then execute the script to create all of the accounts at one time. You can also write a PL/SQL program that would read the list of names and passwords from a file or table and execute the statement to create each account automatically.

The next step is to create the roles of SalesClerk and SalesManager. Right-click the Roles group in the tree hierarchy and select the Create

FIGURE 9.21

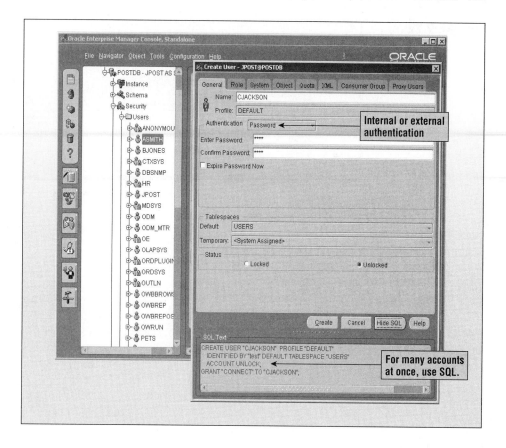

option. Figure 9.22 shows the main editing form. Select the table or view that you want the role to access. Choose the type of access on the right side and grant it by moving it down to the lower form. You can scroll through the form to see the currently assigned permissions. It is also helpful to check the SQL command. Again, if you are creating several similar roles, it is often easier to copy the SQL statement, make a few modifications, and then execute it directly. The GUI approach is useful when you do not want to memorize the SQL syntax, but when you need to assign permissions to many tables, it is often easier to use a text editor to cut and paste simple SQL statements. If you save the text file that generated the roles, it forms a nice reference document of the actual permissions that were granted to each role.

Once the users and the roles have been created, it is relatively easy to assign the roles to each user. Figure 9.23 shows the process using the enterprise manager. However, as shown at the bottom of the figure, the SQL command is also straightforward, so it is easy to automate the process when you have to assign roles to many users at one time. When defining roles and assigning them to users, it is important to remember that users are often assigned multiple roles. Security is more effective when the roles are assigned with relatively small granularity. That is, instead of creating two or three all-encompassing roles and assigning one to a person, it is better to break roles into smaller pieces and assign multiple roles to each person. In the All Powder case, you should consider

FIGURE 9.22

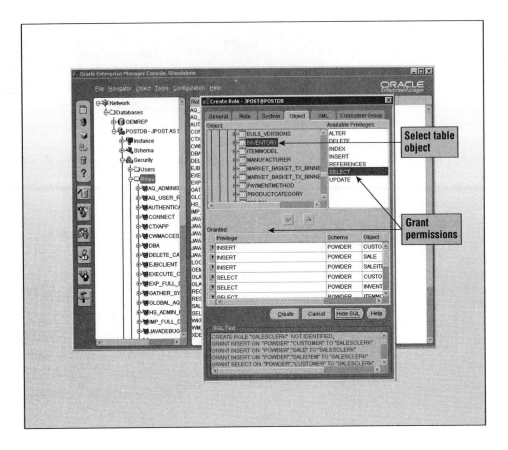

separate roles for Sales, Rentals, Receiving, Adding Customers, and so on. Then sales clerks would be granted the roles for sales, adding customers, and perhaps one or two other tasks. If a person is promoted or moved to a different position, you simply have to change the role assignment to match the new job. It is important that the roles and their names closely match the business jobs.

Of course, you need to test the security assignments. Try the test first using the forms—which is how the sales clerks will generally use the application. Notice that the forms themselves are stored outside the database, so they are not directly subject to the security conditions. However, as soon as the form tries to retrieve data, the security conditions are imposed, so unauthorized users will not be able to see any data. In fact, the first time you try to run a form as a sales clerk, you will probably receive an error message. Remember that Oracle assigns users to schemas and all queries look in the default user schema for tables and views. But the tables needed by the forms are actually stored in the Powder schema (or your schema). You can solve this problem by editing the data sources in all of the forms to include the schema name. For example, use Powder.Customer instead of just Customer. Outside of the forms, such as in SQL Plus, you can change the default schema using the command: ALTER SESSION Set Current_Schema=powder. Then you do not have to continually type the schema name prefix. Another solution is to define synonyms for all of the objects in the database. Synonyms are described in Chapter 10.

FIGURE 9.23

Exercises

Many Charms

Samantha and Madison do not believe that security will be a critical issue at Many Charms. The database will run on one machine and rarely be used by anyone except the two of them. On the other hand, they do need a system on which it is easy to create backup copies. And, for some security, they are willing to use the single database password. On the other hand, they are concerned about performance. Although they do not expect too many orders arriving at one time, they do want to examine some lengthy reports to evaluate sales trends.

1. Run the performance analyzer to improve the performance of the database and identify indexes needed. Also check the performance for the report queries.
2. Create a backup option that makes it easy for the managers to create a backup copy. As much as possible, keep it down to one button. But provide some notices about moving the backup copy offsite in case of fire.
3. Add the security provisions needed by Samantha and Madison.

Standup Foods

Security is a serious concern for Laura. The database contains a large amount of data about employees—and celebrity preferences. Managerial employees will need access to the database to enter a considerable amount of information regarding other employees and the status of the event. Consequently, employee access has to be carefully thought out. Managers should have the ability to enter data on employees who report to them, but should not be able to even see most data on other employees. You will have to use queries to provide this level of security. Assigning access to the entire employee table would give managers too much permission. Instead, you will have to set up queries that retrieve the data for specific approved managers and then give the managers access to the data through that query.

1. Run the performance analyzer to improve the performance of the database and identify indexes needed. Also, check the performance for the report queries.
2. Create a backup option and a written set of procedures that Laura can follow to ensure the data is protected.
3. Create the security provisions needed by Laura. Concentrate on the permissions needed to handle evaluation of employees by a manager—without allowing the manager full access to data for all employees.

EnviroSpeed

The knowledge in the EnviroSpeed database is a major strategic asset to the company. This data represents experience gained over several years and enables the company to be considerably more productive and profitable than its competitors. Tyler and Brennan believe it is critical to protect this asset. On the other hand, it is also critical that employees and hired experts have immediate access to all of the knowledge during a disaster cleanup. Security controls need to be set carefully to protect the database from outside hackers. Fortunately, Brennan and Tyler can trust all of the employees and experts and do not believe it is necessary to track the exact usage by each person to prevent theft.

1. Run the performance analyzer to improve the performance of the database and identify indexes needed. Also, check the performance for the report queries.
2. Create a backup option and a written set of procedures to follow to protect the database.
3. Create the security provisions needed. Concentrate on protecting the data from external attacks.

Final Project

The main textbook has an appendix with several longer case studies. You should be able to work on one of these cases throughout the term. If you pick one or your instructor picks one, perform the following tasks.

1. Run the performance analyzer to improve the performance of the database and identify the indexes needed. Also check the performance for the report queries. Identify the main areas that will be stressed as loads increase.
2. Create a backup option and a written set of procedures to protect the database.
3. Identify the main risk factors and implement the security provisions needed to protect the data, but still ensure users have the access needed to perform their jobs efficiently.

10

Distributed Databases and the Internet

Objectives

- Split a database and link the parts for use on a LAN.
- Replicate a database and synchronize the changes.
- Create Web pages to edit data over the Internet.
- Export and import data as XML files.

Location, Location, Location

Even small companies often need to access data in multiple locations. This distributed access generates several issues in database management. The most important question you will face is where to store the data. The answer depends on how the database is used, how fast the connections are, and whether everyone needs 24-hour access to immediately current data. The first step in designing a distributed system is to answer these questions and determine the most efficient method for handling data updates in the various locations. Note that efficiency also includes cost issues.

Oracle provides several tools to support distributed access to data. The three primary approaches are (1) Internet access, (2) linked databases, and (3) data replication. You could also make the argument that the cluster system is a distributed system on a local scale. The primary purpose of the cluster system is to improve performance and reliability. You can use storage area networks to separate the data files from the processors. Clustering enables multiple processors to work on the same data at the same time. At some level, Oracle treats all of this hardware as a single (really fast) system. On the physical side, you gain flexibility by being able to move, change, and add hardware without altering the database design.

In terms of distributed access, the use of Web-based forms and reports provides considerable flexibility in terms of client access. The database itself has become more centralized, which makes it easier to manage. Yet, managers can access the information from anyplace with an Internet connection. As wireless devices, including cell phones, gain more Internet features, managers will have almost continuous access to the data regardless of location. And this power comes almost automatically when you build Web-based forms and reports. Since the other labs cover these tools, this chapter will focus on database links and replication. Just remember that whenever you encounter the need for a distributed system, you should first ask whether the problem can be solved using the Internet.

Case: All Powder Board and Ski Shop

Initially, you might think that All Powder with only one store would not care much about distributed databases. Certainly, if the owners consider adding a second store, the issues become more complex. This situation will be examined in a second lab exercise. In the meantime, even with one store there are some simplified distributed issues to address. The distributed aspect arises because there will be several locations within the store that need access to the database—the checkout stations, the rental desk, and a couple of offices. Figure 10.1 shows that each of these locations will have a computer that needs to run the forms and share the data.

Distributed questions within a single building are much easier to solve than those spreading across wide geographic areas. The reason is because of the speed of local area networks. Within the store, it is relatively easy to install a high-speed LAN that can transfer data as quickly as a typical computer can transfer data to an internal hard drive. Consequently, it is possible to store the database in one location and share it with all of the other computers—with no noticeable delays. You have already built the system so

FIGURE 10.1

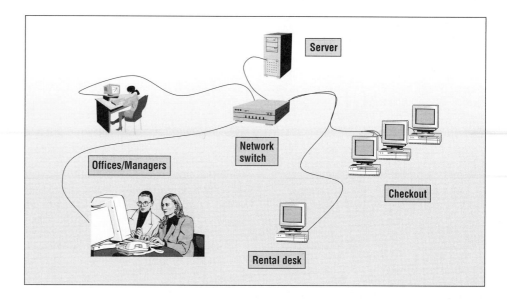

that all of the data files, forms, and reports run on the server. To provide access from multiple locations, all you need to do is ensure that each station has a machine with a Java-enabled Web browser and a network connection back to the server. You might even consider portable wireless devices for some of the employees so they can help customers throughout the store. The key point is that the database will run without any changes.

Lab Exercise

All Powder Board and Ski Shop

The existing single server with network access will work well as long as most of the operations occur in one location. How well would this system work if the company acquires an inventory warehouse or opens another store? The answer depends on how fast of a connection the company is willing to lease between the other locations and the database server. With a relatively high-speed connection, the Web-based approach will work fine. There might be slight delays if everyone opens major reports at exactly the same time, but most of the time, the connection is simply transferring small amounts of transaction data. With only a few users, even a fractional T1 line or frame relay might be sufficient to handle the typical loads. In a real-life situation, you could monitor the amount of traffic and network usage within the existing store to get a better idea of how much bandwidth would be needed to connect to a second store.

> **Action**
>
> If necessary, create a second database, preferably on a different machine.
> Create a small Customer table and load it with four or five rows of data.
> Return to your main database and create a database link to the target.
> Run an SQL statement that retrieves data across the link.

On the other hand, you could eventually reach a situation where you need faster response times at each location. In this case, you might split the database and run two or more servers. The servers would support local operations, but some reports would need to retrieve data from both databases. As long as you have a network connection, you can create a database link that enables forms, reports, and SQL to access data from any connected database. The process is relatively easy, but you will need to think about security issues.

FIGURE 10.2

```
CREATE  TABLE  Customer
(CustomerID  INTEGER,
 LastName     VARCHAR2(15),
 FirstName    VARCHAR2(15),
  Constraint  pk_Customer  Primary  Key  (CustomerID)
);
INSERT  INTO  Customer  (CustomerID,  LastName,  FirstName)
Values  (1,'Smith',  'Adam');
INSERT  INTO  Customer  (CustomerID,  LastName,  FirstName)
Values  (2,'Keynes',  'John');
INSERT  INTO  Customer  (CustomerID,  LastName,  FirstName)
Values  (3,'Samuelson',  'Paul');
INSERT  INTO  Customer  (CustomerID,  LastName,  FirstName)
Values  (4,'Robinson',  'Joan');
Commit;
```

Activity: Create Database Links

The first step is to find or create a second database. It is even better if you happen to have two machines running as Oracle servers. As an example, you can create multiple databases that run on the same server. The easiest way to create a new database is to start the Database Configuration Assistant from the main Windows menu Oracle Home/Configuration and Migration Tools. Once you have the new database created, use Oracle's Net Manager to create an entry in the network table that specifies the host name. Finally, you create a user account or use one of the system accounts. Now you can log on and create a table. To illustrate a database link, you only need a small table with a couple of rows of data. Figure 10.2 shows a small Customer table with a couple of rows of sample data. This new database and table will be the target link.

Log off the target database, start SQL Plus, and log into your main database. In this main database, you want to create a database link to the target you just created. Figure 10.3 shows the SQL statement needed to create the database link. It needs to be issued only one time. Now you can access tables in the other database by adding the name of the link to any SQL commands as shown in the SELECT statement. You should create a descriptive name for the link so you remember which server you are using. In this example, the server would be for the New York store. In general, avoid being too specific about a location, because you might want to move the hardware later. The link name should reflect the business operation. The other tricky part of the link is that it specifies a remote username and password. If you do not specify the CONNECT TO clause, the system will attempt to connect with the current username/password from the local system. This approach would

FIGURE 10.3

```
CREATE  DATABASE  LINK  NewYork
  CONNECT  TO  RemoteUser  IDENTIFIED  BY  t1
  USING  'dbhostname';

SELECT  *  FROM  Customer@NewYork;
```

require that you establish identical user accounts on both machines. From a security perspective, it might be slightly safer to create identical accounts, but it takes time and effort to continually synchronize the accounts and passwords. The USING clause references the hostname of the computer that you entered when you created the network connection to the database. The link needs to be created only one time. From this point, you can reference the table much like any other table in your schema. Of course, if the actual network connect is slow and you try to retrieve thousands of rows of data, you will have to wait quite a while. So, be careful and think about how much data your query might attempt to return over a database link.

Activity: Replicate and Synchronize a Database

Internet pages and linked tables are an efficient and easy solution when all of the computers are connected by high-speed networks, or when you only need to transfer a limited amount of data at one time. They will not work as well when you have multiple locations that are connected by slower links. In particular, when most of the traffic is local, you should consider replication. For example, if the company had stores in two different countries, it is unlikely that workers in the first store would need to share data on a daily basis with the other store. In this configuration, it does not make sense to have one central database and transfer everything back to it. Instead, you would want to install separate database servers in each location that would handle the operations within that area. Yet, on a regular basis, you need to synchronize the data so that managers can still retrieve all of the information to make decisions.

Action
Choose Tools/Replication/Create Replica.
Make a change to a customer name in the master database.
Add a new customer in the replica.
In the master database, choose Tools/Replication/Synchronize Now.
Verify that both databases now contain the same data.

Building replicated databases requires some decisions, but ultimately only two major steps. The decision essentially comes down to whether you want the databases to run as peer-to-peer or if one of the databases will be a master site and the others clones (materialized views) that are updated against the master. In terms of features and capabilities, the two approaches are similar. The peer-to-peer or multimaster approach provides a little more protection against loss, because each of the peer sites has a completely functioning copy of the database. In many ways, the single master approach is easiest and requires less management. It also has a nice template feature so that users can download a template and quickly build a replica of the database. Oracle supports hundreds or even thousands of replicas. Of course, you can always combine the two approaches if you need a few distributed servers. The biggest difference between the multimaster and single master (materialized view) approach is conceptual—the replicas have to synchronize back with a server, and any conflicts have to be resolved at that server.

There are two main steps involved in replicating a database: (1) Create the replica, and (2) synchronize the data between the replica and the server. Of course, there are many options in creating the replica. Also, during synchronization, you might encounter conflicts. Conflicts arise when the same piece of data has been changed on the different copies. Since the copies are not always connected, it is impossible to prevent these conflicts. Instead, the user has to make a decision about which version to accept.

FIGURE 10.4

Start the deployment template.
  Set up master sites.
  Disconnect and log in as RepAdmin.
  Create a master group.
  Create the template.
  Generate the script.
Create materialized view logs on the master site for each table.
On the client, run the script.
  Manually create a materialized view group.
  Create a new refresh group matching the template: CustomerTemplate.
  Select the Customer materialized view (or all).
  Add the materialized view to the refresh group.

The process of creating a replica requires several steps. Figure 10.4 outlines the major steps in the process. Keep in mind a critical element of the process: You must keep notes as you work. You will be asked to create several accounts and passwords. You need to write these down so you can use them later. The easiest way to create a replica and manage the process is to use the replica system built into the Enterprise Manager console. Open the management console and log in with SYSDBA privileges. Expand the database and expand the Distributed node. Under Advanced Replication, you will see the three choices for Administration, Multimaster, and Materialized View. Select the Materialized View Replication option and you will be provided links to instructions for managing the process. Before setting up the replica, you need to understand some of the terminology. You set up a deployment template so users can download the template and create a replica with minimal instructions. A replication group is a collection of related objects such as tables and views that will be replicated together. Replication sites consist of the master site and the materialized view sites (copies). Scheduled links are database links and a time schedule used to automatically synchronize the data. Refresh groups are collections of items that will be refreshed at the same time over the synchronization link.

Begin by creating a deployment template, so select that option on the console screen. The first step is to set up the master site; the next step is to create the master (replication) group; then generate the template. Choose the option to create the master site, and add your main database. Figure 10.5 shows the main screen to add the database. Click the Add button and select your database. You will need the password for the SYSTEM account. You will be prompted to add an administrator user account for the database. It is probably wise to stick with the default username (REPADMIN), but choose a password you will remember. You next have the option to create new schemas to hold the replicated data on the master site. You could use this option to combine data from several other sources, but for this exercise, leave it empty. The next choice is to establish the link scheduling interval. The default is to synchronize the databases every hour. For the exercise, the default value is fine; in an actual situation, you would have to make the decision based on how often the data changes and on whether managers need absolutely current information. Likewise, you should accept the default value of one hour for purging the job schedule—which is invoked to clear the log of successful transactions. You

FIGURE 10.5

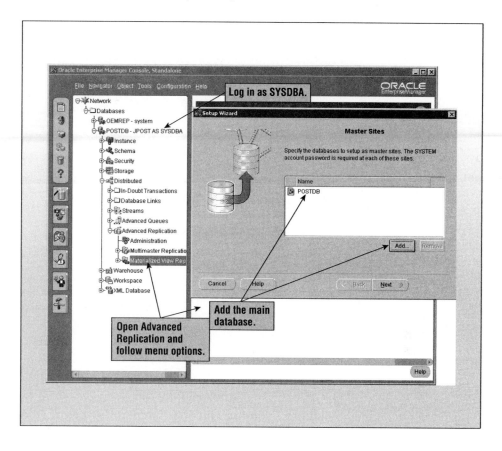

are given a final chance to customize the site settings, so just accept the current values and allow the wizard to make the necessary changes.

As shown on the main deployment menu, the next step is to create the master group to hold the items that will be replicated. But, before you can continue, you must disconnect from the database and log back in as the new replication administrator that you created. Right-click on the database node in the tree view. Reopen the deployment wizard and create a master group. To keep this example small, you will replicate only the customer data, so name this the CustomerReplica. As shown in Figure 10.6, select the Objects tab and choose the Customer table to be replicated. Of course, in a real case, you would usually select additional tables and views. Click the OK button to accept the list, then click the Create button to create the master group.

The next step is to create the template. Click the Create Template link on the main deployment menu. Enter a name (CustomerTemplate) and select your schema. Figure 10.7 shows one of the more important steps in the process—selecting the tables that will be replicated as materialized views. For this example, stick with just the Customer table. Clicking the Next button provides you with additional options that would also be useful in a

Action
Use the Enterprise Manager to open the master database and expand the replication section.
Start the Deployment template.
Set up the Master Site.
Disconnect and log in as RepAdmin.
Create a Master Group.
Create the template.
Generate the script.
Create Materialized View logs.
On the client target run the script.
Manually create a Materialized View group.
Create the Materialized Views.
Add the views to the refresh group.
Refresh the group.
Test a query.

FIGURE 10.6

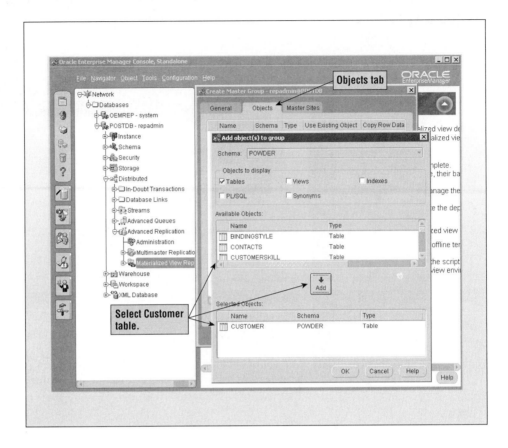

real-life setting. For example, you can use the system to distribute procedures. In this exercise, accept the defaults and do not add other items.

Now that the template is created, you can generate the script that will be
used to create the main accounts on the target databases. Click the Template
Script Generation link and select the template you just created. Create a new
proxy account on the client that the server will use for synchronization. Use
the default name (MVADMIN_PROXY), but enter a password and write both
in your notes. You also need to pick a local user on the target system and
enter the global name of the target database. The global name of the target
database is usually of the form hostname.US.ORACLE.COM. Accept the
default refresh interval of one day. Select your schema that contains the replication objects (Customer table). Figure 10.8 shows the schema selection
screen. This schema will be re-created on the target system. When you reach
the final screen of the wizard, it will show you the name and location of the
script to be created. Copy this name so you can find the script and run it on
the client.

The purpose of the script is to create the accounts and schemas on the
target computer. It can be customized to generate multiple replicas. However, for some reason, the script wizard does not include some important elements that are needed on the client and the server. First, on the server, you
should create Materialized View logs for each table that is being replicated.
In the enterprise manager, expand the database tree for the master server
until you find the Materialized View Log entry in the replication master site

FIGURE 10.7

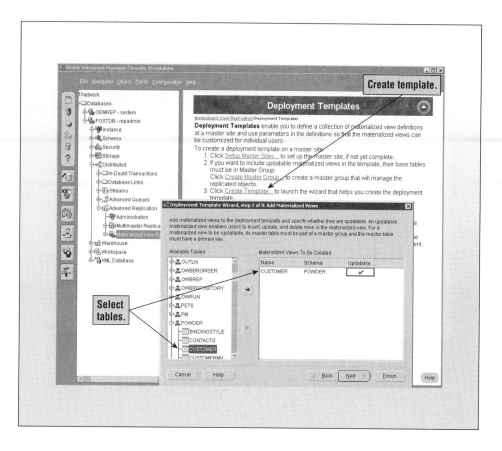

section. Right-click the item and create a new log. Select your schema and the desired table (Customer). Create the log using the default values.

The client site needs two items that are not automatically generated by the template script. They can be created by hand using the enterprise manager, or you can add the SQL commands to the end of the template script. Essentially, you need to create the materialized views to the client and add these views to the new refresh group that you created as well. Figure 10.9 shows the SQL to create the materialized view. Note that you have to enter the name of the link to your host database that was created by the template script. You will also have to add your materialized views to the refresh group.

As long as you can use the enterprise manager to log into the target site, it is relatively easy to create the client materialized view and refresh group. Expand the replication section and find the section labeled Materialized View Site. On the Materialized View node, create a new entry and select the Powder schema and Customer table. In the same manner, add a new refresh group to the client site. As shown in Figure 10.10, once the group is created, select the Materialized View tab to add the view you just created. When the view is added to the group, you can click the Refresh Now button to immediately load the data instead of waiting for the scheduled refresh. The replication link should now be established. Use SQL Plus to log on to the client database and issue a simple SELECT statement on the Powder.Customer table.

FIGURE 10.8

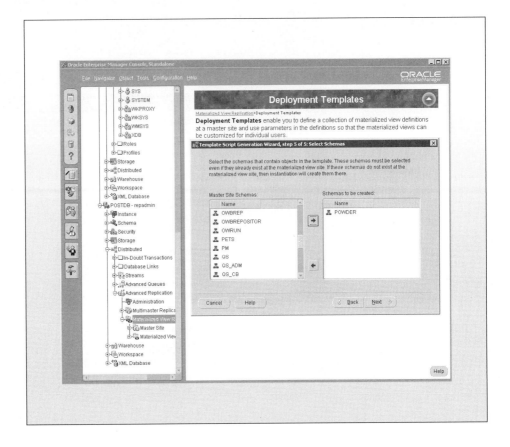

The Internet

Activity: Public Web Pages with Oracle

Sometimes you need to build Web pages that run in straight HTML. In particular, you cannot assume that your customers will have a Java client installed. Also, you would not want to create separate Oracle accounts and passwords for thousands of customers. Consequently, the standard Oracle forms and reports should only be used for internal applications. Yet, you still want to create Web pages for your customers so they can search for products or check on orders or sign up for e-mail specials.

Action

Configure a Data Access Descriptor.
Create two Web pages: GetSale and ListSales.
Load the pages into the database.
Open the first page and test the form.

Oracle provides several tools to build standard Web pages. One of the easiest to use (now that you know PL/SQL) is to create relatively standard HTML pages that have embedded PL/SQL statements to retrieve and update data. Figure 10.11 shows the basic steps. You build these pages using HTML and add the PL/SQL statements. The pages are then compiled and stored in the database schema. Through a link on your main website, users open a form, which passes the data to a results page. You can build relatively

FIGURE 10.9

```
CREATE MATERIALIZED VIEW Powder.Customer FOR UPDATE AS
    SELECT * FROM Powder.Customer@host_database_link;
```

FIGURE 10.10

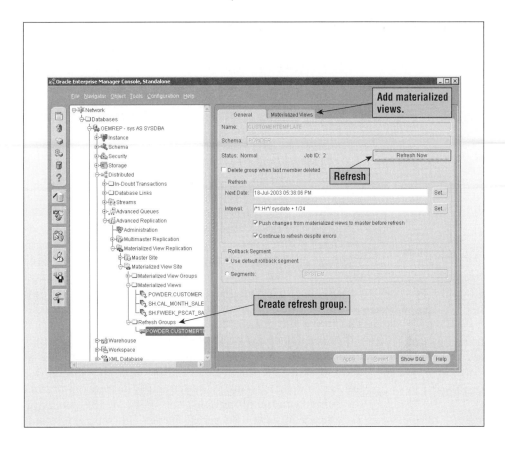

complex forms with sophisticated queries. To highlight the concepts, the example here uses only one table (Sale), a simple input form, and a basic table list as an output page.

The first step is to create a Data Access Descriptor (DAD) that points to your schema and sets up the login with the username and password. In real life, you will want to create a new username and password that the public will use, and give it limited access to specific tables. Everyone using your Web pages will be assigned this account automatically. For this exercise, you can use your personal username and password. The Oracle Web server is based on the Apache engine, which has online administrative pages to control the server. Simply open the main page for your server (for example, http://PostDB), and you will see the main configuration page. Note that it is possible to limit the administrators who can see this page. If you do not see the page, check with the system DBA and ask about the security settings.

FIGURE 10.11

```
(0) Configure the Data Access Descriptor
(1) Create the basic html form to get the SaleID      GetSale.psp
(2) Create the page to display the results            ListSales.psp
(3) loadpsp -replace -user powder/ski1@PostDB GetSale.psp
(4) loadpsp -replace -user powder/ski1@PostDB ListSales.psp
(5) http://PostDB/pls/simpledad/Powder.GetSale
```

FIGURE 10.12

> Modify SimpleDAD
> Schema name: Powder (or your schema name)
> Username: Powder (your username)
> Password: (enter the password)
> Connect String: PostDB (your database name)
> Authentication Mode: Basic
> Leave all other settings at the default values

When the page opens, select the Mod plsql Configuration Menu option and edit the SimpleDAD descriptor. You can also create a new descriptor if you prefer to choose a different name. Figure 10.12 shows the settings you need to make. The descriptor simply lists your schema, the database, and then the username and password. Essentially, the same information you are asked when you log into the database. You only need to perform this setup once, but be sure that you remember (write down) the exact descriptor name.

You are now ready to create the basic Web pages. You could use an HTML editor, or you simply type them into Wordpad and save them as text files. The first page is completely HTML, but you will still want to give it a .psp suffix so that it can be loaded into the database. Figure 10.13 shows the few lines of code that you will need. This page creates a simple form with one text element. Users will be asked to enter the SaleID value and click the Submit button. Be extremely careful with the action parameter. You must include the schema name along with the name of the procedure that will be called. This procedure will be created with the next page, so make sure the name matches. Likewise, you will need to use the SaleID from this form on the next Web page, so be careful to be consistent. Save this page as GetSale.psp and make sure to save it as a text file.

The next Web page will display the results. Figure 10.14 shows the code to produce the page. Before deciphering the PL/SQL statements, notice that it is essentially just an HTML table consisting of three columns: Sale ID, Sale Date, and Customer ID. The values that will be displayed in these columns will come from a database query. The query will currently retrieve only one row because the WHERE clause limits it to a single SaleID value. In real life, most of your forms will retrieve multiple rows, so the example uses a typical loop to be able to display all of the selected rows. To test the loop, you might want to change the SaleID condition to a SaleDate.

FIGURE 10.13

```
<html>
<head><title>Get SaleID</title></head>
<body>
<p align=center>All Powder Board and Ski Shop Sales</p>
<form name='Form1' method='post' action='Powder.ListSales'>
<p>Enter a Sale ID value:
<input type='text' name='SaleID' maxlength='20'/></p>
<input type='submit' name='submit' value='Submit'/>
</form>
</body>
</html>
```

FIGURE 10.14

```
<%@ page language="PL/SQL" %>
<%@ plsql procedure="ListSales" %>
<%@ plsql parameter="SaleID" type="NUMBER" %>
<%!l_SaleID NUMBER := SaleID;%>
<HTML>
<HEAD><TITLE>List Sales Data</TITLE></HEAD>
<BODY>
<p>Sales data for SaleID: <%=SaleID%></p>
<table border=0>
<tr>
    <th>Sale ID</th>
    <th>Sale Date</th>
    <th>Customer ID</th>
</tr>
<%
  for item in
    (select * from sale where SaleID=l_SaleID order by
    SaleDate)
  loop
%>
  <tr>
      <td><%=item.SaleID%></td>
      <td><%=item.SaleDate%></td>
      <td><%=item.CustomerID%></td>
  </tr>
<% end loop; %>
</table>
</BODY>
</HTML>
```

Notice that all **PL/SQL** code is surrounded by special brackets: $<\% \ldots \%>$. Also, notice the three page directives at the top. The first line tells the system which language to use. The second provides the name that should be given to the procedure when it is created in Oracle. The third line identifies any parameters that should arrive from the calling form. In this case, the first form is passing the SaleID value from the text box. To minimize confusion in the query, the fourth line creates a local variable to hold the SaleID and assigns its value when the page is opened. The main code on the form is contained in the line that creates the query and begins the loop (for item in . . .). The "for" statement defines the loop; the "select" statement is a standard query; and the "loop" keyword specifies the start of the loop, which is terminated by an "end loop" statement a few lines below. The query is a simple SELECT statement, but notice the use of the WHERE clause. The values returned are restricted to those that match the incoming SaleID value. The reason for using the local variable (l_SaleID) is to avoid the SaleID=SaleID statement that would be misinterpreted. You can write relatively complex SQL statements within this code, but if they get too complex, you should consider building them as internal procedures. The final aspect of the code is to display the returned column values. The $<\%= \ldots \%>$ statements are the main display commands. The equals sign simply says to display the values. Notice that they are embedded within table column tags so that the

FIGURE 10.15

browser will format them nicely. Save this file as ListSales.psp in the same folder as the GetSale file.

When you have entered and saved the two files, you need to compile them and save them in the database. Oracle provides a command-line procedure to accomplish this task. On the database server, go to the command line (DOS) mode and change to the directory that holds your two files. Issue the two loadpsp commands shown in Figure 10.11 as lines 3 and 4. Of course, you will use your username, password, and database name. The files should compile correctly and be stored in your schema. If you receive any error messages, you will have to double-check the files. If you cannot find any errors, make sure that the server is properly configured to run the Web service. You might have to find and run the owaload.sql script stored in the Apache directory tree. When the procedures have been created, you can exit the command line and open the enterprise manager to see the procedures stored in your schema.

Now that the procedures have been compiled and stored, they are ready for use. However, opening the first procedure requires a slightly tricky URL. Figure 10.15 shows the URL and the basic form. Of course, you will use the name of your Web server and schema, and you might have changed the name of your data access descriptor. The basic format of the URL is: http://WebServerName/pls/DataAccessDescriptor/Schema.procedure. Notice that you must use a dot between the schema name and the procedure, not a slash. Also notice that you must include the pls virtual directory. In general, you will have to place a link on your main website that contains this address.

Once you have the first form open, you can enter a SaleID (try 7000), and click the Submit button. Figure 10.16 shows the results. Although the data is displayed in the three columns, you might want to add some padding to separate the columns a little. Of course, you would need a much better design for a Web page that you display to customers, but that can be handled with HTML. You could even hire a designer to build a good layout, and then go in and add the necessary PL/SQL code.

FIGURE 10.16

Activity: Transferring Data with XML

One issue you will face with distributed databases is the need to transfer data among differing database systems. For example, a supplier might send you product information electronically. Since the supplier does not know what type of database system you have or how your database is organized, it can be difficult to provide the data in a format that your system can read. The process is complicated when suppliers have thousands of customers like your shop. Suppliers have no desire to create thousands of different electronic files. Instead, they should be able to send one file in a standard format, and your system should be able to identify the necessary data, select it, and import it into your database. This dream is not quite reality, but XML (eXtensible Markup Language) was created to make it easier to exchange data among disparate systems.

Exporting data in XML format is relatively easy with Oracle 9i. Oracle has several tools to scan a relational table and produce an XML format. The DBMS_XMLGen package will read an entire table and create the output file in one piece. It also offers some options to control the layout of the file. It can also create nested subsections, such as an items order on an order form. However, it requires a couple dozen lines of setup code. A simpler solution is to use the XMLElement function directly in an SQL statement. Figure 10.17

Action
In SQL Plus, run the SELECT XMLElement command to create an XML file for some of the employee data.
Edit the resulting file to remove the extra title lines printed by SQL.
Add the <?xml...?> tag and the starting and ending <Employees> tag.
Open the file in Internet Explorer.

FIGURE 10.17

```
SET long 20000
SET pages 100
SPOOL D:\Students\AllPowder\Employee10.xml
SELECT XMLElement("Employee", XMLElement("LastName", LastName),
    XMLElement("FirstName", FirstName))
    FROM Employee
    WHERE rownum<10;
SPOOL OFF
```

FIGURE 10.18

```
<?xml version='1.0'?>
<Employees>
<Employee>
    <LastName>Staff</LastName>
    <FirstName></FirstName>
</Employee>
<Employee>
    <LastName>Killy</LastName>
    <FirstName>Jean-Claude</FirstName>
</Employee>
...
</Employees>
```

shows a sample SQL statement that retrieves 10 rows from the Employee table. Notice the use of the Spool command to send the output to a file so that you can edit the file and send it to someone else.

Figure 10.18 shows the part of the resulting XML file with some editing. Before distributing the file, you will have to open the file in a text editor to make some minor changes. First, the Spool command inserts a few lines at the top and bottom of the file. You have to delete everything in the file except the data marked with the <Employee> . . . </Employee> tags. Second, you have to add the <?xml version='1.0'?> tag at the top of the file to indicate that it is an xml file. Finally, you have to add the starting <Employees> and ending </Employees> tag around the entire set of data. Note that each <Employee> data line will be displayed on one row. Figure 10.18 broke up each row and indented the attributes to highlight the layout of the file. Do not take the time to set this indentation in your file—it will take too long.

Figure 10.19 shows that you can open XML files using the Internet Explorer browser. This approach highlights the individual data records and

FIGURE 10.19

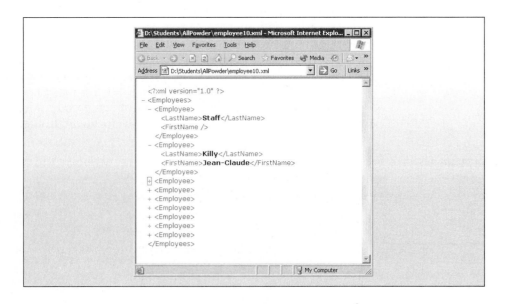

makes it easy to see the structure of the data. You can expand or contract individual segments to focus on individual areas. It is a useful way to quickly check a file to ensure that it is consistent. It is also useful for browsing data sent from an external source so you can check the contents.

Oracle also has several methods to import data from XML files and place it into the database. One of the biggest questions you will face in this situation is whether to store the data in raw XML form or to retrieve the data items from the XML file and store them in relational tables. If you are importing data to be used within your existing database, then you will generally want to extract the data and store it in the relational tables. If you are going to reexport the XML file, or simply need to extract a few items from it, or if it is needed for some other application, you will want to leave it in a special XML table. Oracle 9i supports XML as a data type for a column. You can load an XML table from a data file. Oracle then provides the Extract and ExtractValue commands to retrieve individual items from the XML structure.

Converting from XML to a relational database requires more effort and you will probably need to write Java code to extract the items you want and store them into the proper database tables. The OracleXSU package has several powerful commands to extract, store, and manipulate data in XML. The Oracle text package also has detailed commands for searching and retrieving data from large XML files. Note that you will most likely have to install the Java XDK and the OracleXSU packages. Pay close attention to the installation instructions because the installation process requires several detailed steps.

Oracle 9i has many additional XML features, including the ability to generate Web pages, or even pages for Internet-enabled mobile devices. You can find examples for some of these features within the Oracle documentation. However, if you become heavily involved in XML within Oracle, you will want to pick up a couple of the books specifically targeted to these features.

Exercises

Crystal Tigers

Most of the information for the Crystal Tigers club can be maintained on one computer run by the club secretary. However, the secretary sometimes needs assistance entering all of the data during special events. Although he brings the database on his laptop, it would probably be easier if two or three people brought laptops and handled specific tasks. At the end of the day, the data could be synchronized and available for analysis. It would at least speed up the data entry and give more people access to the critical information needed during the day.

1. Replicate the database and test it on three separate computers, then synchronize the changes a few times to see if this approach will work for the club.

2. The club has talked about making some data available to members over the Internet. Although many of the members do not have Microsoft Office installed, the club would prefer to provide read-only access. Set up a page

that generates activity lists for an upcoming event so members can check the schedule.

3. One of the charitable organizations the club works with is impressed with the database and would like some of the data. Create a query and export an XML file that lists the members and the hours worked for a particular event.

Capitol Artists

Because the system for Capitol Artists collects data from many employees at the same time, the main database needs to run on a central server. All of the computers are connected by a high-speed LAN and are based on the company growth rates. The company is unlikely to open a second office; however, many of the employees have suggested that they would be more productive if they worked from home. The managers have suggested testing this idea by using the database work tracking system. Employees would connect to the database using the Web interface. As they completed client tasks, they would fill out the work table as usual. This data could then be synchronized with the company database at the end of the day. After a month, the managers could see if employee productivity declined or improved.

1. Check the performance of the database using an Internet connection from off-site. If possible, try it with a cable modem connection and with a dial-up connection. Is the performance fast enough?

2. Outline the security issues involved in enabling employees to access the database from home over the Internet.

3. One of the owners travels often and wants to check on daily progress reports over the Internet using her laptop. Create a Web page that displays the work done for the current day and lists the hours and expense of the employees for each project.

Offshore Speed

The Offshore Speed company has some aspects in common with All Powder. In particular, the store needs several computers to access the application that handles sales, orders, and management reports. However, with the Web-based forms, the process is straightforward. On the other hand, the company deals with a huge number of parts, and it seems like vendors constantly change descriptions and prices. The company is trying to work with the vendors to connect to their databases and at least be able to retrieve replicated materialized views.

1. Set up a small new database that would be created by a vendor to hold information on parts. Replicate the table as read-only so the Offshore Speed company can subscribe to it to automatically receive changes on a regular basis.

2. Some of the company's partner firms would like to receive files that they can read into their databases or into Excel. Set up a procedure that will create text files with basic order data for a selected partner.

3. Create a Web page that customers can use to check on the status of their orders. You should create a separate password for the customers that will be stored within the Customer table. Verify that the password and order number are correct before displaying the data.

Final Project

The main textbook has an appendix with several longer case studies. You should be able to work on one of these cases throughout the term. If you or your instructor picks one, perform the following tasks.

1. Describe any distributed features or database links that will be useful to the project and list any problems you might encounter.
2. Create a replica and test all of the forms and reports on both copies. Test the synchronization.
3. Export at least one table into an XML file that could be sent to an outside firm such as a customer or supplier.
4. Create a basic Web form and response page that enables customers (or employees) to enter some identifier and receive additional information. For example, a customer might select a product category and receive a list of products in that category.
5. Create a second database and build a link to that database, so at least one form operates using data in the second database.